Roland Lock

Healing the Sick

A Living Classic

by
T.L. Osborn

Harrison House
Tulsa, Oklahoma

Unless otherwise indicated, all Scripture quotations are taken from the *King James Version* of the Bible.

Bible quotations in this book have been personalized, and sometimes synopsized, to encourage individual application. Abbreviations are as follows:

AR — American Revised

FB — French Bible

LB — The Living Bible

ML — The Modern Language Bible, The New Berkeley Version in Modern English

Ph — The New Testament in Modern English by J. B. Phillips

RS — Revised Standard Version

RV — The Holy Bible: Revised Version

Healing the Sick
ISBN 0-89274-403-0
Copyright © 1951, 1977, 1981, 1986, 1992 by T.L. Osborn, D.D., D.H.L.
T.L. Osborn
P.O. Box 10
Tulsa, Oklahoma 74102

05 04   53

Published by Harrison House Inc.
P.O. Box 35035
Tulsa, Oklahoma 74153

All Crusade Photographs by Dr. Daisy Washburn Osborn.

Printed in the United States of America.

Contents

Introduction

Among the tens of thousands who have been miraculously healed by the Lord under our own ministry in over 70 nations of the world, only a small fraction of them have been individually prayed for. Most of them have been healed through their own faith which came to them while meditating on the Bible truths we presented from the platform or from the printed page.

When we published the first edition of this book, we never dreamed that it would bless such vast numbers of people.

A continual stream of testimonies come to us from all over the world. They are written by those who have been joyfully converted and miraculously healed while reading our literature.

Those who carefully read and act upon the truths we present here obtain a broader understanding and a more solid faith than those who hear only occasional teaching on the subject of healing.

Many who have attended our crusades, but failed to receive healing, have later been miraculously healed while reading this book.

God sent his word and (it) healed them (Ps. 107:20).

The gospel is the power of God to everyone that believes (Rom. 1:16).

When believed and acted upon, any promise of God is transformed into the power of God.

Every promise of God contains the power of God necessary to produce what it promises, when it is believed and acted upon.

God's promises are life to those that find them, and health to all their flesh (Prov. 4:22).

It was when these facts became real to us that we decided to put into print this volume of messages and offer them to the millions of sufferers to whom we may never minister in person.

This revised and enlarged edition is sent out with confidence that those who read and meditate on these Bible truths will receive vital faith, will act on God's promises, and will be miraculously healed.

No literary style is pretended. Our only aim is to make the simplest possible statements which may serve as an anchor for real living faith in the hearts of the humble and sincere, of the **poor in spirit** (Matt. 5:3), who make up the masses of humanity.

I am especially indebted to the writings of F. F. Bosworth and E. W. Kenyon. The material abridged from their writings has been used by special permission.

Dr. Daisy Washburn Osborn, my wife, associate minister and my closest confidante and collaborator in writing, has taken much valued time from her own writing ministry to edit, correct and revise the latest edition of this book, for which I am deeply grateful.

It is my prayer that the reader shall experience great spiritual and physical blessings through the truths I have presented.

— Dr. T. L. Osborn

Chapter 1

HOW MANY WILL GOD HEAL?

I will take sickness away from you. The number of your days I will fulfill.

Exodus 23:25-26

I am the Lord who heals you.

Exodus 15:26

The purpose of this chapter is to acquaint you with what the Bible teaches: If you are sick, God wants to heal you.

Until you are fully convinced that God wants you to be well, there will always be a doubt in your mind as to whether or not you will be healed. As long as there is that doubt in your mind, perfect faith cannot exist; and until faith is exercised, without doubt or wavering, you may never be healed.

> **Without faith it is impossible to please him; for they that come to God must believe that he is, and that he is a rewarder of them that diligently seek him.**
>
> **Hebrews 11:6**

> **But let them ask in faith, nothing wavering. For they that waver are like a wave of the sea driven with the wind and tossed. For let not those [who waver] think they shall receive any thing of the Lord.**
>
> **James 1:6-7**

Once people are fully convinced that God wants to heal them and that it is not God's will for them to be sick, they almost always receive healing when prayed for, if not before. Knowing God's will concerning sickness provides the ground on which perfect faith can act.

God Is Honest

To one puzzled about faith, who said to me, "I just can't seem to get faith to be healed," I asked, "Have you confidence that God will keep His promise to you?"

"Oh, yes," she affirmed.

"That is faith," I assured her, then added, "Isn't it simple?" And she was healed.

> **God is not a man, that he should lie; neither the son of man, that he should repent: has he said, and shall he not do it? or has he spoken, and shall he not make it good?**
>
> **Numbers 23:19**

There has not failed one word of all his good promise.

1 Kings 8:56

For ever, O Lord, your word is settled in heaven.

Psalm 119:89

I will hasten my word to perform it (Jer. 1:12). That word *hasten* means: "to watch over," "to look after," "to protect," or "to stand behind." In all of His unlimited power, God is standing behind His word to accomplish it. Believe that.

There is no reason for doubting God.

F. F. Bosworth said:

Don't doubt God. If you must doubt something, doubt your doubts, because they are unreliable; but never doubt God, nor His word.

D. L. Moody said:

Is there any reason why you should not have faith in God? Has God ever broken one of His promises? I defy any infidel or unbeliever to place a finger on a single promise God ever made and failed to fulfill.

Satan is a liar. Jesus said so. I can open the Bible and show you how, for six thousand years, Satan has lied to people, telling them that God's word is not true. The devil has denied God's word, and promises people everything — but has broken every promise he ever made.

Three Million Healed

God announced Himself to be the healer of His people with these words: **I am the Lord who heals you** (Ex. 15:26). He spoke those words to about three million people. (Ex. 12:37.) Everyone of them believed God's words were true. The result: Everyone of them who needed healing was made perfectly whole.

We are told: **He [God] brought them forth. . . and there was not one feeble person among their tribes** (Ps. 105:37). Can you imagine three million people all well and strong? Not one feeble, not one weak, and not one sick?

If that was true in Israel, under the law, it is much more true for you, who have been redeemed by the blood of God's Lamb and are living under grace, mercy, and truth.

Let this become a settled truth that you know, as well as you know two plus two are four: Healing is for you — all may be healed.

Theological Tradition Hinders

It is God's will for every individual to be well and strong — when His conditions are met and His word is believed. If there is a justified "maybe" in your case, then we are compelled to apply a "maybe" in every case, because **God is no respecter of persons** (Acts 10:34). If God will heal anyone, He will heal you.

In the world today, disease and sickness are claiming a terrible toll of human lives. In spite of the fact that medical science is demonstrating its greatest achievements, disease persists to ravage human lives all over the world.

The tragedy is that these sicknesses and diseases affect the bodies of thousands of Christians, while preachers and teachers, influenced by theological traditions, often stand by with little more than words of sympathy and pity, assuring the sufferer that it must be God's will; that it will work out for the best; that God is teaching the patient some lesson in humility; that possibly it is God's chastisement; or that by it, the sick person is being drawn closer to Him who often works His will in our lives through sickness.

Christians need never be sick, any more than they need to be sinful. (It is always God's desire to heal you.)

Why is disease such a persistent enemy? How is it that sickness has been able to take such a toll among Christians today? In the Old Testament, three million of God's people believed His word when it was spoken, and everyone was completely healed.

Three Million Believed

The only reason those three million Israelites became well and strong was that they believed what God said: **I am the Lord who heals you.** That was said to them, and they believed it.

The only reason disease takes such a toll among Christians today is that many do not believe what God has spoken. They know that God said, **I am the Lord who heals you.** Somehow they have failed to believe that He meant what He said, which is basically what Satan said to Adam and Eve: **God did not mean what he said.** Influenced by tradition (Mark 7:13), people have changed God's **I am** to "I was."

If, under the old covenant, three million of God's people could be well at one time, then how much more may God's people be well today who are living under the new covenant of mercy, grace, and truth, established on better promises, with a better priesthood (Heb. 8:6), through a more excellent ministry.

13

Chapter 2

HEALING FOR ALL

Is it <u>still</u> the <u>will</u> of <u>God</u>, as in the past, to <u>heal</u> <u>all</u> who have need of healing?

The greatest barrier to the faith of many seeking healing in our day is the uncertainty in their minds as to it being the will of God to heal *all*.

Nearly everyone knows that God does heal some, but there is much in modem theology that prevents people from knowing what the Bible clearly teaches — that healing is provided for all.

It is impossible to boldly claim by faith a blessing which we are not sure God offers, because the blessings of God can be claimed only where the will of God is known, trusted, and acted upon.

Read the Will

If we wish to know what is in a person's will, we read the will. If we want to know God's will on any subject, we read His will.

Suppose a lady would say, "My husband, who was very rich, has passed away. I wish I knew whether he left me anything in his will." I would say to her, "Why do you not read his will and see?"

Testament means a person's <u>will</u>. The <u>Bible</u> contains <u>God</u>'s <u>last</u> <u>will</u> and testament, in which He bequeaths to us all of the blessings of redemption. Since it is His last will and testament, anything later is forgery.

If healing is in God's will for us, then to say that God is not willing to heal all as His will states so clearly, would be to change the will — and that, after the death of the testator.

Jesus is not only the testator who died; but He was resurrected and is also the **mediator of the will** (Heb. 9:15; 12:24). He is our **advocate** (1 John 2:1-2), and He will not beat us out of our inheritance, as some earthly advocates might do. He is our representative at the right hand of God.

There is no better way to know the will of God than by reading the Gospels, which record the teachings and the works of Christ. Jesus was the physical expression of the Father's will. His life was both a revelation and a manifestation of the unchanging love and will of God. He acted out the will of God for us.

15

A Faith-Destroying Phrase

When Jesus laid His hands on **everyone of them and healed them,** He was revealing and doing the will of God for all people.

Lo, I come, to do your will, O God.

Hebrews 10:7

I came down from heaven, not to do my own will, but the will of him that sent me.

John 6:38

Everything Jesus did for needy humanity during His earthly ministry was a direct revelation of the perfect will of God for the human race.

F. F. Bosworth says in his book, *Christ the Healer:*

Perhaps no one could be more conservative than the scholars of the Episcopalian church. Yet, the commission appointed to study the subject of spiritual healing for the body, after three years of study and research in both the Bible and in history, reported back to the church: *The healing of Jesus was done as a revelation of God's will for humanity.* Because they discovered that His will is fully revealed, they reported further: *No longer can the church pray for the sick with that faith-destroying phrase, If it be your will.*

Mr. Bosworth goes on to say:

The message taught in the Gospels is one of complete healing for spirit and body, for all who will come to Him. Many today say, "I believe in healing, but I do not believe it is for everyone." If it is not for everyone, then how could we ever pray the prayer of faith?

Among all those who sought healing from Christ during His earthly ministry, there is only one who prayed for healing with the words, **If it be your will.** This was an outcast leper, in Mark 1:40, who did not know what Christ's will was in healing.

Uncertainty Corrected

The first thing Christ did was to correct this uncertainty by assuring him, **I will.**

It is no longer, **If it be your will** — it *is* God's will.

The leper said: **If you will, you can.** Jesus answered, **I will** (Mark 1:41).

Let that settle it forever with you: God will heal the sick. If He wills to heal one, then He wills to heal all.

(He is not willing that **any** should perish.)

Ask

2 Peter 3:9

James asks: **Is any sick among you?** (James 5:14). *Any* includes you if you are sick.

Of those who were bitten by the fiery serpents, the Bible says that **as many as looked to the brazen serpent lived** (Num. 21:9). Even now, *as many as* look to Christ as redeemer are saved — are healed.

When it comes to the benefits of Christ's redemptive work, all are on an equal basis.

The words **whoever** and **whoever will** are always used to invite the unconverted to be saved.

The words **as many as** (everyone, all, and any) are used to invite the sick and the diseased to be healed.

The Universal Invitation

Both invitations are always universal, and the results are always positively promised: **shall be saved; shall have life; shall recover; shall raise them up; healed them all** and **as many as touched him were healed.**

Sometimes parents show favoritism among their children, but God does not. When we meet the same conditions, we reap the same results. When we do our part, God is always faithful to do His part.

The benefits of redemption are for you. If God healed *all* then, He still heals *all;* that is, all that come to Him for healing.

> **Jesus Christ the same yesterday, and today, and forever.**
>
> **Hebrews 13:8**

> **Great multitudes followed him, and he healed them all.**
>
> **Matthew 12:15**

> **As many as touched [him] were made perfectly whole.**
>
> **Matthew 14:36**

> **The whole multitude sought to touch him: [and he] healed them all.**
>
> **Luke 6:19**

> **When the evening came, they brought to him many that were possessed with devils: and he cast out the spirits with his word, and healed all that were sick: that it might be fulfilled which was spoken by Isaiah the prophet, saying, Himself took our infirmities, and bore our sicknesses.**
>
> **Matthew 8:16-17**

Christ is still healing the sick, in order to fulfill the prophet's words: **Himself took our infirmities** [weaknesses], **and bore our sicknesses** [diseases].

17

Always remember: You are included in the **our** of Matthew 8:17, and God is bound by His covenant to continue to heal *all* who are sick and weak, in order to fulfill Isaiah's words.

My covenant will I not break, nor alter the thing that is gone out of my lips.

Psalm 89:34

When the sun was setting, all they that had any sick with various diseases brought them to him; and he laid his hands on everyone of them, and healed them.

HEALING HAPPENS AS SOON AS IT IS SPOKEN Luke 4:40

Healing was for all in those days, and Christ the Healer has never changed.

Healing Is for All and Should Be Preached to All

Philip preached Christ at Samaria:

And the people with one accord gave heed to those things which Philip spoke, hearing and seeing the miracles which he did. For unclean spirits, crying with loud voice, came out of many that were possessed with them: and many with palsies, and that were lame, were healed. And there was great joy in that city.

Acts 8:6-8

Jesus proved to be exactly the same when Philip told the people about Him.

Peter preached Christ to the cripple (Acts 3:6), to the multitude (Acts 5:14-16), to Aeneas (Acts 9:34). All were healed. Jesus was the same for Peter.

Wherever and whenever Jesus Christ is proclaimed as our sacrifice for sin and sickness, *physical healing* as well as *spiritual salvation* will result.

Paul preached Christ.

And there sat a certain man at Lystra, impotent in his feet, being a cripple from his mother's womb, who never had walked: the same heard Paul speak: who steadfastly beholding him, and perceiving that he had faith to be healed, said with a loud voice, Stand upright on your feet. And he leaped and walked.

Acts 14:8-10

Paul must have preached the gospel of healing, because the lame man received faith to be healed while listening to Paul's message.

(This Method Works)

Wherever healing is taught as God's provision for all, faith is always imparted and the people are always healed. This method never fails. Faith cannot fail.

But faith cannot be exercised when one is undecided as to whether or not God will heal all. If He will not heal all, then we are forced to consider in every case: "I wonder if God wills to heal this one? Or is this one of the unfortunate ones whom God wills to remain sick and to suffer?" How could we ever pray the prayer of faith with such uncertainty in our minds?

Let it be a settled fact: It is God's will to heal you. You have a right to healing as well as forgiveness when you believe.

God said: **I am the Lord who heals you** (Ex. 15:26). If God said this, and God cannot lie, He meant it. What God says is true. So, healing is yours.

Healing is part of the gospel and is to be preached throughout **all the world** and to **every creature, to the end of the world** (Mark 16:15; Matt. 28:20).

Being part of the gospel, the divine blessing of physical healing is for *all*.

Chapter 3

REASONS FOR FAITH

Many recognize the fact of divine healing, but have no personal knowledge of Jesus the Savior of the body. They see that others are healed, but question whether healing is God's will for them.

They are waiting for a special revelation of the will of God concerning their case. In the meantime, they are doing all within the power of human skill to get well with the use of natural means, not thinking that from their own standpoint they might be opposing the will of God.

The Bible reveals the will of God in regard to healing. God need not give any special revelation of His will when He has plainly given His revealed will in His word.

A careful study of the scriptures will show that God has declared that His will includes healing for His children. He has declared Himself to be the healer of His people.

Ordinance for Healing

When God called the Israelites out of Egypt, He gave them a statute and an ordinance for healing:

> **If you will diligently hearken to the voice of the Lord your God, and will do that which is right in his sight, and will give ear to his commandments, and keep all his statutes, I will put none of these diseases upon you, which I have brought upon the Egyptians — for I am the Lord who heals you.**
>
> **Exodus 15:26**

The Hebrew text reads: **I will permit none of these diseases upon you which I permitted upon the Egyptians.**

This covenant was repeated at the close of the forty years' wanderings of Israel.

All through their history, in sickness and pestilence, the Israelites turned to God in repentance and confession and received healing in answer to their prayers. If healing in answer to prayer was God's way under the old covenant, it is much more prevalent under the new covenant.

> **Great multitudes followed him, and he healed them all.**
>
> **Matthew 12:15**

Fulfilling God's Will

Christ's healing was not to prove His divinity alone, as some suppose, but to fulfill His commission — to fulfill the will of God.

Lo, I come to do your will, O God.

Hebrews 10:7

Jesus Himself is a revelation of the will of God. He *did* the will of God; He healed *all* who came to Him. He has an unchanging priesthood: **Jesus Christ the same yesterday, and today, and forever** (Heb. 13:8).

He is the same in *love* as when, in compassion, He healed the multitudes.

He is the same in *power* as when He healed all manner of diseases.

Wherefore in all things it behooved [was necessary for] **him** [Jesus Christ] **to be made like his brethren, that he might be a merciful** [compassionate] **and faithful high priest.**

Hebrews 2:17

During His earthly ministry, Jesus was always **moved with compassion. and healed all them that had need of healing,** and He is our faithful and merciful high priest today.

Christ's Commission To Heal

In the scriptures, compassion and mercy mean the same thing. The Hebrew noun, *rachamin,* is translated both "mercy" and "compassion." The Greek verb, *eleeo,* is translated "have mercy" and "have compassion"; likewise, the Greek adjective, *eleemon,* is defined "merciful — compassionate."

Christ commissioned the *twelve disciples* to heal (Matt. 10:7-8). Later, He commissioned the *seventy.* His commission was given to *all who believe* (Mark 16:17-18). It was given to *the church* (James 5:14-16). These commissions have never been revoked.

The Thread of Healing

Healing, in answer to the prayer of faith, was the only way of healing known to the early church. A thread of healing has run through all the ages to the present day; and now this truth, almost lost in the spiritual darkness of the Middle Ages, has been discovered during the great outpouring of the Holy Spirit in these last days. Christians in every land are now proving God is the healer of His people.

God has provided healing through Christ's redemptive work. (Is. 53:4-5; Matt. 8:16-17.) The Hebrew word which is rendered *griefs* in Isaiah 53 is said to be everywhere else in the Bible translated *sicknesses.* Also, **by his stripes** (bruises) **we are healed.**

22

The word "bore" in Matthew 8:17 implies substitution — suffering *for*; not sympathy, as in suffering *with*. If Christ has borne our sicknesses, why should we bear them? NO

There are types of Christ's redemptive sacrifice for our healing in the Old Testament: the cleansing of the leper (Lev. 14); the healing of the plague (Num. 16:46-48); the brazen serpent (Num. 21:7-9); the healing of Job (Job 33:24).

In Deuteronomy, chapter 28, disease and sickness were a part of the *curse*. But Galatians 3:13 declares: **Christ has redeemed us from the curse of the law.**

Healing Is Promised

Sin and sickness are intimately connected throughout the scriptures (Ps. 103:3). From both sin and sickness, we have redemption through the blood that was shed and the stripes borne by Jesus.

All that God has given us is given through Christ Jesus our Lord for whoever will — whoever will meet the conditions and believe the word. We may exempt ourselves, saying, "It is not His will"; but God leaves no one out. He is no respecter of persons. His promises are to all.

Is *any* [not some] **sick among you?** (James 5:14).

Ask, and it shall be given you (Matt. 7:7).

If you shall ask *any thing* in my name, I will do it (John 14:14).

Whatever *you* desire when you pray, believe that *you* receive it, and *you* shall have it (Mark 11:24).

Healing is promised through the power of the Holy Spirit. (Rom. 8:11.)

All these scriptures clearly make known God's will to heal whoever comes to Him in faith. This is His will, His Way. No other way of healing is recommended in the Bible. God has no other way for His people.

He has willed us healing, health, and strength in Christ. This is our right and privilege in Him. We please and glorify Him by accepting His way. He wills that we be well. Will we accept this provision of His love? Will we obey Him, in taking His way, that His will may be done in us, and that we may glorify God in our bodies?

Positive Knowledge in Prayer

With positive knowledge of the will of God, we do not pray: "Lord, heal me, if it be Your will." That implies doubt, and doubt cancels faith.

An invalid said to me: "I believe in praying for God to heal, if it be His will." Then to illustrate the thought, he said: "A child may ask a parent for something; and the parent will give it, if it will be good for the child; and so, in this way, I pray for healing."

I answered: "If the parent had promised to give the child a certain thing, the child would have a right to expect it. Our Father has promised us healing, and we have a right to expect Him to keep His promise."

Not knowing the will of God in a certain matter, we may pray in faith that God will do this for us, if it be His will; and He will do what is best for us.

But where God has revealed His will, by promising to do a certain thing, we need not be in ignorance of it or in doubt concerning it.

The Bible reveals physical healing to be His will, just as spiritual healing is His will, if we fulfill the conditions and believe His promise.

The faith that appropriates God's promise rests on the knowledge of His will. His known will is the basis of our faith. We could not take healing by faith, believing that we had received it, if there was any question as to whether or not it was for us.

We must know the will of God; then we may take by faith whatever He has promised in His word, believing that when we ask we receive.

Our will also has a part in the question of healing: Will we take that which God wills for us? **If you live in me, and my words live in you, ask what you will, and it shall be done to you** (John 15:7). When our *will* meets His *will*, the work is done.

Chapter 4
WHY MORE DO NOT GET HEALED

Faith comes by hearing the word of God (Rom. 10:17). Faith is never derived through sympathy. Faith never comes through discussing with people their pains and aches, weaknesses and sicknesses.

Faith is born when we hear the word of truth.   M/F

Jesus said: **You shall know the truth, and the truth shall make you free** (John 8:32). He is the truth.

If we want to see people delivered from the bondage of disease, we must teach them the part of God's word that sets them free from disease. The truth is: Christ wills every person (you) to be healed, or He would not have taken the stripes by which **you were healed.**

Then one may ask, "Why do not more get healed?"

The answer: Because of the lack of teaching and preaching the Bible truth of healing.

Let us not stand by the bed of sick people to sympathize with their pains. Let us never insinuate that it must be God's will to "take them"; or that "it will teach them patience"; or that perhaps, "they will be drawn closer to the Lord" through their sickness.

Let us rather declare war on every form of sickness, and take authority over every form of demon power through the name of Jesus Christ. Let us minister deliverance to those in need of healing.

If Salvation Is for All, Healing Is for All

We are never in doubt as to God's willingness to save the most hopeless human being. Why can we be so certain? Because we have been taught the Bible truth in this regard.

We have been taught from childhood that salvation is for all who believe, because **God so loved the world, that he gave his only begotten Son, that whoever believes in him should not perish, but have everlasting life** (John 3:16).

Had we been taught the truth in regard to healing for the body as positively as we have been taught the truth in regard to spiritual salvation, people would believe for healing in the same way that they believe for regeneration.

If God worked miracles and healed in times past, but will not do the same today, it must be that He is a God who *was* and not a God who *is*. But the Bible says, **I am the Lord who heals you.**

Right now God is saying, **I am the Lord who heals you.** Tomorrow He will be saying exactly the same thing. He will be healing the sick who look to Him tomorrow. There is no maybe; He heals all who come to Him believing His promise.

Because of your faith it will happen (Matt. 9:29). **So, ask in faith, without wavering** (James 1:6).

Spiritual and Physical Healing

Healing in the Bible is physical as well as spiritual.

Sin and sickness which proliferate in the human race are both the result of the disobedience of Adam and Eve.

The two redemptive blessings which Christ brought to the world are salvation and healing — deliverance from sin and sickness.

Salvation from sin and sickness or healing from sin and sickness are both blessings included in our redemption, provided by one sacrifice and by one substitute. To say *healed* or to say *saved* means the same. If we say *healed*, or if we say *saved*, that is for the body as well as for the spirit.

It would be incomplete for an unsaved person who is sick in body to be saved from sin and not be healed of sickness, after they had heard and believed this truth of the gospel.

For you to be healed and not to be saved would be incomplete. God wants your spirit to be regenerated when your physical needs are met. Why? Because that is what redemption is. How could you be blessed physically and not be blessed spiritually, after you heard this truth? You discover Jesus as your own substitutionary sacrifice, bearing both your sins and your sicknesses in your place, and you are set free.

This is the truth that sets people free in their bodies as well as in their spirits. (John 8:32.)

The Dual Provision

In our gospel crusades worldwide, we always preach the two-fold provision. We tell the unsaved to accept Jesus Christ as healer and Savior at the same time — to believe that He heals them of sickness at the same time that He saves them from sin. This brings a perfect deliverance to spirit and body alike. Body and spirit are delivered together when people believe it.

Paul says: **You are bought with a price: therefore glorify God in your body and in your spirit, which are God's** (1 Cor. 6:20). We are told to use both body and spirit to glorify God. Both are bought with a price.

26

No wonder Jesus said to the man who was sick with palsy, **Son, be of good cheer; your sins are forgiven** (Mark 2:5; Matt. 9:2). When he took up his bed and walked, his sins were left behind with his sickness.

That is why Jesus asked: **Which is easier to say to the sick of the palsy, Your sins are forgiven; or to say, Arise, and take up your bed and walk?** (Mark 2:9).

Had Jesus told this man that his sins were gone, his sickness would also have had to leave, because the remedy for both was provided in the same sacrifice.

Isaiah declared: **He was wounded for our transgressions and with his stripes we are healed** (Is. 53:5). Had Jesus told the man to rise up and walk, then his sins also would have had to leave.

Always see your two-fold deliverance in Jesus Christ.

The word *saved* in Romans 10:9 is the same Greek word used by Mark when he said, **as many** [sick people] **as touched him were made whole** (Mark 6:56). Both words, *saved* and *made whole*, were translated from the Greek word, *sozo*.

Each of the words found in the following scriptures are translated from the same Greek word, *sozo: healed* — Mark 5:23; *saved* — Mark 16:16; *healed* — Luke 8:36; *saved* — Acts 2:21; *healed* — Acts 14:9; *saved* — Ephesians 2:8; *saved* — Luke 18:42; *save* — James 5:15; *made whole* — Mark 5:34; *be whole* — Mark 5:28; *whole* — Luke 17:19; *whole* — Acts 4:9; *saved* — Acts 4:12; *made whole* — Mark 6:56.

Christians Need Not Be Sick

We do not tolerate sin in our lives because Jesus bore our sins. Neither do we need to tolerate sickness in our bodies because Jesus bore our sicknesses.

> **Himself took our infirmities** [weaknesses], **and bore our sicknesses** [diseases].
>
> **Matthew 8:17**

> **Surely he has borne** [carried away] **our griefs** [sicknesses and diseases], **and carried our sorrows** [pains].
>
> **Isaiah 53:4**

By these scriptures we know that **Jesus bore our sicknesses.** According to 1 Peter 2:24, **Who his own self bore our sins in his own body on the tree,** we know that **Jesus bore our sins.** If He bore them, we need not bear them. If we have to bear them, then Jesus need not have borne them. If we must bear them, then it was useless for Jesus to bear them.

The gospel very clearly shows that **Jesus Christ bore them** — that is, carried them away — and that, therefore, we are redeemed from them. So we need **never bear them.**

Christians are often taught that, although they were redeemed (from their sins) they must continue to suffer their sicknesses, because (it may not be God's will to heal them.) They know He healed others, but perhaps those were the more fortunate ones on whom He bestowed this mercy.

If it were only His will to do so, they know He could heal them; but since they are not sure of His will, they will "be patient" and continue to "bear the cross" of their physical suffering.

Disease destroys the very body that has been bought with a price — the price of the body of the Son of God. This is not reasonable.

God Wills To Keep His Promise

How unlike God's word this doctrine is.

Rev. F. F. Bosworth wrote:

When I ask people if they think it is God's will to heal them, and they reply that they do not know whether it is or not, I then ask them if it is God's will to keep His promise.

The reason more people are not healed is because of a lack of preaching and teaching these truths.

Since **faith comes by hearing the word of God**, then, if we expect the people to have faith to receive God's divine blessing of physical healing, we must teach them these scriptural truths which alone can build faith for this blessing.

How many would be saved if they never heard a message on salvation? Or if, when the subject of salvation was addressed, the main points expounded were:

(1) Maybe it isn't God's will to save you.
(2) Perhaps your sin is for God's glory.
(3) Perhaps God is using this sin to chastise you.
(4) Be patient in your sin until God wills to save you.
(5) The day of miracles (conversion) is past.

How many would receive faith to be saved through such messages?

Yet these are about the only points many sick people hear concerning God's provision for physical healing. It is easy to understand why many are not healed today.

LIES TAUGHT BY THE CHURCH

NEVER LET THIS BE SO

Chapter 5

ASKING THE FATHER IN JESUS' NAME

Whatever you ask in my name, that will I do, that the Father may be glorified in the Son.

John 14:13

Whatever you shall ask the Father in my name, he will give it to you.

John 16:23

According to these scriptures, we have a right to ask the Father for healing, in the name of Jesus Christ, and receive healing. If we believe God's word, we may ask, in Jesus' name, and we shall receive that for which we ask; that is, as John said in 1 John 5:14: **If we ask any thing according to his will** — and, certainly, healing is His will for all.

If you are suffering from sickness, you have a right to ask the Father for healing. **Whatever you desire, when you pray, believe that you receive it, and you shall have it** (Mark 11:24).

However, note that our asking must be in Jesus' name.

The Power of Jesus' Name

There is power in the name of the Lord Jesus Christ.

It is written in Philippians 2:9,10: **God also has given him a name which is above every name: that at the name of Jesus every knee should bow, of things in heaven** [angels], **and things in earth** [men], **and things under the earth** [demons].

Beings in all three worlds must bow to the name of Jesus. That name holds dominion over Satan and his entire kingdom.

Smith Wigglesworth tells of ministering to a man who was dying from tuberculosis. He said that, while standing beside the bed, they did nothing but repeat the name of Jesus over and over. The presence of God began to fill the room; healing flowed into that dying man's body; and he arose, perfectly whole.

Peter said to a crippled man: **In the name of Jesus Christ of Nazareth rise up and walk,** and the man walked (Acts 3:6).

Paul said to a demon: **I command you in the name of Jesus Christ to come out of her,** and the insane woman was perfectly restored (Acts 16:18).

29

Jesus left His name with us. We have the right to use it. Satan is commanded to respect that name **which is above every name**, and his entire kingdom is compelled to obey our command when given in the name of Jesus Christ. (Luke 10:17.)

The Resources of Heaven

Remember, it was this Jesus who conquered sin, Satan, disease, death, hell, and the grave; and we use His name by His authority.

As E. W. Kenyon writes:

> When Jesus gave us the right to use that name, the Father knew all that name would imply when breathed in prayer by oppressed souls; and it is always His joy to recognize that name.

The possibilities involved in that name are beyond our understanding.

When Jesus says, **whatever you ask the Father in my name**, He is giving us a signed check on the resources of heaven, and asking us to fill it in. What a privilege.

If you are in need of healing, begin a study of the resources of Jesus, in order to obtain a measure of the wealth which that name holds for you today. It is yours to use today. Jesus said so. Only believe and begin to use His name in prayer today.

Jesus is saying in effect: "You ask the Father in My name. I will endorse the petition, and the Father will give you anything I have endorsed."

As we accept our rights and privileges in the new covenant, and pray in Jesus' name, it appears that the request and the petition passes out of our hands into the hands of Jesus. He then assumes the responsibility of that need, and we know that He said, **Father I thank you that you hear me, and I know that you hear me always** (John 11:41-42).

In other words, we know that the Father always hears Jesus, and when we pray in Jesus' name, it is as though Jesus Himself were doing the praying. He takes our place. The answer is sent to us, from the Father; and we rejoice.

Irrevocable Provision

If you need healing, you may ask the Father for it, in Jesus' name, believe that He hears you, and you will find your sickness will leave. Why?

> **This is the confidence that we have in him, that, if we ask anything according to his will, he hears us: and if we know that he hears us, whatever we ask, we know that we have the petitions that we desired of him.**
>
> **1 John 5:14-15**

30

It is yours. You have a right to it. Ask Him for it and receive your health, in Jesus' name, because Jesus gave us permission to use His name in prayer.

Whatever you shall ask in my name, that will I do, that the Father may be glorified in the Son. If you shall ask any thing in my name, I will do it.

John 14:13-14

Up to this time you have asked nothing in my name: ask, and you shall receive, that your joy may be full.

John 16:24

If you need healing, you may ask the Father for it, in the name of His Son, and you shall receive it, and your joy will be full.

Peter took Jesus at His word, and to the lame man needing healing, he said, **In the name of Jesus Christ of Nazareth rise up and walk** (Acts 3:6).

Jesus Touches Every Phase of Life

That name has never lost its power. You may receive healing through that name.

People are saved through that name, for **there is no other name whereby we must be saved** (Acts 4:12).

You can pray and make your petitions to the Father in that name. (John 14:13-14; 16:24.)

In that name the lame, impotent, and helpless are made to walk again.

Jesus said, **In my name they shall cast out devils** (Mark 16:17).

Paul proved this prophecy of Jesus to be true several years after Jesus had spoken it. Paul said to the evil spirit, **I command you in the name of Jesus Christ to come out of her. And he came out the same hour** (Acts 16:18).

What power that name has for the church today. It touched every phase of the early church.

According to Colossians 3:17, we are taught: **Whatever you do in word or deed, do all in the name of the Lord Jesus.**

In Ephesians 5:20 we learn that we should always be **giving thanks for all things to God and the Father in the name of our Lord Jesus Christ.**

In Hebrews 13:15 we are told to **offer the sacrifice of praise to his name.**

In James 5:14 we are instructed to **anoint the sick in the name of the Lord.**

In I John 3:23 we are informed: **This is his commandment, that we should believe on the name of his Son Jesus Christ.**

We see by these scriptures that the name of Jesus touches every phase of the life of the Christian and that it must fill a place in our thoughts, in our prayer lives, in our teaching and preaching — a place about which many are altogether unlearned because they have been untaught today.

Chapter 6

IF TWO OF YOU SHALL AGREE

> If two of you shall agree on earth as touching any thing that they shall ask, it shall be done for them of my Father which is in heaven.
>
> Where two or three are gathered together in my name, I am there in the midst of them.
>
> Matthew 18:19-20

It is proverbial that there is strength in unity.

> Two are better than one. For if they fall, the one will lift up the other: but woe to the one that is alone when he or she falls; for that one has no other to help him or her up. Again, if two lie together, then they have heat: but how can one be warm alone? And one standing alone can be attacked and defeated, but two can stand back to back and conquer; three is even better, for a triple-braided cord is not easily broken.
>
> Ecclesiastes 4:9-12

From Deuteronomy 32:30 and Joshua 23:10, we conclude that **one can chase a thousand, but two shall be able to put ten thousand to flight.**

Jesus had a reason for doing so when **He appointed seventy other disciples, and sent them** *two by two* **before his face into every city and place** (Luke 10:1).

Agreeing in Faith

God must have had the same reason in mind when He said: **Separate me Barnabas and Saul for the work** [for which] **I have called them** (Acts 13:2).

We notice that it was Peter and John who were seen by the lame man; and through the strength of their united faith, the miracle was done in his body. (Acts 3.)

We are mentioning these things to show you that where any two of you **shall agree on earth as touching any thing that they shall ask, it shall be done for them of my Father which is in heaven** (Matt. 18:19).

We have proven this to be true in many cases where the victims of disease were unable to grasp faith for themselves. In such cases when two shall agree — not only in words, but in spirit — the sick recover.

This is not necessary when one person, who is mentally responsible, can hear the word of God and exercise his or her personal faith. This is always the best.

Faith comes by hearing the word of God. (Rom. 10:17.)

Individual Faith Possible

Give heed to the word and have your own faith. Tens of thousands of people have testified of receiving healing during our crusades by hearing and believing the word of God as we preached or taught it to the multitudes.

A man, who had been engrossed in hearing the message as we preached, arose to find his rupture gone. A lady discovered her arthritis and varicose veins were healed. A blind woman received her sight; innumerable others have been healed of every kind of disease while hearing and believing the word of God.

Anytime you hear the word of God and give heed to it, you will have your own faith — the faith that will set you free. That is always better than depending on the faith of someone else.

However, there are cases in which the person is unable to reason, or is too sick to grasp these truths or listen to the word of God. In such cases, two believers can agree in prayer, and the promise is: **It shall be done for them of my Father which is in heaven.**

Thank God for His promise, and for His interest in our physical health as well as in our spiritual health.

John coupled these things in his letter to his friend, Gaius, saying: **I wish above all things that you may prosper and be in health, even as your soul prospers** (3 John 2), and John, who leaned on Jesus' bosom, knew what the will of God was.

Christians do not doubt that God wills to save and regenerate every unsaved person, regardless of how hopeless the case may be.

It is also God's will to heal every sick person, regardless of how incurable, if the sufferer will look to Him and believe His word. God's will is to heal all.

How can anyone doubt God's healing love and compassion for His children when He has given us so many promises for our healing.

You have a scriptural right to be healthy and strong.

"Well," you may ask, "how then can one ever die?"

According to the Bible, it is very simple. Listen to God's prescription for the death of His child: **You take away their breath, they die, and return to the dust** (Ps. 104:29). That does not mean that you must die with a cancer, does it? Or any other form of disease or sickness?

The child of God is **redeemed from the curse of the law,** a part of which is disease (Gal. 3:13; Deut. 28:58-61).

The Bible ideal for the death of a child of God is: **You shall come to your grave in a full age, like as a shock of corn comes in its season** (Job 5:26). That was how Abraham, Sarah, Isaac, Jacob, Moses — and many others — died.

Chapter 7
ANOINTING WITH OIL

James tells us in the fifth chapter and fourteenth verse of his epistle: **Is any sick among you? Call for the elders of the church; and let them pray over the sick, anointing them with oil in the name of the Lord** (James 5:14).

This is an unmistakably clear promise of healing for the sick.

From Mark 6:13 we learn that the disciples did this, for it says: **They cast out many devils, and anointed with oil many that were sick, and healed them.**

Affliction Defined

Just preceding this promise to the sick, James mentions the *afflicted*. This has caused much speculation as to what form of sickness may be termed an affliction.

According to *Strong's Concordance*, this word translated *affliction* has no reference whatever to physical disability.

Webster tells us that, in common use, the word affliction has the meaning of physical ailment, but that is not true of the Greek word from which affliction was translated. It is a word which means trouble, persecution, hardship, or tribulation.

Those enduring persecution, or some other kind of trouble or hardship, should never call for the elders and expect the elders to pray their troubles and tribulations away. Instead, James says **Is any afflicted? let the afflicted one pray** (James 5:13).

A Bold Declaration

Notice what James asks: **Is any sick among you?** That does not infer that healing is for only a few favored ones. He is bold to declare the promise of healing to any sick.

Every person who is sick has a Bible right to call for the elders of the church and to be healed — and, if necessary, to be saved at the same time. That should make you rejoice, especially if you have been taught that healing is just for the lucky ones, or just for those whom God happens to want to heal.

Healing is for you. You have a right to health in your body, as well as to health in your soul, because James says in chapter 5, verse 15: **The prayer of faith shall save the sick, and the Lord shall raise them up; and if they have committed sins, they shall be forgiven.** Verse 16 says: **Confess your faults one to another, and pray one for another, that you may be healed.**

James then adds: **The effectual fervent prayer of the righteous avails much.**

This is a clear promise, and easy to understand. By acting upon these words, millions have been healed down through the ages, and millions more are healed in this century.

Notice in verse 15 James says: **The prayer of faith shall save the sick.** The prayer of faith is the only prayer that will be effective in obtaining healing for the sick.

The Prayer of Faith

How could one pray the prayer of faith while entertaining the thought, "Maybe it is God's will to take this person home by means of this disease," or, "Maybe God is working out something precious in this life by means of this sickness"; and "Perhaps I should encourage them to patiently endure it, and so learn the lesson that God is seeking to teach." One could never do so. This is the attitude in which many prayers for the sick are prayed.

Is it any wonder that so many fail to receive healing when prayed for?

Paul says: **Christ is the savior of the body** (Eph 5:23). He also says: **The body is for the Lord; and the Lord for the body** (1 Cor. 6:13).

Then he asks: **Do you not know that your bodies are the members of Christ?** (1 Cor. 6:15); and again: **Do you not know that your body is the temple of the Holy Ghost?** Then he adds: **Therefore glorify God in your body, and in your spirit, which are God's** (1 Cor. 6:19-20).

The body is for the Lord. It is not for ourselves or anyone else — especially Satan. It was not created for disease and sickness.

If Christ has become **savior of the body**, and **the body is for the Lord**, then we need not tolerate sickness and disease in it. We need not have sickness in the body, any more than sin in the spirit. Sickness is sin to the body. Sin is sickness to the spirit. Realize your full deliverance. Take your liberty.

Stand fast therefore in the liberty by which Christ has made us free (Gal. 5:1).

Settle it forever: It is God's will for you to be well. Claim the promise; then act on His word; and arise out of your doubts and fears to find **health springing forth speedily** (Is. 58:8).

Remember, James asked: **Is any sick among you?** It is true that any sick person may call for the elders to pray the **prayer of faith** for them.

The prayer of faith cannot, and never will, be prayed while the elders are wondering if it is God's will to heal this one or that one.

James says: **Ask in faith, nothing wavering. For the one that wavers is like a wave of the sea driven with the wind and tossed. Let not that person think that they shall receive any thing of the Lord** (James 1:6-7).

Chapter 8

THE LAYING ON OF HANDS

Jesus gave the commission to His followers to **go into all the world and do as He commanded** (Mark 16:15). This commission is still in effect. Jesus promised: **They shall lay hands on the sick, and they** [the sick] **shall recover** (Mark 16:18).

Just before He said this, Jesus had said: **These signs shall follow them that believe,** and added, **In my name they shall cast out devils; they shall lay hands on the sick, and they shall recover.**

Any believer can lay hands on the sick, and the promise is: **They** [the sick] **shall recover.** A believer does more than merely agree that the word is true. A believer is one who acts on the word of God.

(God never tells us to do something that we cannot do.)

Obtaining the fulfillment of His promise is more a matter of obedience than of conscious faith. Faith is doing what God tells us to do, then expecting God to do what He tells us He will do.

Noah built the ark — God flooded the earth.

Moses stretched out the rod — God parted the waters.

Joshua marched around the walls of Jericho — God pushed them down.

Elijah smote the waters — God parted them.

Elisha threw the stick in the river — God made the iron to swim.

Naaman dipped seven times — God healed the leprosy.

Jesus said it is the believer who may lay hands on the sick. It is God who will make them well.

James said that the believers may anoint any sick with oil, and pray the prayer of faith on their behalf. He says it is the Lord who shall raise up the sick.

God says, "You do a small thing; I will do a large thing. You do a foolish thing; I will do a wise thing. You do something that only a human being can do; I will do something that only I, God, can do."

Do what God tells you to do, then expect God to do what He said He would do. That is faith.

41

When Jesus Visited Our House

When we were very young, my wife Daisy and I went to India as missionaries; but we could not convince the Hindus and Moslems that Jesus Christ is God's Son and that He was raised from the dead. They asked us to prove it. I read verses from our Bible to them; but they had their Koran which they claimed was God's word, given by the mouth of His prophet, Mohammed.

Both books, the Bible and the Koran, were beautiful black books with gold embossed letters on their covers.

Which Was God's word?

We could not prove the Bible to be God's word, because we did not understand faith and the need for miracles at that time. So we returned to America in what seemed to be defeat.

But we had seen the masses, and we knew they needed to believe the good news of Jesus Christ in order to be saved. We fasted and prayed many days for God to show us His answer to our dilemma. How were we to help non-Christians to believe on Jesus Christ, to be convinced that He is more than just another religion? God answered our prayer.

One morning at 6:00 o'clock, Jesus Christ awakened me in our bedroom. I lay before Him as though I were dead, unable to move a finger or a toe. Water poured from my eyes, yet I was not conscious of weeping.

After a long while, I was able to crawl from my bed to the floor where I lay on my face until the afternoon.

When I walked out of that room, I was a new man. Jesus became Lord and Master of my life. I knew this truth: He is alive! He is more than a religion!

Soon after that awesome experience, a man of God came to our area. He had an amazing gift of healing. As we attended his meetings, we saw hundreds accept Christ; and right before our eyes, we watched him cast out devils and lay hands on the sick in Jesus Christ's name. The blind, deaf, dumb, and cripples were healed instantly.

A thousand voices whirled over my head, saying, *You can do that. That is what Peter and Paul did. That is what Jesus did. That proves that the Bible is true. You can do that.*

As we walked out of that packed auditorium, we were overwhelmed.

We began fasting and praying again. Daisy and I made a new pact with God. We resolved that we would read the New Testament as though we had never read it before in our lives; and we would believe everything we read.

Whatever Jesus told us to do as His followers, we would do. Whatever He said He would do, we would expect Him to do.

We would act upon His written word, just as prophets of God acted upon His spoken word in Bible days.

We would do as the first disciples of our Lord had done.

If He said we could heal the sick, we would expect to see the sick healed.

If He said we could cast out devils, then we would do it in His name and expect them to obey us.

I can never tell you what that step meant to us. The Bible became a living, pulsating, thrilling book of truth.

We disregarded all of the teaching we had ever had. We accepted God's word as being true and began to act on it exactly like the early Christian believers did.

Through that decision, we discovered the authority we have in the name of Jesus and the power we have over the kingdom of Satan, as well as the virtue that flows through every true believer.

As this latest edition of this book goes to press, I can witness that, for nearly four decades, in 70 nations of the world, Daisy and I have gone in Jesus' name and have acted on the written word of God.

We have preached to multitudes — from 10,000 to over 200,000 souls daily in these mass crusades — and have seen tens of thousands of the most amazing miracles perhaps ever witnessed in any Christian ministry.

God's word becomes very simple when we regard every word as true and act accordingly. Its staggering truths of power and authority granted to the church become a living reality.

How thrilling it is to share a gospel that works.

As we constantly witness the deliverance of the deaf and dumb, the restoring of sight to the blind, the healing of the lame, the crippled, the sick and diseased, we rejoice over the truth of Jesus' words: **All things are possible to them that believe** (Mark 9:23).

They Shall Lay Hands on the Sick

Everywhere that believers lay their hands on the sick in faith, the sick recover. We should expect nothing less than this.

The Bible records incidents of faith in the laying on of hands: **My little daughter lies at the point of death: I pray you, come and lay your hands on her and she shall live, said Jairus, a ruler of the synagogue, to Jesus** (Mark 5:23-41).

Jesus went and **took the damsel by the hand, and said to her, Arise, and she arose.**

Jesus saw a woman bowed over with **a spirit of infirmity** and He laid His hands on her: **and immediately she was made straight, and glorified God** (Luke 13:11-13).

43

The father of Publius lay sick of a fever and of a bloody flux: Paul went in and prayed, and laid his hands on him, and healed him (Acts 28:8).

If you are a believer, the nature of God is in you. The Spirit of God dwells in you as His temple. The power of God is in you, and it is this power of God that heals the sick when hands are laid on them in Jesus' name.

Sometimes this is accompanied by manifestations: You may feel the life of God pouring through your body, making it whole. At other times, you may feel nothing.

It makes no difference whether or not you have a feeling. The word of God is superior to your feelings.

It is written, **They shall lay hands on the sick, and they shall recover.** That word is always true. Whether feeling comes or not, healing always comes.

A lady came to us for prayer. After the meeting, she was asked how she felt.

"Well, I never got blessed," she replied, "but I got healed."

A few moments later, as she was thinking about her wonderful healing, she became happy and felt "blessed." Many people, such as this lady, expect some type of feeling or sensation when prayed for, instead of expecting healing.

One may be healed by the power of God and never feel anything. Others may feel great surges of God's healing power — a heat, a coolness, or a shock as of a current of electricity. But take my advice: Do not expect feeling — expect healing.

A minister said to me, "I used to pray for God to cause people to fall when I prayed for them and He did just what I asked Him to do. Most everyone I laid my hands on fell.

"But I discovered that many of them would find they were not healed. I then began to pray for God to heal them instead of slay them."

He said he found that God was faithful to do what he asked Him to do. "Now, whether they fall or not," he said, "I expect them to get healed, and it is done according to our faith."

He was a man who had wanted feeling instead of healing. He came to realize this, and now his ministry is far more effective. Healing is always better than feeling.

When the sick learn to base their faith on the word of God exclusively, they have won the victory. It then becomes true that nothing in the realm of feeling can ever separate them from what the word of God says.

As long as you talk in terms of what you feel, you do not yet comprehend the meaning of faith in the word of God.

Faith Involves the Word of God

Let us suppose that you come to us for prayer to be healed. After we have prayed for you, you say, "I believe I got healed — I feel so much better," or, "I can't feel a pain."

You are talking in terms of what you feel.

Sooner or later if you get a bad feeling, you will still talk in terms of what you feel and will say, "Well, I thought I got healed, but I feel so bad. I guess I'll have to be prayed for again."

You nullify your healing by believing in what you feel more than in God's word.

You will notice that the people who determine whether or not they are healed by their feelings, will never credit God's word. If they feel good, they say they are healed. If they feel bad, they say they are not healed. They never give credence to God's word.

I was taken to the room of a sick man; and when I encouraged him to look to God for deliverance from his lifelong sickness, he replied, "I feel like I'll be healed some day."

I asked him why he felt that way.

"Well," he replied, "several have received the witness that I would be healed some day. Even the pastor thinks I'll get well, and I remember that a long time ago the Lord blessed me and gave me a witness that I was going to be healed."

He was struggling to believe for healing on the basis of someone's "witness" or "feeling." You see, he never mentioned the word of God as having any promise for him.

Practice believing God's word. Faith in His word wins every time.

Faith Is Never Feeling — Feeling Is Never Faith

Faith has nothing to do with feeling. Feeling has nothing to do with faith. Faith constantly attributes everything to what the word of God says, irrespective of pains, symptoms, or feelings.

Suppose you come for prayer with your faith based on the word of God instead of feelings. You are ministered to, according to the scriptures, by the laying on of hands, and perhaps you are anointed with oil.

Then someone asks: "How do you feel?"

You answer: "I am healed because the Bible says, **They shall lay hands on the sick, and they shall recover.**

But the inquirer insists: "Do you feel any better?"

Your answer is very positive, knowing that God's word is back of what you say: "I know I'm healed, because it is written, **With his stripes, I am healed.**" You may add, "God said, **I am the Lord who heals you,** and that means me."

The work has been done, because you attributed your healing to the power and authority and faithfulness of the word of God.

You may ask: "But what about feelings? Must we continue to carry our pains?"

No, you need not carry your pains and aches with you, ignoring them; neither will you be untruthful about your pains.

Always speak the truth. But here is the secret: Answer the inquirer with the word of God. Say just exactly what the Bible says: "**By his stripes, we are healed**. They laid hands on me, and I shall recover. Jesus said it and He cannot lie."

Faith disregards everything but God's word.

When the hands of believers are laid upon you, you will recover, if you will only believe. Stand by God's word, and God will stand by you.

There has not failed one word of all his good promise (1 Kings 8:56).

I am the Lord: I will speak, and the word that I shall speak shall come to pass (Ezek. 12:25).

The word which I have spoken shall be done, says the Lord God (Ezek. 12:28).

For all the promises of God in him (Jesus Christ) **are yes, and in him** (Jesus Christ) **Amen, to the glory of God by us** (2 Cor. 1:20).

When a believer lays hands on you in Jesus' name and earnestly prays for your healing, believe the word of God; believe that Jesus spoke the truth when He said, **They shall recover**.

It is written, **They shall recover**; and in 2 Corinthians 1:24, the Bible says, **By faith you stand**. Faith in God's word always brings the answer. Thank Him for healing from the very moment that the hands of believers are laid on you in Jesus' name.

Chapter 9

SPECIAL MIRACLES BY FAITH

The people in Asia believed that, by taking cloths from Paul's body, sick people would be healed and evil spirits would depart from those possessed of them.

God did special miracles by the hands of Paul: so that from his body were brought to the sick handkerchiefs or aprons, and the diseases departed from them, and the evil spirits went out from them.
Acts 19:11-12

God is no respecter of persons. This ministry of sending forth cloths from God's servants is still in effect today, and thousands of miracles are taking place through this simple act of faith.

When the sick receive these cloths and lay them on their bodies in faith, as though the servant of God had laid hands on their bodies and had prayed, the same results will follow today.

When Paul sent these cloths and aprons to the sick, they were laid on sick bodies with the same faith that they would have exercised had Paul come personally and laid hands on them and ministered to them.

Sometimes we send cloths, in the name of Jesus, to people whom we cannot visit personally. If a sick person will believe God's promises and will consider that when such a cloth is laid on their sick body, it is as though we had come and prayed for them and had laid our hands on them personally, and if the sick person will believe then that God has heard the prayer and granted healing, the sickness will leave.

We receive testimonies almost daily from those who have been healed through this act of faith.

Chapter 10

HEALING IN REDEMPTION

Surely He has borne our griefs [sicknesses and diseases], **and carried our sorrows** [pains].

But he was wounded for our transgressions, he was bruised for our iniquities: the chastisement of our peace was upon him; and with his stripes we are healed.

Isaiah 53:4-5

First Peter 2:24 says: **Who his own self bore our sins in his own body on the tree, that we, being dead to sins should live in righteousness; by whose stripes you were healed.**

By these scriptures we know that healing for the body is provided in the same redemption as salvation for the spirit. In redemption, there is both physical and spiritual healing. If you are saved, you should be healed. If you are healed, you should be saved.

Healing Is Part of Salvation

When you realize that healing is part of your personal salvation, you need not **call for elders**; you need not have **hands laid on you**; you no longer need to **ask in Jesus' name** for what you already possess; neither do you need to have **two** [believers] **agree in prayer for you**. You accept Christ's life for both body and spirit.

You know that you are free from the bondage of both sickness and sin.

You see your substitute, Jesus Christ, made sick and sinful for you. You come to know that neither sin nor sickness can ever be laid on you again because Jesus bore them all on the cross for you.

You comprehend the truth of the statement: **Himself took our infirmities** [weaknesses], **and bore our sicknesses** [diseases] (Matt. 8:17).

You know that Jesus, your substitute, has delivered your body from sickness as well as your spirit from sin.

You see your sicknesses, as well as your sins, laid on Jesus at Calvary; and you know that if Jesus bore your infirmities and your sicknesses, you no longer need to bear them.

If you need to bear them, then it was useless for Jesus to bear them; but since He has borne them and the Bible says they were yours then certainly you do not have to bear them.

49

Christians do not need to be sick. God wants them to be well and strong.

See your sins forgiven and your sicknesses healed. See deliverance for your body as well as for your spirit.

Begin to sing with David: **Bless the Lord, O my soul, and forget not all his benefits.** [Many have forgotten some of the benefits of redemption; David had not.] **Who forgives all your iniquities; who heals all your diseases** (Ps. 103:2-3).

Complete Deliverance

David says **forgives all** and **heals all** in the same breath.

At last you have come to know why Jesus said: **Which is easier to say, Your sins are forgiven you; or to say, Arise, and take up your bed, and walk?** (Mark 2:9).

At last the joy of a full salvation has become real to you. You realize complete deliverance.

You join with Peter in saying: **Who his own self bore our sins in his own body on the tree; by whose stripes you were healed.**

You understand that it was all accomplished in your redemption. You are a free person. No more sin — no more sickness. Both have been taken away by your substitute.

It is when you come to know these vital truths that your sickness begins to melt away, your deformed limbs begin to straighten. You find yourself freed in body as well as in spirit.

No Glory in Suffering

You no longer take your place with Job of the Old Testament, thinking you must suffer sickness because Job suffered. You have learned that you are living in the post-Calvary epoch under grace and truth which sets you free from the curse of the law (Deut. 28:58-61).

A minister told me some time ago: "Every time I pray for the sick, either myself, my wife, or my child becomes ill." Then he went on to tell me that he believed he must have these tests to prove his faith; that it was his duty to prove himself faithful in sickness in order for God to use him in the healing of others who were sick.

I asked him if he felt that he should prove himself faithful in sin in order for God to use him in preaching salvation to sinners.

Then I told him: *The difference between your preaching and mine is that you are preaching and believing that you must suffer and be faithful before you can tell others that they can be healed. I tell the people that Jesus has already suffered for them and for me — that, therefore, we all can enjoy the redemption which He has provided for us — that Jesus is the substitute, not me.*

Righteousness — A Certainty

E.W. Kenyon says:

Jesus bore our infirmities, our diseases and our sicknesses, and what He bore, we do not need to bear. What He took upon Himself, we do not need to suffer.

Always remember: Satan cannot legally lay on us what God laid on Jesus.

Christ became sick with OUR diseases that we might be healed. He knew no sickness until He became sick for us.

The object of Christ's sin-bearing was to make righteous all those who would believe in Him as their sinbearer. The object of His disease-bearing was to make well all those who would believe in Him as their disease-bearer.

Christ's sin-bearing made righteousness a certainty to the new creation. He took our sins, and so made us righteous.

His disease-bearing made healing a certainty to the new creation. He took our diseases, and so made us well; He took our infirmities, and so made us strong; and He now trades us His success for our failures.

Disease Is Cruel

Disease makes slaves of the people who care for the sick. The loved ones who are up day and night, working over the sick ones, are robbed of joy and rest. Sickness is not of love, and God is love.

Disease steals health; it steals happiness; it steals money that we need for other things. Disease is our enemy; it is a robber. Look at what it has stolen from the tuberculosis patient. It came during youth and has burdened the family; filled them with anxiety and doubt, fears and pains, and robbed the patient of faith.

Do not tell anyone that disease is the will of God. It is the will of hate; it is the will of Satan. If disease has become the will of love, then love is turned into hate. If disease is the will of God, then heaven will be filled with sickness.

Jesus was the exact image of the Father (Heb. 1:3), and **He went about healing all the sick** (Acts 10:38).

Disease and sickness are never the will of the Father. To believe they are, is to be deceived by the adversary. If healing had not been included in the plan of redemption, then it would never have been placed in the great substitutionary chapter of Isaiah 53.

Faith Becomes Natural

This is the deliverance we desire for you to find as you read this book. Act on it, and you will discover new health returning to your body.

Faith in God's word is never ignored by the Father. Instead, it always brings His complete answer. This is the faith He longs to see you exercise. It will become a part of you. It will become as natural to your spirit as seeing and hearing is to your physical body.

God said, **I am the Lord who heals you** (Ex. 15:26). If three million people could believe it and find perfect health and strength under the law, cannot we, who are living under grace, mercy, and truth be the healthy body of Christ?

Chapter 11

BASIS FOR STEADFAST FAITH

A man came to me asking that we pray for him to be healed. He had been deaf in one ear for over twenty years.

He seemed to be very uncertain regarding his healing, because as he put it: "I've been prayed for by the greatest people of faith in our country during the last twenty years, and I have never received help." Then he asked, "Why cannot my ear be healed?"

"It can," I replied, "if you will believe."

"But they have all told me that," he said, "and I have never received help from any of them."

"My friend," I interrupted, "do you think God is willing to heal a fellow like you?"

"I don't know," he answered; then added, "I know that if it is His will to do it, He is able, but well, I guess that's just one of those things we aren't supposed to know."

I said, "That is why you have never been healed. You have never read the word of God for yourself, nor have you received the faith that has been taught to you. You do not know whether or not God has said He would heal you; therefore, you do not know whether or not it is His will to heal you."

I asked, "Do you believe it is God's will to keep His promise?"

"Of course," he replied.

"Well," I said, "He has promised to heal you; and if I can quote you His promise, then you should believe Him and be healed right here and now."

God Included You

I quoted a few scriptures regarding the healing of our bodies, which are applicable to everyone individually, such as **I am the Lord who heals *you*** (Ex. 15:26), which was spoken to over three million people; **By whose stripes *you* were healed** (1 Peter 2:24), and **Is *any* sick among you? let that person call** (James 5:14). Then I asked, "Now, in the face of all of these scriptures, which are statements made to all who will believe them, do you think God included you?"

"Yes," he said, "I guess He did."

"Well then," I asked, "is God willing to heal you, seeing that He has made provision for the healing of every sickness and every disease among all the people?"

"Yes," he said, very firmly. "I do believe healing is for me tonight. I have never seen it like this before."

There seemed to be a glitter of faith in his eyes when he saw that God's word was for him personally.

I knew the circumstances were right for prayer on his behalf. I had hardly touched his deaf ear before sound burst into it and he could hear me as well with that ear as with the other.

When, at last, he knew what God had said regarding all sickness and disability, and dared to step out on that word, declaring himself as being included in the *any* of James 5:14, the *you* of Exodus 15:26, and the *our* of Matthew 8:17, then what God's word had said was accomplished in him. He was healed.

That illustrates so well the purpose for which this book is written: that you may see that the promises in God's word are for you and that, realizing this, you will act upon God's word and expect Him to make it good in your life.

What Faith Is

Now faith is the substance of things hoped for, the evidence of things not seen (Heb. 11:1). This is sometimes quoted: Faith is the title-deed for things you have hoped for, the putting to proof of things unseen," or "Faith is the title-deed to the property you know you possess, even though you have not yet seen it."

One of the most helpful and enlightening expressions of faith is this: *Faith is expecting God to do what you know He has said in His word that He will do.* Faith is believing that God speaks the truth.

God has never asked that we exercise faith for something that He has not first promised to do for us.

One writer said, "God deals with His children like this: First, He gives us a promise. Then when that promise creates faith which produces action, He fulfills it!"

Always remember: God never asks us to believe He will do something for us unless He has promised to do it. Because of this fact, Paul has stated, **Faith comes by hearing the word of God** (Rom. 10:17). How could faith possibly come any other way?

How am I to know that a millionaire will make me a gift of a thousand dollars unless he says that he will do so? His ability to do it would not prove his willingness. I must have his promise before I can expect such a gift from him.

The only way for your daughter to know that she will receive a new dress tomorrow is for you to promise it to her. She believes that you will not fail to keep your word; yet there is the possibility that you could die before tomorrow; or that you may not have been honest with her. But not so with the Lord.

Balaam, a true prophet of the Lord, said, **God is not a man, that he should lie; neither the son of man, that he should repent: has he said, and shall he not do it? or has he spoken, and shall he not make it good?** (Num. 23:19).

Christ the Healer

F. F. Bosworth, who wrote one of the most outstanding books ever to be published on the subject of divine healing, begins with these words:

Before you can have a steadfast faith for the healing of your body, you must be rid of all uncertainty concerning God's will in the matter. Appropriating faith cannot go beyond your knowledge of the revealed will of God.

Before attempting to exercise faith for healing, you need to know what the scriptures plainly teach; that it is just as much God's will to heal the body as it is God's will to heal the spirit. It is only by knowing that God promises what you are seeking that all uncertainty can be removed and a steadfast faith can be possible.

His promises are each a revelation of what God is eager to do for us. Until we know what God's will is, there is nothing on which to base our faith.

Mr. Bosworth then goes on to say:

Jesus said, **The word is the seed** (Luke 8:11). It is the seed of divine life. Until you are sure from God's word that it is His will to heal you, you are trying to reap a harvest where no seed has been planted. It would be impossible for a farmer to have faith for a harvest before seed was planted.

God Is Faithful

It is not God's will that there be a harvest without the planting of seed — without His will being known and acted upon. Jesus said, **You shall know the truth, and the truth shall make you free** (John 8:32). Freedom from sickness comes from knowing the truth. God does nothing without His word.

He sent his word and it healed them are the words of the Holy Spirit (Ps. 107:20 FB). All his work is done in faithfulness to His promises.

If you are sick, knowledge that it is God's will to heal you is the seed which is to be planted in your mind and heart. And it is not planted there until it is known and received and trusted. You cannot become a Christian until you know that it is God's will to save you. It is the word of God planted and watered and steadfastly trusted, which heals both spirit and body. The seed must remain planted and be kept watered before it can produce its harvest.

Able and Willing

For you to say, "I believe the Lord is able to heal me," before you know from God's word that He is willing to heal you, is like a farmer saying, "I believe God is able to give me a harvest," without any seed being planted and watered.

God cannot regenerate your spirit before you know His will in the matter, because salvation is by faith — that is, by trusting the known will of God. Being healed is being saved in a physical sense.

Praying for healing with the faith-destroying words, "If it be your will," is not planting the seed; it is destroying the seed. **The prayer of faith** which heals the sick is to follow (not precede) the planting of the seed (the word) upon which faith is based.

This is the gospel which the Holy Spirit says **is the power of God to salvation**, in all its phases, both physical and spiritual. And all the gospel is for **every creature** and for **all nations**. The gospel does not leave a person in uncertainty praying, "If it be Your will"; it tells you what God's will is.

The Holy Spirit's words, **Himself bore our sicknesses** (Matt. 8:17) are just as truly a part of the gospel as His words, **Who his own self bore our sins in his own body on the tree** (1 Peter 2:24).

Neither the spiritual nor the physical phase of the gospel is to be applied by prayer alone. Seed is powerless until it is planted.

Instead of saying, "Pray for me," many should first say, "Teach me God's word, so that I can intelligently cooperate with Him for my recovery." We must know what the benefits of redemption are before we can appropriate them by faith.

Purpose To Be Whole

David specified, **Who forgives all your iniquities, who heals all your diseases.**

After being sufficiently enlightened, our attitude toward sickness should be the same as our attitude toward sin. Our purpose to have our body healed should be as definite as our purpose to have our spirit healed. We should not ignore any part of the gospel.

Our substitute, Jesus, bore both our sins and our sicknesses that we might be delivered from them. Christ's bearing of our sins and

sicknesses is surely a valid reason for trusting Him now for deliverance from both.

When in prayer, we definitely commit to God the forgiveness of our
sins, we are to believe, on the authority of His word, that our prayer is
heard. We are to do the same when praying for healing.

**Attend to my words; incline your ear to my sayings. Let them not
depart from your eyes; keep them in the midst of your heart. For they
are life to those that find them, and health to all their flesh.**
                                                          Proverbs 4:20-22

In this comprehensive passage, God tells us exactly how to **attend** to
His words. He says, **Let them not depart from your eyes**. Instead of
having your eyes on the symptoms and being occupied with them, let
not God's words **depart from your eyes**; that is, look at them continually and, like Abraham, be strong in faith by looking at the promises of
God and at nothing else.

Good Seed Grows

When we attend to God's words by not letting them depart from
before our eyes and by keeping them in the middle of our hearts, the
seed is in **good ground**, the kind of ground in which Jesus says, **it
brings forth fruit**, and where Paul says, **it works effectively**.

When the farmer puts seed into the ground, he does not dig it up
every day to see how it is doing. He believes that the seed has begun
its work.

Why not have the same faith in the imperishable seed, Christ's
words, which He says are **spirit and life**, and believe that they are
already doing their work, without waiting for visual evidence.

When your eyes are on your symptoms and your mind is occupied
with them more than with God's word, you have planted the wrong
kind of seed for the harvest that you desire. You have in your mind
seeds of doubt. You are trying to raise one kind of crop from another
kind of seed. It is impossible to sow tares and reap wheat. Your symptoms may point you to death, but God's word points you to life, and
you cannot look in these opposite directions at the same time.

After you plant seed, you believe it is growing even before you see
it. This is faith, which is **the evidence of things not seen**. In Christ, we
have perfect evidence for faith.

Any person can get rid of their doubts by looking steadfastly and
only at the evidence which God has given for our faith. Saying only
what God says will produce and increase faith. This will make it easier
to believe than to doubt; the evidences for faith are much stronger than
those for doubting. Don't doubt your faith; doubt your doubts, for
they are unreliable.

God Is Waiting on You

A lady said to me, "Mr. Osborn, I would give anything to have my mother healed. I know God is able to completely restore her, and I believe I have the faith that God would heal her if I only knew it was His will to do so."

I asked her, "Do you believe it is God's will to save a sinner?"

"Oh yes," she replied.

"How do you know?" I asked.

"Well," she answered, "if for no other reason, the golden text of the Bible John 3:16 proves that, for it says, *Whoever* **believes in him, shall not perish, but have everlasting life.**"

She was willing to believe that God would save the vilest sinner because she could quote *one* Bible verse which promised what she believed. I asked her: "Do you not believe it is God's will to heal your mother?"

"Well, I do not know that we can tell," was her reply.

"Will God keep His promise?" I asked her.

"Yes, of course, He will," she said.

"Well," I answered, "the same Bible that invites **whoever** to be healed of sin also invites **any** to be healed of sickness."(James 5:14.)

Then I continued, "The same Christ, who always forgave sins, always healed sicknesses. It was the same deliverer who said, **Arise, and take up your bed and walk** (Mark 2:9), who said, **Son, be of good cheer; your sins are forgiven you**" (Matt. 9:2).

I continued, "The same scripture that says, **Who forgives all your iniquities,** also says, **Who heals all your diseases** (Ps. 103:3). The same scripture that says, **Who his own self bore our sins in his own body** also says, **By whose stripes you were healed** " (1 Peter 2:24).

Christ came to rid us of sickness as well as sin. He took our sicknesses as well as our sins; He redeemed us from one, the same as from the other.

I told the woman, "Both sin and sickness are hateful in God's sight. Jesus Christ always defeated both, while here on earth, and He still wants to do the same. If you can be so sure that God is willing to save the sinner, then you can be just as sure that He is willing to heal your mother who is sick."

Faith Within Reach

The woman was amazed and thrilled beyond measure at the simplicity of the word of God, and was very happy to discover that Christ is healer for all, just as He is savior for all.

Faith is only believing that God will do what He said in His word that He would do. This fact places faith within the reach of the simplest child.

When once we conclude that the written word is God's revealed will to us for everything that He longs to do for us, then we will treasure that word and stand upon it, fully expecting God to make it good, without wavering, doubting, or worrying.

Healing From Heaven

Lilian B. Yeomans, M.D., begins chapter two of her wonderful book, *Healing from Heaven*, with these words:

I believe that one of the greatest hindrances to healing is the absence of certain, definite knowledge as to God's will. There is lurking in most everyone, who has not properly studied God's word, a feeling that God may not be willing, that we have to persuade Him to heal us.

People often say, "I know that God is able; He has the power to heal me if He only will — like the leper in the eighth chapter of Matthew, who said to Jesus, **If you will, you can make me clean.**"

Many of us have been taught to pray, "If it be Your will, heal me." That wasn't the way David prayed; he cried in Psalm 6:2, **Have mercy on me, O Lord, for I am weak: O Lord, heal me, for my bones are vexed.** Then he adds in the ninth verse, **The Lord has heard my supplication; the Lord will receive my prayer.** There are no "ifs" or "buts" in David's prayer.

The prophet Jeremiah, too, had no doubt about God's will as to healing, for he cried, **Heal me, O Lord, and I shall be healed; save me, and I shall be saved** (Jer. 17:14).

And we, God's people of this day, should be free from doubt regarding our Father's will for our bodies, for it is as clearly revealed in the word as is His will concerning our spiritual salvation.

His Works Not in Vain

In a sense, the whole Bible is a revelation, not only of God's willingness to heal our spiritual ailments, but our physical ones also. One of His covenant names is Jehovah-Rapha, the Lord who heals, and He is also the changeless, healing, health-bestowing, life-giving Lord, undisputed Sovereign over all the powers of the universe.

Jesus is the exact image of the Father, the perfect expression of God and His holy will. He could say, **You who have seen me have seen my Father also,** and He declared that His works were not His own, but the

Father's that sent Him. He healed all who came to Him, never refusing a single individual. You cannot find a case where He said, "It is not My will to heal you," or "It is necessary for you to suffer for disciplinary purposes." His answer was always, **I will**, and this fact settles forever what God's will is in regard to sickness and health.

Salvation Includes Physical Healing

The word salvation, if properly understood, shows beyond a shadow of a doubt that healing for the body is always the will of God for any and all who have accepted Jesus Christ as Savior.

Webster tells us that *salvation* is deliverance from sin and sin's penalty. A prominent part of that penalty is sickness. (Deut. 28:15-61.)

The word saved is the Greek word *sozo*, which, when properly translated, carries the meaning of physical and spiritual healing. It is the same word Jesus used when He said to the leper: **Your faith has made you whole** (Luke 17:19). It is the same word used in Luke 8:36: **He that was possessed of the devils was healed.**

The word salvation is an all-inclusive word which means full deliverance, complete safety, preservation, and soundness — spiritually, mentally, and physically. What a miracle — salvation from sin and from sickness.

Salvation Is Healing

Dr. John G. Lake, a great missionary evangelist in South Africa at the turn of the 20th century, had a ministry which resulted in the healing of thousands. In an article entitled, *The Dominion of a Christian,* under the subhead of *Divine Healing Not Something Separate from Salvation,* Dr. Lake writes these words:

One of the difficulties concerning healing that God has to remove from the human mind, is this wretched thing that often prevails in the best of Christian circles where healing is taught and practiced the idea that divine healing is something disassociated or separate from Christ's salvation. It is not.

Healing is simply the salvation of Jesus Christ having its divine action in one's body, the same as it had its divine action in one's spirit. When Christ healed the body, He healed the spirit also. All a person needs to do is receive the Lord by faith. Doing this, one's defective eyes receive sight, the dormant mind becomes active, and the sick body is healed.

Dr. Lake wrote, further:

I want to fix this thought in your minds. The healing of an individual is God's demonstration to that soul that their sins have been forgiven; and so James states, after affirming that the prayer of faith shall save the sick, **that if the sick person has committed sins, they shall be forgiven.**

If only the victim of sin and sickness, who has come to Jesus for deliverance, will have faith enough to believe it, he or she will be free in body, free in spirit, healed within and healed without.

The word of God is written so that we can understand and be sure what the will of God is.

Our Enjoyable Freedom

From Genesis to Revelation it especially emphasizes one thing: That the will of God is to free the body, mind and spirit from sin, and the effects or penalty of sin which are disease and death.

When the will of God is completed in the human race, sin, sickness, and death will have disappeared.

The beginning of immortality is when God breathes His life into you and me, and our spirits become the recipients of eternal life in Jesus Christ.

How simple it should be for people who have this confidence and faith in the Lord Jesus Christ and His salvation to add faith for the body as well as for the spirit. It works identically the same for sickness as for sin. Had this truth been preached, the sickness question would have vanished, once and for all, when the sin question was taken care of.

One of the most enjoyable freedoms in the world is the mental and spiritual freedom that comes with escape from the bondage of fear. The fear of sickness need never be tolerated by the redeemed, recreated, and delivered child of Jehovah-Rapha, the Lord, the Great Physician or Healer.

It might be thought that this truth has been somewhat overemphasized, but if you could stand by our sides as we proclaim these truths and hear the warnings — "Beware of false prophets who will deceive you with miracles"; "It may not be the Father's will to heal you"; "Sickness is often His divine blessing"; "Healing is not for today"; and so forth then you would understand why we underscore the fact that according to God's word, it is always His will to heal those who will obey Him, believe Him, and act boldly on His word.

Chapter 12

LOOKING AT GOD'S WORD

To understand what God's will is regarding our sickness or infirmity, let us look at some of God's promises to us in His word.

To the children of Israel on their way to the promised land, God said, **I am the Lord who heals you** (Ex. 15:26). In this statement, He gave them one of His redemptive names. He said, *I am Jehovah-Rapha,* that is, *I am the Lord, your physician, your healer.* What a wonderful, universal promise this is regarding physical or mental trouble of any kind.

There were some three million to whom Jehovah-Rapha gave that promise. That it was meant for every one of them is proven by the fact that **there was not one feeble person among their tribes** (Ps. 105:37).

Remembering His Benefits

Remember, the word of God is a revelation of God's will for every one of us.

Note the psalmist's praise in which he says, **Bless the Lord, O my soul: and all that is within me, bless his holy name. Forget not all his benefits: who forgives all your iniquities; who heals all your diseases** (Ps. 103:1-3).

As long as Jesus Christ will forgive all of our sins, He will heal all of our diseases. As long as He is a sin-forgiver, He will be a sickness-healer. Both sin and sickness are hateful in His sight. He was, is, and always will be as willing to heal all who are sick as to save all who are sinful.

The benefits which the Lord was to bring to the world, says David, were *salvation to the sinful and healing to the sick.*

Forget Not All His Benefits

Many have forgotten the benefits of **Who heals all your diseases**. The benefits of healing for those who are diseased have been forgotten through the traditional preaching and teaching of those who have brought to us the traditions of men rather than the truth that sets people free.

Every promise of God in His word is a revelation to us of what He is eager to do for us. His promises to heal all reveal His will to heal everyone. Had He not promised to heal all diseases, then in some instances He might not be willing to heal. But seeing that He has promised to heal all our diseases, then it is His will to heal all who ask Him.

Believe His word. Accept it as a revelation of His will for you. Act accordingly, and healing will be yours.

Healed With His Stripes

Consider the words of Isaiah when, in the 53rd chapter of his prophecy, verses 4 and 5, he says, **Surely he has borne our griefs** [sicknesses], **and carried our sorrows** [pains]. **He** [Jesus] **was wounded for our transgressions, and with his stripes we are healed**.

There can he no doubting the truth of Isaiah's statements because **When the even was come, they brought to him** [Jesus] **many that were possessed with devils: and he cast out the spirits with his word, and healed all that were sick: that it might be fulfilled which was spoken by Isaiah the prophet, saying Himself took our infirmities, and bore our sicknesses** (Matt. 8:16-17).

If Christ has borne our sicknesses and pains (Is. 53:4), and if He took our infirmities and bore our sicknesses (Matt. 8:17), that proves that we need not bear them. He, as our substitute, has borne them in our place, so we are set free.

God's word reveals His will for us. If He wanted some of us to be sick, then Jesus would not have borne our sicknesses and diseases for us; because, in so doing, He would have liberated us from the very thing God wanted some of us to bear.

But since Christ could say, **Lo I come to do your will, O God** (Heb. 10:9), then when He bore our sicknesses and our diseases and suffered the stripes by which we are healed, we have the will of God revealed concerning the healing of our bodies.

Faith steps out on that word, and the effects of perfect healing are soon manifested in our bodies.

Commanded To Heal

Jesus Christ was always as ready and willing to heal the sick as He was to forgive the sinful. So many seem to think we, who are sharing the gospel of healing for the sick, are off on what the critic and unbeliever often term a side issue of the Bible.

I remind myself that Jesus spent more of His three years of ministry healing the sick and casting out devils than in any other phase of His ministry. There are more cases recorded of His having healed the sick than there are of His having forgiven the sinful.

Every person whom Jesus sent to preach the gospel was commanded by Him to do exactly as He had done while here on earth; namely, heal the sick, raise the dead, cast out devils, cleanse the lepers, and freely give (Matt. 10:1, 7-8; Mark 3:14-15; 6:7,13; 16:15-18; Luke 9:1,6; 10:9; John 14:12-14; 15:7).

The same commission in which Jesus commanded His disciples to **Go to all the world, and preach the gospel to every creature,** adding that **the one that believes and is baptized shall be saved,** also commands us saying, **they** [believers] **shall lay hands on the sick, and they** [the sick] **shall recover** (Mark 16:15-18).

As long as it is scriptural to preach water baptism and salvation by believing on the Lord Jesus Christ, it is also scriptural to lay hands on the sick so that they may recover.

It is strange to me that so many say that the days of miraculous healing of the sick are past, but they still baptize in water those who profess to believe on the Lord Jesus Christ. Both are in the same commission. I wonder who told them that the days of laying hands on the sick for healing are over and that, therefore, the sick should no longer expect to be healed by the power of God?

The word of God says, **They shall lay hands on the sick, and they shall recover.** That reveals to us the fact that it is God's will for the sick to recover. If it were not, He would not have said, **They shall recover.**

Faith is believing that God will do what you know He said in His word that He would do. If you do not know what He said about healing the sick, then you will not be able to have faith for healing. But when you read God's will (the Bible), it is easy to believe that He will do what He said He will do.

Since God said He will heal the sick (Ex. 15:26; Ps. 103:3; 1 Peter 2:24), then He is willing to heal the sick. Since He is willing to heal the sick, then He will heal the sick, Since He will heal the sick, then He will heal the sick now. In fact, what He wills to do, He would rather do now than later. He would rather do it today than tomorrow. **Now is the accepted time; now is the day of salvation** (2 Cor. 6:2).

Religious Forgery

There are always some who dare to re-word the will. This is really committing forgery, since no will may be changed after the death of the one who made it.

Before leaving this world, Jesus left us His Father's will regarding the sinful and the sick, by stating, **They that believe and are baptized shall be saved, and they** [believers] **shall lay hands on the sick and they shall recover.**

Some may cheat you out of the benefits of redemption by misinterpreting God's will to you; but you can read the will for yourself. If you are in need of healing, do not accept the ideas of those who tell you that you must suffer for God's glory.

Read the will. Take advantage of it. Claim its benefits. Use your rights declared in it. All heaven stands ready to enforce every covenant right of yours, when you dare to be bold in claiming them. Satan is a liar and the father of lies. He delights in blinding men and women to their covenant rights and to their redemptive benefits. But Jesus said, **You shall know the truth, and the truth shall make you free** (John 8:32).

Believe His promises right now. No time is better than now for God to do for you what He has promised to do.

Chapter 13

THE NATURE OF FAITH

Many people get the wrong idea about the nature of faith in God's word. They imagine that faith is for almost anyone except themselves. They think that, in order to exercise faith, one must wonderfully and rigorously exercise the mind, to strain and worry or go through certain rituals in order to appropriate the promises of God and secure His blessings.

Many will say they believe the word of God, but they are still sick. They will say, "I have all the faith in the world; but until I see some change, I do not believe I am healed. I refuse to claim something I do not have. 1 believe that if a person is healed, they will know it."

This is the wrong idea of the nature of faith.

There are just two platforms on which to stand: One is belief; the other, unbelief. Either the word of God is true, or it is not. God will either do what He has promised, or He will not. His promises are either reliable, or they are not.

Will you believe that the word of God is true? Or will you believe that it is false? If you believe that God is truthful, then you need not hesitate to obey and act upon His promises, regardless of whether or not you can see the immediate results.

Faith: A Decisive Act

Genuine faith in God and in His word is stepping out upon what He has said, regardless of what one sees or feels or senses in the natural. Faith is a decisive act, depending only upon God's word. Faith ignores every natural symptom or evidence which is contrary to what God's word states.

When you pray the prayer of faith and call upon God for what you need, then you leave the results with Him, knowing that, according to His word, it shall come to pass.

You know what God has promised in His word; you do not seek after "signs and wonders" in order to verify God's promises, or to give evidence that He will fulfill His promises.

You know that the word of God says, **These signs shall follow them that believe,** not those who have to *see* something before they will believe (Mark 16:17).

David said, **I had believed to see** (Ps. 27:13). He did not say, "I had to *see* before I would believe." Yet many are demanding a sign of healing before they will believe that they have received healing.

Those who believe they have received healing according to the word of God, invariably *see* the healing manifested in their bodies.

Believe the Word of God

Suppose a person, bound hand and foot and cast into prison, were to make an appeal for pardon; and the jailer were to come and present the paper showing that a pardon had been granted. Would the prisoner feel grateful toward those who had granted the pardon?

The jailer reads the pardon, takes off the fetters, unlocks the prison doors, throws them open, and says,

"You are free: go your way in peace."

But the prisoner says: "I know the pardon says I am free, and I believe every word of it, but I am in prison."

"The doors are open. Walk out," says the jailer.

"I know the doors are open, and I know I would be free if I were out; but I am not out."

"Well, walk out," persists the jailer. "Do you not believe that what the pardon says is true?"

"Yes, I believe every word of it, but it seems as if I never will get out of here."

A pardon would be of no benefit to such a person. By choice, the prisoner remains in prison instead of acting on the authority of the pardon.

The gospel of healing for the body is of no benefit to those who will not act upon it.

The scripture, **I am the Lord who heals you**, is of no value to those who will not accept that promise of God and act upon it.

Who heals all your diseases is of no benefit to the person who will not step out on that statement and act his or her faith.

With his stripes you were healed is worthless to you if you refuse to believe that all of your sicknesses were borne by Christ. You refuse to believe that you are healed because you can still feel a pain, so you say, "I know that does not mean me; it cannot mean that I was healed because I am sick." So you refuse to believe the word of God because of what you can see or feel, forgetting that the very nature of faith is **the substance of things hoped for, the evidence of things not seen** (Heb. 11:1).

Act on the Word

A lady in the state of New York, who had been in bed with tuberculosis for several months was musing on the scriptures one afternoon.

She was a wonderful Christian, but had never heard the truth about divine healing.

As she lay in bed meditating on the second chapter of I Peter, she came to verse 24: **Who his own self bore our sins in his own body on the tree.**

As she read this, she wept for gratitude for the salvation that Jesus had provided for her. She rejoiced because He had borne her sins and because of the wonderful experience of salvation she had enjoyed.

She knew that when her tuberculosis had run its course, she would be ready to die.

While rejoicing over this great mercy of forgiveness, she decided to read further: **By whose stripes you *were* healed.**

She looked back at the first part of that verse and noticed that Jesus had borne her sins. He had already done it. It was in the past. It was over, and so she was saved. She knew it. It was real to her. No one could make her doubt it.

But what about these other words in the same verse? **By whose stripes you *were* healed.** Could it he true? Did it mean what it said? Yes, she thought, it must be true. It is the word of God.

Promise Turned to Practice

"Mother," she called in a voice weakened by the ravages of tuberculosis, "did you know that God has said in His word that I was healed?"

Her mother replied, "Why, dear, what do you mean?"

"Look here," the daughter said, with tears of joy flowing down her cheeks. "Listen to this. The Bible says, **By whose stripes you were healed.** That must mean me. It's wonderful! I never saw that before. Just look at it! **By whose stripes you were healed.** Mother, it has already been done. I'm healed! Get my clothes. Bring them here. I'm healed. Oh, this is wonderful!"

The mother did everything she could to calm her daughter and to keep her in bed. She avoided bringing her clothes to her.

But the daughter asked, "Haven't you taught us to believe all of the word of God? Haven't you brought us up to believe every word of the Bible?" and the mother could not control her daughter's joy.

The former tuberculosis patient arose by herself, put on her clothes, left her bedroom, shouted through the house, and was completely healed. In less than three weeks, she was normal in weight and was completely restored.

What had happened? She had come to treat the word of God as a direct revelation of what He was eager to do for her. When she saw what He had said in His word and believed it, it produced faith: **Faith**

comes by hearing the word of God. God's healing power went through her body and she was delivered.

Rev. E. E. Byrum relates the following incident that occurred in his life around 1885 when the ministry of healing was almost unknown among Christians:

Shortly after the Lord called me to work for Him, I learned a very precious lesson. There was much sickness in the community in which I lived.

Three of our family had been stricken down with fever and passed through a severe siege of sickness. I soon felt the dread disease taking hold of me. I withstood it for several days, but was finally overpowered by it.

Lying in bed for a few hours, burning with fever and suffering excruciating pain, I began to commune earnestly with the Lord. I told Him that He had called me to a ministry, which in my present condition I was unable to fulfill.

The Move Is Yours

As there were no elders to call upon, I began to refer my case to the Lord and to quote His many wonderful promises, among which was John 15:7: **If you live in me, and my words live in you, you shall ask what you will, and it shall be done to you.**

I examined my consecration and then asked Him to search me. I was willing to do anything for Him, and I said, "Lord, I am living in You, and Your words are living in me, so the promise is mine. I give my case entirely into Your hands and I pray You, heal me."

Then I waited for the work to be done, but no change came.

Finally I said, "Lord, why am I not healed?"

The answer came at once: "Take Me at My word and arise."

I said, "Amen, Lord, I will." And without hesitation I began to get out of bed.

It seemed as if my head would burst with pain, but in my weakness I began to dress myself.

When half-dressed, a slight change came over me and, dropping upon my knees, I thanked the Lord for it. After dressing, and giving thanks again and again, I was much better and walked into another room declaring that the Lord had healed me.

Within twenty minutes, the fever had entirely left my body. Immediately, I went to work and was well from that very hour.

I am sure that had I lain in bed and refused to act on the Lord's word, I would have had to pass through a long siege of sickness. To God be all the glory.

It taught me a very valuable lesson of trusting Him and His word. I found that when faith is acted, in spite of every contradictory sense, God will always fulfill His word, and make it good to us.

Real faith is taking God at His word and stepping out upon His promise with all confidence and sincerity, without a doubt or fear.

Divine Healing for All by Faith

Real faith cannot exist, nor can you claim healing for your body, until you know that God wants to heal you. How can you know this? Read God's will as it is revealed in the Bible. You may know that He wills to heal everyone who is sick in exactly the same way that you may know that He wills to save everyone who is sinful.

The very minute you realize that the promise of God to heal all who are sick pertains to you personally, then your faith is ready to act and healing will come.

Because of so much wrong teaching regarding this great mercy of healing, many have failed to boldly claim the promise as theirs personally and have, consequently, failed to receive the healing which was clearly God's will for them to enjoy.

Chapter 14
SOME UNSCRIPTURAL TEACHINGS

What About Afflictions?

Many are the afflictions of the righteous: but the Lord delivers them out of them all.

Psalm 34:19

Because of teachers and preachers who misinterpret this scripture, making it applicable to sickness and disease, Christians have often forfeited their covenant rights to physical healing. They have remained subservient to diseases, conceding to the will of Satan rather than identifying with the will of God.

This verse does not say, "Many are the sicknesses and physical disabilities of the righteous." It says, **Many are the afflictions of the righteous.**

The word affliction, used in this case (in the original text), has nothing to do with sickness or physical disability. It means trials, hardships, persecutions or temptations.)

It would be unreasonable to say that Christ has borne our sicknesses and taken our infirmities; that by His stripes we were healed; that He heals all our diseases; but also to say that there are many sicknesses which God expects us to bear, until such time arrives or circumstances develop when He wills to deliver us.

The message of substitution is that Christ bore our sins so that we need not bear them, but be saved from them. In the same way, Christ bore our sicknesses so that we need not bear them, but be healed of them.

Christ did not bear our trials, persecutions, hardships, or troubles; but He did bear our sins and sicknesses. He bore them so that we need not bear them. That is why He is our substitute. He took our place. What He has borne, we are forever set free from if we will only believe that He did it for us.

Until this becomes personal, you will never benefit from it. The moment you believe that Christ bore your sins, you can be saved. The moment you believe that He bore your sicknesses, you can be healed.

Others quote James 5:13: **Is any among you** *afflicted?* **let the afflicted one pray**. They have decided that their long-standing physical disability is an affliction. So they go through life praying, instead of being healed.

This word affliction has the same meaning as is used in the verse mentioned above. It has no reference to sickness, disease or physical disability. It has to do with hardships, sufferings, trials and persecutions.

"If you are persecuted," James says, "pray." He does not say, "Call for the elders and ask them to pray for God to remove your troubles." But he does say that if you are sick, you may call for the elders and be healed.

If you are persecuted, God's word says, **God is able to make all grace abound toward you** (2 Cor. 9:8) and, **He gives more grace** (James 4:6).

Through your trials, you will gain great victories; so, again, as James says, pray. You pray. Don't ask the elders to pray for you.

One young man came to us for prayer. He said, "Please pray for me. I have a bad temper; and besides this, I have one temptation after another. So many troubles come my way. I wish you would just cast out the whole thing."

I replied, "Is any among you afflicted? Let him pray."

Then I said, "Some things have to be cast out and some things have to be overcome. I am not here to pray all your troubles away because, through your trials and temptations, you can learn to be an overcomer. If you are sick, I will pray for you and Jesus will heal you; but if you are just having some problems, you pray. If you are merry, sing psalms. If you are sick, be healed. But if you are afflicted, pray" (James 5:13-14).

What About God's Chastisement?

Another scripture that is often used to justify sickness is this:

> **Whom the Lord loves he** *chastens*, **and scourges every child whom he receives. If you endure chastening, God deals with you as with children; for what child is there whom the parent chastens not? But If you be without chastisement, whereof all are partakers, then are you bastards, and not legitimate children.**
>
> **Hebrews 12:6-8**

This scripture does not say: "Whom the Lord loves He makes sick, or smites with disease."

It does not say: "God imparts disease to or makes infirm every child whom He receives."

The word chasten comes from a Greek word which means "instruct, train, discipline, teach or educate," like a teacher instructs a pupil or like a parent teaches and trains a child.

When a teacher instructs a student, various means of discipline and training may be employed in the education process, but never sickness.

When parents train a child, there are many ways to correct and to guide it in the right way, but no parent would impose a physical disease or affliction upon their child.

However, theological tradition would have us believe that when God trains His child, His chastening is supposed to be a cancer, tuberculosis, blindness, a crippled limb, or some other form of infirmity. Instead of causing obedient and consecrated believers to rise in authority, demanding their redemptive and covenant rights, the idea of sickness as chastening leaves the sick in uncertainty, wondering for what particular wrong they are being punished.

Good parents never punish their child until, first, they clearly explain the reason for the punishment. **How much more, our heavenly Father** (Matt. 7:11).

Most people who believe their sickness to be God's chastisement have no idea why God is punishing them.

I am not speaking of those who are rebellious, disobedient and contrary toward the Lord. I simply wish to encourage those who do believe and who are obedient to God's will, to no longer allow the devil, who is the deceiver, to condemn and lie to them. He wants to keep them sick and physically infirm and unfit to **abound to every good work** (2 Cor. 9:8), by telling them that their sickness is God's "chastening rod"; that God is correcting them for some mistake or error, or is perfecting some defective thing in their lives.

Satan will constantly condemn you by bringing to your mind every mistake you have ever made, offering his lying suggestion, "That is why you are sick. That is why you do not get healed. Your God is chastening you with His 'rod of sickness,' and there is no hope for you to try to be healed."

Your adversary, the devil, therefore succeeds in causing you to blame God the healer of sickness for the very sickness Satan has put upon you.

I heard a theologian say that ninety percent of the Christians who are sick, are sick because God is using sickness as a "chastening rod" to express His love for them and is molding their lives to His perfect will. He said that Christians who are not brought under the "chastening rod" of sickness by God once in a while are "bastards" and not "legitimate children."

If such a preacher will be consistent, people will remember when they are sick or suffering never to resort to medical treatment, or to be prayed for to be healed. In so doing, they may be endeavoring to hinder their loving Father's will, who allegedly is seeking to bless them by means of their sickness or so-called "chastisement."

Theological tradition is never consistent in this matter. In one breath, they tell the sick to humbly and patiently submit to God's "chastening rod" of sickness.

In the next breath, however, they are likely to advise them, if they have not already done so, to fight against God's "chastisement" by placing themselves in the hands of the doctor they think best qualified to rid them of their Father's correction.

This would mean rebellion instead of submission.

If you believe that sickness or infirmity is God's chastisement for some wrongdoing, you should make no attempt, either by medical means or by prayer, to get rid of the sickness or infirmity.

You should endeavor to find out what your wrongdoing consists of, and if successful you should concentrate on righting the wrong. Then having righted it, you should leave it to your heavenly Father, not to a doctor, to discontinue His "chastisement."

Even if it were true, the idea of sickness as God's chastisement, if consistently and reasonably followed to its logical conclusion, requires divine healing instead of medical treatment after all.

The loving heavenly Father, who is said to use sickness as a chastening rod, would surely remove His "rod of chastening" — sickness — when His purpose had been accomplished.

What About Suffering?

Another scripture which is so often used is 1 Peter 5:10: **But the God of all grace, who has called us to his eternal glory by Christ Jesus, after that you have *suffered* a while, make you perfect, establish, strengthen, settle you.**

This does not say: "After you have been sick and have suffered with disease for a while, God will make you perfect and stable." However, it does say: **after that you have suffered a while.**

Is it possible to suffer any other way than by being sick or diseased?

In the second book of Corinthians, Paul enumerates his hardships: reproaches, necessities, persecutions, distresses, stripes, imprisonments, tumults, labors, watching, fastings, dishonor, evil report.

He writes: **As unknown, and yet well known; as dying, and, behold, we live; as chastened, and not killed (2 Cor. 6:9); in stripes above measure, in prisons more frequent, in death oft. Of the Jews five times received I forty stripes save one. Thrice was I beaten with rods, once I was stoned, thrice I suffered shipwreck, a night and a day in the deep (2 Cor. 11:23-25).**

These were Paul's sufferings for Christ's sake and it is such suffer-ings as these to which Peter refers in this verse, as the context shows. No one has the right to include sickness or disease here.

It was because he had endured these sufferings for Christ's sake that Paul could say, **Henceforth there is laid up for me a crown of righteousness** (2 Tim. 4:8).

You will never receive a **crown of righteousness** for having been sick. If a sick person believed that, they would not call in a doctor to cure the sickness, nor ask God to heal it.

It is said of the apostles that after they had been beaten because they had preached the gospel and healed the sick in the name of Jesus, **They departed, rejoicing that they were counted worthy to suffer shame for his name** (Acts 5:41).

If you believe you are suffering for your Lord, you should not try to alleviate the pain, but should bear it gracefully and even rejoice that *you have been counted worthy* also.

The Ministry of Suffering

Dr. Charles S. Price wrote:

I want you to understand that the healing of your body — not merely the bodies of the people that were suffering when Jesus was on earth, but your bodily suffering today — was included in the great redemptive work consummated by Jesus on your behalf.

I believe that in order to clear up a question that sometimes arises in the mind because of modern teaching, I ought to point out one great error over which many sincere people stumble; an error received by tradition.

Have you not heard people talk about the ministry of suffer-ing? Of course you have.

There is such a thing as the ministry of suffering, but it cer-tainly does not mean that it is a ministry of sickness.

There is the matter of tribulation also, but neither does that refer to sickness.

We are told that, if we suffer with Christ, we shall also reign with Him; but that does not say or mean that, if we be sick or infirm with Christ, then we shall reign with Him.

When teachers who deny divine healing attempt to prove their argument that it is God's will for some to be sick, they immediately take the scriptures regarding the ministry of suffer-ing and make them applicable to sickness. The Bible does not do that.

Always remember that when Jesus spoke of sin and sickness, He spoke of them as evils from which He came to deliver us.

But Jesus did not speak of suffering in this manner.

Has it occurred to you that Christ bore our sins and sicknesses but did not bear our sufferings?

He told His disciples that they would have to bear their cross, but He did not mean that it was to be a cross of sickness.

He very clearly taught that we should resign ourselves to the carrying of our burden, to the weight of our cross, and sometimes even to a load of suffering, but never did He tell His disciples or us that we should resign ourselves to sickness and to disease. On the contrary, He fought it, He cast it out; and everywhere He went, the sick were healed by Him.

John J. Scruby says:

Peter has much to say about this suffering in his first epistle, in which he was seeking to comfort the believers who were passing through a *fiery trial*.

If you will read such passages as these 1 Peter 1:3-7; 3:13-14; 4:1,12-19; (and there are many others like them in the New Testament) you will see that suffering in its scriptural sense has nothing to do with sickness.

As to suffering with Christ, in the sense of being sick, that is unreasonable. Christ was never sick except as His redemptive *stripes* made Him sick; and He voluntarily took these stripes in order that we might not be sick. Peter, who speaks so much about Christ's sufferings, says, **By whose stripes you were healed** (1 Peter 2:24).

Since Christ, as our substitute, **took our infirmities, and bore our sicknesses** (Matt. 8:17), to the extent that anyone has been sick, it is to that same extent that one has not realized the physical benefits of Christ's redemptive work.

What About Paul's Thorn?

The scriptures which tell us of Paul's *thorn in the flesh* have been extremely misinterpreted. You will find our detailed answer to some widely taught traditions concerning Paul's thorn in chapter 37 of this book.

Tradition Binds — Truth Liberates

Jesus said, **You shall know the truth, and the truth shall make you free** (John 8:32).

All of these, and many other unscriptural teachings, tend to hold sick people in bondage. When the people are given the facts that Christ bore our sins and diseases in our stead, it is then that the will of God in the matter of healing for the sick is revealed, and the sick can exercise faith to be made whole.

God wants to heal all who are sick just the same as He wants to save all who are sinful.

Theological tradition says, "Be faithful in your sickness; be patient. Keep waiting on God, and He will heal you in His own good time."

But the fact is, you are not waiting for God to heal you. God is waiting for you to accept the healing He has already provided for you.

The Lord would have saved you long before He did, but He had to wait until you believed on His Son, Jesus Christ, as savior and accepted His free gift of salvation.

The Lord would heal you today. In fact, He would have healed you as soon as you became ill had you given Him the chance. But He must wait until you accept Jesus Christ as healer. Until you do that, your own healing is delayed.

Believe God's word today. Be healed right now. Look up and say:

THANK YOU, *Lord, for bearing my sickness and for setting me free. Thank You for Your stripes by which I was healed. Thank You that I am redeemed from sin and sickness. Thank You for deliverance, both for my spirit and for my body. I believe it, and I praise You for it.* AMEN.

Chapter 15

THE PRAYER OF FAITH

The prayer of faith shall save the sick, and the Lord shall raise them up (James 5:15). This promise was made to "any" who are sick.

I am grateful every time I think of the two all-inclusive words that march hand-in-hand across the pages of scriptural truth. They are the **whoever** of salvation and the **any** of divine healing.

If either of those words do not include you, or anyone else, then I do not understand the English language.

On the other hand, if the word **any** does include you, and everyone else, then we should rejoice that healing is for all.

The prayer of faith can never be offered while you are wondering whether or not God is willing to do the thing which you are asking Him to do.

Daring To Violate God's Will

Real faith comes by hearing the word of God, that is, by hearing God say through His word what He wants to do. Praying the prayer of faith is merely asking God to do the thing which He promised to do.

If it is God's will for you to be sick, we could not pray the prayer of faith. If it is God's will for you to be sick, then it is wrong to ask someone to pray for your healing, for you should not want to violate your heavenly Father's will.

If it is God's will for you to be sick, you should not seek help from doctors, nurses, or any other kind of medical aid. You would be saying, in effect, "It is Your will, Lord, that I should be ill, but I am going to call a doctor or do some other things so that I may avoid Your will."

To be perfectly logical, if you think it may not be God's will for you to be healed, you should make no effort whatever to get well, but should resign yourself to your "fate" and tell the world that you are suffering sickness for the sake of the Lord Jesus Christ.

But, when did He say that He wanted *you* to suffer sickness for Him? *He* suffered for you.

If you really think it may be God's will for you to be sick, and you doubt His willingness to heal you, then I would suggest that you be content with your lot and suffer bravely.

81

If you believe that it is God's will for you to suffer, then I would suggest that you use your medical money for the good of others.

If God is not willing to heal you, and you want His will more than anything else in the world, I should not think it advisable to trust your case into the hands of a physician who would immediately seek to break God's will for you.

Positive Prayer Brings Results

Concerning the prayer of faith, many people have the idea that this always means an immediate answer. They think that unless instant results are manifested, the prayer of faith has not yet been offered.

No doubt many have failed to receive our Lord's healing in their bodies because they have dictated to Him just how and when they wanted to be blessed.

Praying the prayer of faith does not necessarily mean that the answer is seen or felt immediately. It is the prayer offered by one who knows what God's word declares, is positive that God has heard that prayer and knows that God is bound by His own covenant to answer and manifest the results asked for.

God may do this instantly or He may do it gradually, but one thing is certain: God will answer the prayer of faith.

Once the prayer of faith is offered and the disease is rebuked, the case is in the hands of the Lord and He does the restoring. Whether it is done instantly or by a gradual healing does not matter. His word stands true, and it is for us to believe and doubt not, trusting Him to completely and thoroughly take away the disease.

Faith Versus Symptoms

When you have fully complied with the word of God and offered the prayer of faith, you can from that very moment declare yourself healed by the power of God, because His word says, **If we know that he hears us, whatever we ask, we know that we have the petitions that we desired of him** (1 John 5:15).

Although in some cases the symptoms of a sickness may linger for a while, faith declares that it is done because God's word says so.

Faith is not afraid to take its stand upon the word of God. Faith has nothing to do with anything but the word of God.

The tempter whispers, "You dare not claim your healing. You are not healed — just look at those symptoms."

But the true believer rests secure in the promises of God, believing, trusting, giving Him the glory, realizing that God is true to His word and that Satan is not only a liar, but the father of lies.

Faith in the Word of God

If you have faith, Jesus said, **Nothing shall be impossible to you** (Matt. 17:20).

He said, **If you live in me, and my words live in you, you shall ask for whatever you desire, and it shall be done to you** (John 15:7).

He also says, **If you shall ask anything in my name, I will do it** (John 14:14).

Again, **Whatever you desire, when you pray, believe that you receive it, and you shall have it** (Mark 11:24).

This is why you can pray the prayer of faith and leave the results with God, regardless of circumstances.

I could relate hundreds of incidents that have taken place in our gospel crusades across the United States and around the world. But if I only relate these experiences to you, your faith might be based on what happened to other people instead of on what the word of God says. Chapter 55 of this book is included, however, as our witness that *Jesus Christ is the same today* for anyone who believes the Bible. (Heb. 13:8.)

Relating experiences will encourage your faith, but only hearing the word of God *creates* faith.

Faith and Our Five Senses

While God's word alone creates faith, if we only related experiences, we would appeal to the natural senses.

Your natural senses have nothing to do with faith and true faith must ignore them.

If you walk by faith, you cannot walk by sight. If you are to consider the word of God as true, then you cannot always consider the evidences of your senses as true.

Feeling, smelling, tasting, hearing, and seeing are the senses by which the natural person is directed. The word of God and faith are the two factors by which the spiritual person is directed.

The natural person walks by the senses, but the spiritual person walks by faith in the word of God. (2 Cor. 5:7.)

Sight and feeling belong to the natural person.

Faith and obedience belong to the supernatural person.

Every Christian is a supernatural person.

It seems unreasonable to some people not to believe the natural senses. They have accepted them as conclusive evidence for so long that it is difficult for them to realize that there is other evidence besides that of the five natural senses.

People have been taught that the final court of appeal is the natural senses. "Seeing is believing," they say. They have based their lives on that premise and have failed to take into account the higher source of knowledge. This higher knowledge is revelation faith, which comes through the word of God and through prayer.

The word of God should be the final court of appeal for the Christian — the super-person.

Often when Christians are told that they are to walk by faith and not by sight, and to disregard the evidence of the physical senses, they think this is unreasonable. "Do you mean to say," they ask, "that I cannot depend on what I see? I could never accept such an absurdity. When I hold a book in my hand, I see it and feel it and can smell the printer's ink on its pages. If I drop it, I can hear it fall. Do you mean to tell me that the book is not real and that it is not here?" No. We do not mean that.

We may accept the evidence of our senses as true in natural things; but in spiritual things when this evidence contradicts God's word, then we ignore our physical senses and believe what the word of God says.

What Witnesses to Our Healing?

I have often wondered why people who think it's absurd to believe that God's word is true if their senses testify to the contrary, have such faith in a contagious disease to which their child has been exposed. They believe that their child will manifest the symptoms of the disease in a certain number of days because a child, sick with the disease, was in their class at school.

They have no physical evidence that their child will have this disease. They are expecting it purely by faith — faith in Satan's disease. Without feeling it, they believe it — they have faith in it.

The child has no apparent symptoms of the disease. It is as well as ever, but they believe it will have the disease in a few days.

Why do they believe that?

They have what we call "faith" — faith in the disease. They believe the disease has begun its work, in spite of the fact that they cannot see, feel, smell, taste, or hear anything of it with their senses. That is faith.

The only fault here is that this is faith in the wrong thing but it certainly is faith.

They trust in diseases completely and with unquestioned confidence, yet they may feel we are being unreasonable when we lay hands on them and tell them, "Your sickness will leave. It must go because God has said it will go. He said, You shall recover, so nothing can stop it."

Seeing Is Not Believing

Many say, "Seeing is believing," yet they believe in the power of disease *before* they see its effects. According to the word of God, believing is seeing.

Others say, "I will never believe it until I see it."

I reply, "You will never see it until you believe it."

As soon as you believe it, God delights to let you see it, since **faith is the evidence of things not seen** (Heb. 11:1).

Faith brings the unseen things into being and makes the unfelt things real to the senses.

It pleases God when you look only at His word. It pleases Him when you base your faith on His promise. By this kind of faith, **people of God obtained a good report from Him** (Heb. 11:2), and you will, too.

Faith in God's word is always pleasing to Him.

When Jesus was here in human form, He recognized the evidence of the senses, but He never allowed Himself to be dominated by them. The senses were His servants; He lived above them.

He pronounced the blind man healed and the leper cleansed, when apparently they were still blind and still leprous.

He called the things that were not as though they were — and they came to pass.

Jesus cursed a fig tree one day, and its roots died. But its death was not evidenced until the next day when it was seen to have died from the roots — not from the visible branches down, but from the invisible roots up. (Mark 11:20.)

Sense Knowledge Is Deceptive

Our senses relate to the natural person in the natural world; but in obtaining blessings from the spiritual world, faith relates to the spiritual person.

We may accept the evidence of our senses as long as it does not contradict the word of God. However, when God's word differs from our senses, we are to ignore the evidence of our senses and act on the word. When we do this, the Father honors His word and makes it good in our lives.

We are always safe when we believe God, no matter how convincing the evidences of our senses may be. What God says is always true.

Let God be true, but every person a liar (Rom. 3:4).

Sense knowledge is a deception when it does not agree with the word of God. When we are walking by faith, we delight to cast aside the senses and enjoy the Father's already-provided blessings.

Abraham's Faith

The greatest example one could ever study on this subject is that of Abraham's faith.

Of Abraham, Romans 4:18-21 says:

Who against hope believed in hope, that he might become the father of many nations, according to that which was spoken, So shall your seed be.

And being not weak in, faith, he considered not his own body now dead, when he was about an hundred years old, neither yet the deadness of Sarah's womb;

He staggered not at the promise of God through unbelief; but was strong in faith [not grumbling or complaining because the answer was not manifested immediately, but], **giving glory to God;**

And being fully persuaded that, what he [God] **had promised, he was able also to perform.**

Abraham completely ignored the evidences of his physical senses, which testified to the fact that he was almost one hundred years old.

Sarah felt old, looked old, and was old, according to the natural senses; but Abraham ignored that fact, too.

Why did he ignore these facts? Because they contradicted what God had said. God said Abraham would have a son. His physical senses said, "Impossible," but he ignored his natural senses and believed the word of God. That is faith.

The scriptures say that Abraham believed God. (Rom. 4:3.)

The word "believe" is a verb, and a verb shows action. I would say, "Abraham acted like what God said would indeed come to pass."

Sarah's Faith

Sarah did not "feel" like she had the strength to conceive seed and to be delivered of a child; but she ignored her feelings, and **through faith also, Sarah herself received strength to conceive seed, and was delivered of a child when she was past age** (Heb. 11:11).

How did this come about to a woman who was nearly a hundred years old? It was not by the evidence of her senses — not by her "feeling" — but **because she believed God was faithful who had promised** (Heb. 11:11).

Faith Not Natural

Faith does not consider what the natural eye can see, what the natural ear can hear, or what the physical body can feel. Faith heeds only God's promise.

The natural eyes see only the great walls of Jericho; the natural ears hear only the taunting of the enemy; but faith sees the walls fallen and the enemy conquered. (See Joshua, chapter 6.)

The natural body feels the gnawing pains of the cancer, but faith sees it dried up and consumed by the healing power of Jehovah-Rapha — **the Lord who heals you** (Ex. 15:26).

The natural eye sees the blackness of the clouds hanging low overhead. The natural ears hear the blast of the thunder. But faith quietly commands: **Peace, be still** (Mark 4:39).

The natural eye sees the flesh consumed by disease. The physical hand feels the fever burning away the tissues of the body.

But faith sees the sickness as a part of the **curse of the Law** (Deut. 28:22). Faith sees the power of sickness abolished at Calvary where every sufferer was redeemed (Gal. 3:13). In the name of Jesus, faith commands the disease to leave its victim, then walks out of the room with the quiet assurance that what the Bible says shall come to pass: **They shall recover; The Lord shall raise them up** (Mark 16:18; James 5:15).

Faith Versus Reason

One would almost think that faith is blind to physical conditions. When reason argues with it, faith does not waver.

Faith sees Satan defeated, even when he is seen ruling in power. In the mind of faith, diseases are healed, even before a prayer is offered.

Faith moves and acts as God moves and acts. Reason is troubled, excited, and nervous; faith stands unmoved. Faith knows that God cannot lie, so faith never argues, but takes it for granted when a request has been made according to the word of God. Faith considers a work as finished, even before it is manifested.

Faith and the Word Are Victors

Read God's word. Feed on His word. Live in His word. Let it produce faith in your heart.

The psalmist David says, **The entrance of your words gives light; it gives understanding to the simple** (Ps. 119:130).

Know the integrity of God's word and step out on that word. It will not fail you, because God will not fail you.

David also says, **Your word have I hid in my heart, that I might not sin against you** (Ps. 119:11).

Charles H. Spurgeon quoted that scripture like this: "This is a good thing in a good place for a good purpose."

87

We may change this scripture a little and use it in reference to sickness — Your word have I hid in my heart, that I may be kept from sickness by You — and it will still be what Spurgeon said it is: "A good thing in a good place for a good purpose"; for **faith comes by hearing** (knowing) **the word of God** (Rom. 10:17), and healing comes through faith in the promises of God.

Real faith in God and in His word is never discouraged. Real faith always thrives on a test.

Faith lives in the light of anticipated results. It does not look at or live in bondage to present circumstances, but rather it overrules circumstances and determines destiny by walking in the light of promised accomplishments.

Persistent faith always wins. Let nothing discourage you. Let nothing change you. Allow no symptoms to change your attitude toward God's word. Settle it forever in your heart that God's promises will be fulfilled.

It may require seven trips around the walls (Josh. 6:15-16), or seven dips in the river (2 Kings 5:14), but the victory will come through persistent faith in what God has spoken.

Faith is the victor. Faith comes by hearing God's word, so read His word and enjoy a life of victorious faith.

Faith Is a Possessor

Every place where your foot shall step, I have given it to you for an inheritance (Josh. 1:3) was the inspiring promise which greeted the Israelites as they faced the Promised Land. Footprints mean possession, but it must be their own footprints.

In possessing your New Testament blessings provided in redemption, every promise that you put your feet upon is yours.

The rich plain of healing is yours to the extent that you tread upon it.

The fertile valley of deliverance is yours, if you will go in and possess it.

The highlands of spiritual power are yours, if you will imitate grand old Caleb and, by faith, drive out the Anakims of unbelief that dwell there. (Josh. 14:6-15.)

Any or all of these blessings are yours to possess in the name of Jesus.

All of the promises in the Bible are yours, so do not be slack to go up and possess your land. Between you and your possessions are powerful enemies, but gather your forces of prayer and faith in that all-sufficient name of Jesus and go against them. Do not stop until the last enemy is conquered.

The size of your inheritance depends on how much land you have stood on, walked on, and really claimed. If you have not claimed it all, then as much more of it is yours as you dare possess.

Put on the whole armor of God, which will make you invulnerable and take the **sword of the Spirit** (Eph. 6:10-17), which will make you invincible. **Fight the good fight of faith** (1 Tim. 6:12). **Endure hardness, as a good soldier** (2 Tim. 2:3). **Resist the devil**, and you will find the promise true: **he will flee from you** (James 4:7).

To most people, faith is merely a word or a theory. You can make it a fact and a power.

Satan knows that in the matter of healing, God's interests and yours are identical. He knows that God and you are allies. He knows that God cannot let you fail, while you are trusting His word, for He could not do that without seeing Himself fail; and this He cannot do.

When the **prayer of faith** has been prayed, **stand fast in the faith and be strong** (1 Cor. 16:13).

Do not give up. Trust for a well body. Believe that you will recover. Lay claim to your covenant rights. Then God will get the glory, and you will get the victory.

Faith is the victory (1 John 5:4).

Chapter 16

IS FAITH ESSENTIAL TO HEALING?

You may ask, "Dr. Osborn, do you believe that I must have faith? Do you not think I could be healed through your faith?"

The Bible says, **Without faith it is impossible to please God** (Heb.11:6).

We walk by faith, not by sight (2 Cor. 5:7).

Being healed through another person's faith is the scriptural exception, not the rule. I would advise you to abide by the rule rather than by the exception. I am certain that when you have heard the word of God until faith has been born in your heart (and the word, if given heed to, will always produce faith), you will be healed through your own faith.

The Father planned that every believer should be a conqueror — not just a few who are favored.

God wants you to discover that you have power over the devil. He wants you to know that you have power over sickness, that you are a victor, that you are a conqueror, that you can rebuke disease and sickness and see the symptoms melt away.

You will never be able to walk in this victory as long as you are depending on the faith of someone else.

Neither can the faith of another person set you free from sin. You must hear the gospel and be forgiven of your sins. You must personally believe on the Lord Jesus Christ as savior. Then you will be saved.

You must hear the word of God. You must believe on the Lord Jesus Christ as healer. Then *by his stripes*, you are healed.

Faith Can Be Seen

In most cases Jesus did not heal anyone until after He had obtained that person's confession of faith, or until He had observed some act of faith for healing.

This was so in the case of the centurion. (Matt. 8:5-10.)

The Bible says of the palsied man who was let down through the roof on a cot: **And Jesus seeing their faith said to the sick of the**

91

palsy, **Arise, and take up your bed, and go your way** (Matt. 9:2; Mark 2:11).

If you were bedfast, would you allow four men to carry you up onto a roof and then let you down, cot and all, through a hole in the roof? Not unless you believed that something would happen to you when you were placed before the Lord.

Faith is better seen than heard. Jesus saw their faith in their actions.

Faith without works (or actions that correspond) **is dead** (James 2:26).

In the case of the two blind men who **followed him, crying, Jesus, Son of David, have mercy on us. Jesus said to them, Do you believe that I am able to do this? They said to him, Yes, Lord. Then he touched their eyes, saying, According to your faith be it done to you. And their eyes were opened** (Matt. 9:27-30).

Faith Always Honored

To the woman of Canaan who sought mercy from the Lord for her daughter who was lying at home **grievously vexed with a devil,** Jesus replied, after He had seen her persistent and unwavering faith, **O woman, great is your faith: be it done to you even as you will. And her daughter was made whole from that very hour** (Matt. 15:22,28).

To the woman who had an issue of blood for twelve years, and who pressed through the crowd, saying within herself, **If I may touch but his clothes, I shall be whole,** Jesus said, **Daughter, your faith has made you whole; go in peace, and be whole of your plague** (Mark 5:28,34).

To the blind man in Mark 10, Jesus said, **Go your way; your faith has made you whole** (Mark 10:52).

To the one leper who returned to give thanks, Jesus said, **Go your way; your faith has made you whole** (Luke 17:19).

When a certain man asked Jesus to come to his house and heal his son because **he was at the point of death,** Jesus said, **Go your way; your son lives,** and the Bible says, **The man believed the word that Jesus had spoken to him, and he went his way.**

And while on his way home, **his servants met him, and told him, saying, Your son lives** (John 4:47-53).

There are many cases in the gospels that do not state whether or not the people who were healed had faith, such as the woman bowed over with an infirmity (Luke 13:11-13), the man with a withered hand (Matt. 12:10,13), the man by the pool at Bethesda (John 5:5-9), the multitudes (Matt. 12:15; 14:14, 35-36; Mark 6:56), and many others.

But it is certain that they had faith to be healed, because when Mark says, **and he (Jesus) could do no mighty work there, except that he**

laid his hands upon a few sick folk, and healed them. His inability to do mighty work there was because of their unbelief (Mark 6:1-6).

When Paul was preaching the gospel at Lystra, one of his hearers was a man whose feet were crippled. He had been born in this condition. No doubt Paul desired that the man be healed immediately. Instead Paul waited until the lame man had heard the word of God and had obtained faith for healing. (Rom. 10:17.)

Then Paul **steadfastly beholding him, and perceiving that he had faith to be healed, said with a loud voice, Stand up right on your feet. And he leaped and walked** (Acts 14:9-10).

During our gospel crusades around the world, I have seen tens of thousands of sufferers of disease and sickness completely healed while in the audience listening to the message we were preaching.

The preaching of the word always produces faith when believed.

The Bible says that, **by faith**, people of God **obtained a good report** (Heb. 11:2). God was pleased with the patriarchs and matriarchs of old when they demonstrated great faith.

Without faith it is impossible to please him [God] (Heb. 11:6).

Individual Faith

God's promises are for you personally. You have an individual right to pray for and receive every blessing promised to the believer.

Jesus says, **Everyone that asks receives**. He emphasizes this fact six times, so that you will clearly understand that He wants you to feel free to ask Him for what you want.

He says, **Ask, and it shall be given you; seek, and you shall find; knock, and it shall be opened to you: for every one that asks receives; and the one that seeks finds; and to the one that knocks it shall be opened** (Matt. 7:7-8).

All through the Bible, God seeks to impress every one of His children that we all have equal rights. He respects none above another. He has no favorites. He expects each one of us to have faith.

Jesus says: **The one who comes to me I will not cast out** (John 6:37). That means you. Christ is saying: "Those that come to Me for any need, whatever it may be, I will not refuse them."

Jesus says: **If you live in me, and my words live in you, you shall ask for what you desire, and it shall be done to you** (John 15:7).

Jesus says: **Whatever things you desire, when you pray, believe that you receive them, and you shall have them** (Mark 11:24).

Paul said: **If you shall confess with your mouth the Lord Jesus, and shall believe in your heart that God has raised him from the dead, you shall be saved** (Rom. 10:9).

Speak for Yourself

To be saved, you must do your own repenting, your own believing, your own confessing, your own accepting, your own receiving; then you will be saved.

To be healed, you have the right to do your own asking, your own believing, your own claiming, your own receiving; then you will be healed.

Thousands of Christians are spending their lives depending on the prayers and the faith of other people, as though others were closer to God than they; as though others could pray better than they; as though God will hear the prayers of others quicker than their own prayers.

Every Christian has equal rights, and it is God's will and desire that each of His children claim and accept all of His blessings.

Every person can pray and receive the answer.

Jesus said, **Everyone that asks receives** (Matt. 7:8).

Every sinner who has ever been saved had to prove Christ's statement to be true; otherwise, they never could have been saved.

If the privilege, **Everyone that asks receives**, is available to the unconverted, how much more is it available to God's children. That is, if this privilege was available before we were saved, how much more is it available after we are saved.

Even Babies Can Ask

Every child can do its own asking from its parents.

Every baby does its own asking, even before it can speak a word. Unable to do anything but cry, it does its own asking. Certainly the other children in the family do not have to beg the mother to please feed the baby. The baby asks for itself.

There are thousands of Christians who have never learned the privilege of asking for themselves. They spend their time writing and calling on others to pray for them, to do their praying for them, to ask God for them.

Others may pray with you; but never substitute the prayers of others for your own asking, because Jesus said, *everyone* **that asks receives**.

Everyone who has a bank account can use it personally. How unreasonable it would be for me to ask someone across town to go to the bank and try to get some money out of my account. It is my money. I can draw my own check without any problem. I have a right to demand the money because it is mine.

He Said It, You Believe It

Every blessing which Christ died to provide is the private property of every person for whom He died.

The Bible tells us that every snake-bitten Israelite, **when they looked on the brazen serpent, lived** (Num. 21:8-9). Everyone of them had to do their own looking at the brazen serpent.

The people were near to death; but when they cried to the Lord, **He sent his word and healed them** (Ps. 107:20).

Tens of thousands of times in our great campaigns, people have been healed of all manner of sicknesses, diseases and infirmities while they were in the audience — healed through their own faith, which they had received through hearing the word of God.

Faith is believing that God will do what He has said in His word that He will do. God has never asked anyone to believe Him for anything that He has not promised to do.

God has said: **I am the Lord who heals you.**

The prophet Isaiah said: **He [Jesus] was wounded for our transgressions, and with his stripes we are healed.**

Jesus said to the leper: **I will; be clean** (Matt. 8:3).

He said to the centurion: **I will come and heal him** (Matt. 8:7).

To the blind man, He said: **Receive your sight** (Luke 18:42).

Peter said: **His own self bore our sins; by whose stripes you were healed** (1 Peter 2:24).

Jesus said: **They shall lay hands on the sick, and they shall recover, and in my name they shall cast out devils** (Mark 16:17-18).

James said: **Is any sick among you? The prayer of faith shall save the sick, and the Lord shall raise them up** (James 5:14-15).

Faith is merely believing that God will do these and other things, which He said in His word that He would do if we would only believe.

If you can believe, all things are possible to them that believe (Mark 9:23).

Have Faith in God

We could sum up the matter by quoting the command of Jesus: **Have faith in God** (Mark 11:22).

Faith will always move the hand of God. Faith always possesses. Faith is a persistent force. Faith relies on the ability of God. Faith knows no defeat. Faith thrives on a test. Faith never argues. Faith never gets excited. Faith never brags on itself. Faith is never nervous. Faith never trembles. Faith is never overpowered.

Faith looks directly to the word of God. Faith knows what God has said, because it has been born by the word of God. Faith knows that what God says is a revelation of what it is His will to do.

Faith accepts God's word as final. Faith claims that word and steps out on it. Faith possesses the promises. Faith demands results. Faith claims its covenanted rights.

When reason argues; when one fears, trembles and becomes nervous; faith stands steadfast and immovable because it knows what God has said. That settles the matter with faith. Faith is invincible. Faith is irresistible.

Be grounded in the word of God. Know His word. That way you will know His will.

Bring your request to Him and leave the results with Him. Give Him a chance to do for you what He has been waiting so long to do, but could not until you were ready to act on His word in faith.

Do as Abraham did. He believed God. **And being not weak in faith, he staggered not at the promise of God through unbelief; but was strong in faith, giving glory to God; being fully persuaded that, what he [God] had promised, he was able also to perform** (Rom. 4:19-21).

Right now, go to God and quote any of His promises that you want Him to fulfill for you. Ask Him to do it. Pray the prayer of faith for that promise; place your order in the letter-drop of faith and turn it loose. Trust it to the heavenly authorities to take it through and to bring you the order properly filled.

Don't keep praying again and again for the thing desired. Release your faith and let it bring you the answer.

Maintain this attitude of faith. Refuse to be moved. Let nothing budge you from your stand on the promise of God, and your prayer will be answered to the fullest extent; for God will say to you: **Go your way; and as you have believed, so be it done to you** (Matt. 8:13).

Chapter 17

THE IMPORTANCE OF YOUR WORDS

You said that you could not do it — and the moment you said it, you were defeated.

You said you did not have faith — and at that moment, doubt arose like a giant and bound you.

Perhaps you never realized that to a great extent you are ruled by your words.

You talked failure, and failure held you in bondage.

You talked fear, and fear increased its grip on you.

Solomon said: **You are snared with the words of your mouth, you are taken [captive] with the words of your mouth** (Prov. 6:2).

Testifying — Witnessing — Confessing

Few Christians have recognized the importance of their words and the place they hold in their lives. Our words form our confession of what we believe or do not believe. Whenever the word "confession" is used, some people automatically think of confessing sin, weakness, and failure. But this is only the negative side of the subject. The negative confession of your sin was only to open the way to the positive confession of God's word.

Nothing in your walk as a believer is more important than the words of your confession, though this is hardly ever mentioned in traditional theology.

Christianity is called the "confession," according to Hebrews, chapter three. The Greek word, which has been translated **profession** in the King James Version, is rendered "confession" in other cases; and the word **profession** in Hebrews 3:1 is "confession" or "acknowledgment" in the original.

The two words are closely related, yet the difference is important. The Greek word from which the word "confession" is translated actually means, "saying the same thing." It means, *saying what God says.* It means to agree with God in your testimony: saying what God says in His word about your sins, your sicknesses, your apparent failures, your health, your salvation, your victories, or about anything else in your life. In other words, testify to — or acknowledge — what God says.

Confession in Trial

For example: Sickness is pressing to overthrow your health. Symptoms of some disease are beginning to appear. Satan is desiring to destroy your health and to render your life ineffective in Christian service.

But God has made provision for your health. He has made a covenant of healing with you. He has promised **You shall serve the Lord your God, and [He] will take sickness away from the midst of you** (Ex. 23:25), because He promised, **I am the Lord who heals you** (Ex. 15:26).

God's word says **He heals all your diseases** (Ps. 103:3).

Jesus Christ has redeemed you from your diseases, because **Himself took your infirmities, and bore your sicknesses** (Matt. 8:17) at the whipping post (Matt. 27:26; John 19:1) and, therefore, **by his stripes, you were healed** (1 Peter 2:24).

Knowing all of this provides a basis for your faith. You know that Satan cannot lay a disease on your body, because Christ has already borne your diseases for you.

Therefore, you resist Satan and his lying symptoms of disease. You do not fear them. You know that your redemption is a fact. You know that your diseases were laid on the body of Christ and that He has borne them for you. You have no fear.

You boldly and firmly rebuke Satan, your adversary with the word of God, in the name of Jesus Christ who died to set you free. You take a firm stand.

Speak as Jesus Spoke

You do exactly as Christ, your example, did when tempted by Satan in the wilderness: You say, **Satan, it is written** (Matt. 4:4,7,10). Then you quote him the word: **By his stripes, I am healed. He heals all my diseases. Christ himself took my infirmities and bore my sicknesses** (Is. 53:5; Ps. 103:3; Matt. 8:17).

This is confession.

Confession is *saying what God says — talking the language of the Bible at all times*. It is resisting Satan with *the Lord says*. It is claiming your rights and confessing God's word — God's promises.

The Greek word from which confession is translated means, "saying the same thing"; that is, "saying what God says," or "agreeing with God in your conversation"; "acknowledging the word."

Your Attitude Like Christ's

A friend comes to you during your trial of faith and suggests: "Oh, you must be careful. I know a person who died of this sickness. You must go quickly to bed and call for help."

But you speak God's language, because you believe what God says. You use His words in your lips — in your conversation. You boldly confess, **The Lord is the strength of my life, of whom shall I be afraid? Christ has borne my diseases: and by His stripes, I am healed** (Ps. 27:1; Is. 53:5).

Under all circumstances at all times, you speak God's language. You harmonize your language and your thoughts with His. His attitude as set forth in His word is developed into your life until Satan cannot prevail against you because God's word is part of your very life and nature. (2 Pet. 1:4.)

You become as irresistible as God because of God's word that comes to control your prayers, your words, your thoughts, and your actions.

Confession is affirming something that you believe. It is testifying of something that you know. It is witnessing of a truth which you embrace. God's word is the exclusive subject of your confession of your testimony.

Words Are the Medium

Jesus planned that this great message of Christianity should be given to the world through words; that is, through the confession of those who believe in Him.

Testifiers, witnesses, and confessors have been the great leaders and agencies of the new and revolutionizing life of Jesus Christ (Christianity) in the world.

The major problem that we face, then, is to know what our words are to be: simply God's word, at all times, in the face of all adversities, under all circumstances.

Confession is affirming Bible truths. *Confession is repeating with our lips (from our hearts), the things God has said in His word.*

What to Speak

You cannot confess or witness of things you do not know. You must confess what you know personally about Jesus Christ and about what you are in Him. You know these facts through His word.

The secret of confession and of positive faith lies in getting a true understanding of:

1. What Jesus actually did for you;
2. What you are in Him as a result of it;
3. What the Bible promises that you can do as a result of His finished work in you.

This knowledge, coupled with a firm confession of these facts and actions which correspond, develops the highest kind of faith. This knowledge comes through the word of God.

Simply to admire these facts in the Bible and to say that you believe them, but to refuse (or neglect) to confess them boldly and to act on them, robs you of faith when you need it most.

You Become the Victor

When you know who Jesus is, what He did for you, what actually belongs to you now, and what you may enjoy in your daily life, it makes you a victor.

To know that Satan is defeated by your substitute, and that his defeat is eternal, makes your redemption a blessed fact and reality.

You can know that Satan's defeat was administered by your own substitute; that this defeat was credited to your account; that in the records of the supreme court of the universe you are now the master of Satan; Satan recognizes that, in the name of Jesus, you are his ruler. When your heart knows this, as well as you know that two plus two are four, then dominating faith, coupled with a new confession of authority, becomes natural.

You automatically talk like Jesus talked. You understand the facts of your redemption. Faith becomes as natural as fear was before you were enlightened.

You know that God Himself put Satan and all his kingdom beneath your feet and that you are considered by the Father and by Satan, as the victor. You have been liberated.

Your language becomes that of a superperson. You talk like someone of another race or kingdom; and that you are — **a chosen generation, a royal priesthood** (1 Peter 2:9).

You have authority. God is backing you. You are bold. *You speak God's language as commonly as unbelievers talk their fears.*

Salvation Instant and Definite

What a miraculous change would be produced in the church today if Christian believers would rise to the place God has given them and would talk the language God desires His people to talk.

Not long ago, a Christian who boldly claimed present salvation was considered sacrilegious. For someone to firmly believe and confess salvation as a finished work, and that it is a definite fact, was considered irreverent. But gradually the light began to shine, and we have come to the knowledge of present salvation — once and for all, an instant and definite work of God's boundless grace.

But how few Christians dare to confess boldly to the world what the word declares they are.

Take this sample scripture: **Therefore if any one be in Christ, that one is a new creature** (2 Cor. 5:17).

That does not mean that we are just forgiven sinners — poor, weak, staggering, sinning church members. It means what it says: We are new creatures now. We have been created in Christ Jesus, with the life of God, the nature of God, and the ability of God within us.

Old things are passed away; behold all things have become new (2 Cor. 5:17). Confess it. Believe it. It means what it says. We are new. All things are new. Old things are gone. Those old earmarks of sin, sickness, disease, failure, weakness, and fear have all passed away.

Your Command Honored

Now we have God's nature — His life, His strength, His health, His glory, His power. We have it now.

What a revolution would take place if Christians believed those things and began to talk like that, live like that, and act like that. Yet that is exactly what the heart of God our heavenly Father yearns for.

See yourself as a believer in a sick room where sickness had almost seized the life of a loved one: You are bold. You are a master, and you know it. You boldly confess "Greater is He that is in me than this disease that is stealing my loved one." You command that disease to leave; you speak in the name of Jesus and order Satan to release his hold. You calmly order that loved one to arise and be made whole. The sick one is healed.

What made the difference? You knew your position, your authority, and your rights. Satan had to honor your command, and God confirmed His word.

Take Colossians 1:13-14 for another example: **Who has delivered us from the power of darkness, and has translated us into the kingdom of his dear Son: In whom we have redemption through his blood, even the forgiveness of sins.**

That would mean that Satan's dominion ended and Jesus' dominion began. Satan's dominion was broken over your life the very moment you were born again. You received a new Lord to reign over your life — Jesus Christ.

Control Your Life

Disease and sickness, weakness and failure can no longer rule over you. Old habits can no longer control your life. You are redeemed. You are saved.

What a stir there would be if this scripture became a reality: **Fear not; for I am with you: be not dismayed; for I am your God: I will strengthen you; I will help you; I will uphold you with the right hand of my righteousness** (Is. 41:10).

If God be for us, who can be against us? (Rom. 8:31).

This is the most revolutionary thing that has ever been taught. Scriptures such as these must be your confession as you stand before the world.

You believe and say, "God is with me this morning."

You are of God, little children, and have overcome them: because greater is he that is in you, than he that is in the world.

1 John 4:4

You fearlessly say, "God is in me now; the Master of creation is with me." What a confession that is.

Revolutionizing Results

You face life fearlessly. You know that greater is He that is in you than all the forces that can be brought against you.

You face bills that you cannot pay. You face enemies that you have no ability to conquer. You face them fearlessly. You affirm with triumph: **He prepares a table before me in the presence of my enemies** (Ps. 23:5).

You are filled with joy and victory because God has taken over your problems. He is fighting your battles.

You are not afraid of circumstances, because **you can do all things through Christ which strengthens you** (Phil. 4:13). He is not only your strength, but He is by your side. He is your salvation. Whom should you fear? He throws light upon life's problems so that you can act intelligently. He is your salvation and deliverance from every trap that the enemy sets for you, from every snare in which he would enslave you.

God is the strength of your life; of whom shall you be afraid? (Ps. 27:1).

You are not afraid of anything. You have no fear because God is on your side. This is your confession.

The Family Language

Jesus' continual bold confession is your example. He continually confessed what He was.

You are to confess what you are in Christ. You are to confess that you are redeemed, that your redemption is an actual fact, that you are delivered out of the dominion and authority of Satan. You confess these facts boldly, with absolute certainty, because you know they are true.

You confess that you are a new creature, recreated in Christ Jesus; that you are a partaker of His divine nature; that sickness, disease, fear, weakness, and failure are things of the past.

Your language amazes your friends; it seems absurd and presumptuous to them. But to you, it is simply stating facts which are written in the Bible: it is the language of God's family.

You dare to stand in the presence of human evidence which contradicts God's word, and calmly declare that the word of God is true.

For instance, let's say that physical evidence declares you to be sick with an incurable illness. You boldly confess that God laid that disease on Jesus, that He bore it away for you, that Satan has no right to put it on you, that **by his stripes you are healed**. You believe that firmly and, therefore, you hold fast your confession in the face of contradictory evidence which says it is not true; *but your confession of God's word wins, and you are healed.*

The High Priest of Our Words

In Hebrews 3:1, Jesus Christ is called the **High Priest of our confession**. The next verse declares that He is faithful to Him that appointed Him (as the **High Priest of our confession**) as Moses was faithful.

In times of sickness, we boldly confess His promises to heal us. When we confess His words, then our high priest, Jesus Christ, acts on our behalf, according to our confession of His word, and intercedes to our Father for the benefits of the promises which we are confessing. He is the **High Priest of our confession**.

Between the time that we ask God for some benefit provided for us, and the time our Father grants that blessing to be manifested, we **hold fast the profession of our faith without wavering; [for he is faithful that promised]** (Heb. 10:23).

We know that the **High Priest of our confession** is faithful, as was Moses, to intercede for us until the answer is granted, according to the promise which we are faithfully confessing in our prayer, our conversation, our testimony, our thoughts, and in our actions.

Wrong Words Are Powerful Too

A wrong confession is the confession of defeat, failure, and of the supremacy of Satan. Talking about your combat with the devil — how he has hindered you, how he is holding you in bondage and keeping you sick — is a confession of defeat.

It is a wrong confession. It glorifies your adversary. It is an unconscious declaration that God, your heavenly Father, has failed you. Most of the confessions we hear today glorify the devil. Such a confession continually saps the very life out of you. It destroys faith and holds you in bondage.

The confession of your lips that has grown out of faith in your heart will defeat the adversary in every battle.

The confession of Satan's ability to hinder you and to keep you from success gives him advantage over you. He fills you with fear and weakness.

But if you boldly confess your Father's care and protection, and declare that He that is in you is greater than any force around you, you will rise above satanic influence.

Every time you confess your doubts and fears, you confess your faith in Satan and deny the ability and grace of God. When you confess your weakness and your disease, you are openly confessing that the word of God is not true and that God has failed to make it good.

God declares: **With his stripes you were healed**; and, **Surely he has borne our griefs** [sicknesses], **and carried our sorrows** [diseases]. Instead of confessing that He has borne your diseases and put them away, you confess that you still have them and take the testimony of natural evidence instead of the testimony of the word of God. In this way, you fail.

As long as you hold fast to the confession of weakness, sickness and pain, you will still have them. You may search for years for some man or woman of God to pray the prayer of faith for you, but it will be of no avail, because your unbelief will destroy the effects of your faith.

As long as you confess your sins and your weaknesses, you are building weakness, failure, and defeat into your very system.

Read the word. Talk the word. Confess the word. Act on the word, and the word will become a very part of yourself.

Chapter 18

EMANCIPATION PROCLAMATION

Christ has redeemed us from the curse of the law, being made a curse for us.

Galatians 3:13

What was that curse?

It is recorded in Deuteronomy, chapter 28, where we are told that the following diseases came upon the people because of disobedience to God's law: **pestilence, consumption** [or tuberculosis], **fever, inflammation, extreme burning, botch, emerods, scab, itch, blindness, smiting in the knee and in the leg,** and **failing of the eyes.**

If your case has not been definitely stated in this list, then listen to verses 60-61 of this chapter: **all the diseases of Egypt, and also every sickness** and **every disease which is not written in the book of this law.**

These words include you and your case.

Redeemed From Curses

Paul says that **Christ redeemed us from this curse of the law, because he was made a curse for us** (Gal. 3:13). The curse of the law includes **all diseases, every sickness, and every plague** known throughout the history of the world (Deut. 28:60-61).

In order for Christ to redeem us from this terrible curse of the law, He was made a curse for us; that is, He bore for us the punishment prescribed by the law. That is why He had to take **our infirmities, and bear our sicknesses** (Matt. 8:17).

Adam and Eve sold us into slavery to the devil and put us in bondage to his power, under his jurisdiction. But *Christ has redeemed us.* He has bought us back.

He has purchased us with the price of His own body and blood, and freed us. **You are bought with a price: therefore glorify God in your body, and in your spirit, which are God's** (1 Cor. 6:20).

Abundant Life

What a thrill to know that God so loved us that He paid a great price for our redemption. He gave His Son as our substitute, who assumed our guilt, bore our judgment and endured our condemnation in order to absolve us of all debt and obligation to Satan's regime, so that we could be restored to God as though no sin had ever been committed. He legally *redeemed* us. He proved how much He values us and wants to be able to share His best with us — His abundant life.

God so loved the world, that he gave his only begotten Son.

John 3:16

That was the kind of love we cannot understand — God's love.

Salvation is your emancipation from everything outside God's will for humankind. Now you can act accordingly. You may speak the language of a winner.

Confess your freedom, instead of your bondage. Confess: **With his stripes, I am healed**, instead of your sickness. Confess your redemption from all disease (Ps. 103:3). Confess that your redemption is complete — from sin and sickness.

Confess that Satan's dominion over you ended at Calvary, because it was there that God freed you. God's word states all of this, so confess it.

Slaves Set Free

When the slaves in the United States were emancipated, they were still living in slaves' quarters. They still looked like slaves. They still felt like slaves. But when they heard the Emancipation Proclamation read, they had a legal right to say, "I am free," and to act on that liberty.

Believe in your proclamation of freedom: **Stand fast therefore in the liberty by which Christ has made us free** (Gal. 5:1).

You are free. Confess that. Tell the devil that you have found the truth. He has known it all the time, but has lied to you and blinded your eyes to it. He has kept you from knowing your legal rights in Christ, your redeemer. **The god of this world (Satan) has blinded the minds of them which believe not** (2 Cor. 4:4).

Tell Satan you have found the truth — the truth that sets you free from him. Let him know, by your confession of God's word, that you are free from his dominion and that you know it.

The statement, **He [Jesus] has borne our griefs** [sicknesses], **and carried our sorrows** [diseases], is God's check for your perfect healing. Endorse that check with your confession, and perfect health will be manifested in your body.

An End to Chronic Ailments

The diseases of your body were laid on Jesus. You need never bear them, because He has borne them for you. All you need to do is believe this and begin to confess it.

Refuse to allow sickness to stay in your body, because you were healed with His (Jesus') stripes.

If Christians would believe this, it would be the end of so-called chronic ailments in their bodies. Always remember: Satan is a deceiver, a liar.

Sickness, disease, sin, and infirmities, all were laid on Christ. He bore them. He carried them away, leaving us free and well. We should rejoice in this liberty of ours.

Redemption has not become a reality to many. It has been only a theory, a doctrine, or a creed. Satan has taken advantage of this lack of understanding.

We are redeemed from all the power of Satan. That means we are *bought back* from the hand of the enemy. We are *born again*. We are the *new creation*. We are freed from the *kingdom of darkness*. We are no longer slaves of Satan. Sin and sickness no longer rule over us.

You are bought with a price: therefore glorify God in your body, and in your spirit, which are God's.

1 Corinthians 6:20

No Trespassing

How can you glorify God in your body when it is weakened by disease? It is just as impossible to glorify God properly in your body when it is full of sickness as it is to glorify God in your spirit when it is full of sin.

Tell the devil, "Satan, you are a liar. You know I am redeemed, because I have accepted Jesus as my redeemer. I am no longer dwelling on your territory, and you have no legal right to trespass on my property. It is no longer yours, neither is it under your jurisdiction. I have been redeemed from your authority by Jesus Christ."

Say to your enemy, "This sickness you have put on me was cursed on the cross of Calvary for me (Gal. 3:13), and you know that I do not have to bear it. I command you, in Jesus Christ's name, to leave my body. I am free from your curse, for it is written: **With his stripes, I am healed**, so I am healed. God said so. Satan, you are a liar; your pains are lies, your symptoms are lies, and your words are lies. You are the father of lies, Jesus said you are."

Then, thank the Lord for your deliverance.

Satan knows all of that. It is only when he knows that you have discovered it that he must respect your words. So few realize that they are free from the dominion of Satan. He knows it, but until you discover it, he will continue his assault on your life. Many have died prematurely because they have not known their rights in Christ.

Crucified, Buried, and Raised With Christ

When Jesus was crucified, we were crucified with Him. **I am crucified with Christ** (Gal. 2:20).

When Jesus was buried, we were **buried with him** (Rom. 6:4; Col. 2:12).

When Jesus arose from the grave as conqueror, we arose with Him (Col. 3:1; Rom. 6:4-5). **He has quickened us together with Christ; and has raised us up together in Christ** (Eph. 2:5-6).

When Jesus went back to the throne and **sat on the right hand of God** (Mark 16:19), [He] **made us sit together** [with Him] **in heavenly places** (Eph. 2:6).

We are his (God's) **workmanship, created in Christ Jesus** (Eph. 2:10). Through Jesus Christ, God made us what we are — a new creation.

> **If any one be in Christ, that person is a new creature; old things are passed away; behold, all things are become new.**
> **2 Corinthians 5:17**

We are now a new creature, made in the likeness of God through the power of Jesus Christ. God gives us His nature, His love, His faith, His life, His Spirit, His power. We are re-created.

All that Jesus did was for us. Everything He conquered was for us. He had no need to conquer Satan for Himself.

He had no sins of His own to carry away, because He had no sin until He *took our sins*. He did this for us.

He had no need to put away sickness for Himself, because He had no sickness until He was made sick for us. He did this for us. He conquered for us; and now that we are recreated in Christ Jesus and are made partakers with Him, we become conquerors through Him.

In all these things, Paul says, **we are more than conquerors, through him that loved us** (Rom. 8:37).

All Was for Us

All that Jesus did was for us, and we are now partakers of His victory.

We were captives, but Christ has freed us from captivity.

We were cursed by sin and sickness; but Christ, our redeemer, has freed us from that curse and loosed us from its dominion.

We were weak, but the Lord has become our strength, so now we are strong.

We were bound and imprisoned, but Christ has freed us from slavery.

We were sick, but Christ has borne our sicknesses and carried them away, so now, **with his stripes we are healed.**

Remember, you were slaves of Satan. You were bound by sin and sin's penalty, sickness. You were subject to Satan's authority. But now you are free. You now have Christ's emancipation proclamation — the Bible — and it is YOURS.

Do not be a slave any longer. Do like the slaves in the United States did when they heard their Emancipation Proclamation read: Claim your liberty; act on your deliverance.

You are free. Shout your freedom. Confess your freedom. Believe in your freedom. Redemption is a fact. Act on your liberty. Your bondage is past. Your prison is open. Your freedom is granted.

The spirit of the Lord God is on me; because the Lord has anointed me to preach good tidings to the meek; he has sent me to bind up the brokenhearted, to proclaim liberty to the captives, and the opening of the prison to them that are bound.

Isaiah 61:1

Moffatt's Translation reads: **to tell prisoners they are free, to tell captives they are released.**

Chapter 19

SATAN'S DEFEAT

Take a look at 1 John 3:8: **For this purpose the Son of God was manifested, that he might destroy the works of the devil.** Now look at Colossians 2:15: **Having spoiled principalities and powers, he made a show of them openly, triumphing over them in it.**

According to these scriptures, Jesus has *destroyed* the works of the devil, *spoiled* his power, and *triumphed* over him. Since Satan's works have been *destroyed*, his power has been *spoiled*, and he has been *triumphed* over, he must be a *defeated foe*.

Jesus' triumph was our triumph. His victory was our victory. He did nothing for Himself — He did it all for us. He defeated Satan for us. He spoiled his power for us. He destroyed his works for us. He conquered him for us.

Illegal Possession

But Satan (who was defeated) holds his master (the church, which is the body of Christ) in bondage. The defeated one is binding his own master. According to the New Testament, the church is given power and authority over an already conquered Satan.

Can you afford to subject yourself to Satan's dominion any longer? Never. Arise from his bondage. Confess that you are the conqueror. Then be sure you **hold fast your confession of faith without wavering; [for he is faithful that promised]** (Heb. 10:23). Maintain your confession of God's word.

"Every believer can become a devilmaster overnight," says F. F. Bosworth.

When Jesus arose from the dead, He left an eternally defeated Satan behind Him. Always think of Satan as an eternally defeated foe. Think of Satan as one over whom Jesus — and you in Jesus' name — have entire dominion and authority.

The Bible declares: **We are his workmanship, [re]created in Christ Jesus** (Eph. 2:10).

If any one be in Christ, that one is a new creature (2 Cor. 5:17).

We are positively "made new" in Christ.

We become **members of his body, of his flesh, and of his bones** (Eph. 5:30).

The Believer's Authority

On the basis of these scriptures, we have become what Christ is. We are what He is. We are in Him. He confirmed this when He said, **Those who believe on me, the works that I do shall they do also** (John 14:12). We now have the authority to work the same works that Jesus worked, by doing them in His name.

If this is true of our works, then it is true in regard to our standing with God.

God has placed us in Christ: **In whom we have redemption** (Eph. 1:7).

God sees us in Christ: **Of his fullness we have all received** (John 1:16). These facts constitute our confession. We think, speak, pray, and act accordingly.

To tell what Satan is doing in your life is to deny what you are in Christ. When you know that you are what Christ says you are, then you act accordingly, confessing what He has made you. This glorifies God and His word.

When Jesus said in Mark 9:23, **All things are possible to them that believe**, He meant that all things are possible to the believer. What masters He has made us to be!

We believe in Him — but who is He? What is He? If we are created in Him, what does that mean? If it is in Him that we live and move and have our being, then we must find out all about Him.

The Christ Who Lives in Us

The Man at the right hand of God, who loved me and died for me, now lives for me. He was God's answer to the universal cry of humanity — God manifest in the flesh.

Jesus was not a philosopher searching for truth; He was truth. He was not a mystic; He was reality. He was not a reformer; He was a re-creator. He was not a visionary; He was the light of the world. He never reasoned; He knew.

He was never in a hurry. He was never afraid. He never showed weakness. He never hesitated. He was always ready. He was sure. There was sureness in all He said or did.

He had no sense of sin or need of forgiveness. He never sought or needed advice. He knew why He came. He knew from whence He came. He knew who He was. He knew the Father. He knew about heaven. He knew where He was going. He knew humankind. He knew Satan. He had no lack. He had no limitation.

And we are re-created in Christ Jesus. We are in Christ. We are members of Him.

Jesus had no fear. He had no defeat. He did not shrink from pain or brutal treatment. He was the master when they arrested Him. He was the master at His trial. He was almighty, yet just a man. And He is in us.

Christ lives in me (Gal. 2:20).

That Christ may dwell in your hearts by faith (Eph. 3:17).

Christ in you, the hope of glory (Col. 1:27)).

Christ, who is our life (Col. 3:4).

But of him are you in Christ Jesus (1 Cor. 1:30).

Jesus Christ is in you (2 Cor. 13:5).

Are not these facts almost staggering?

When Christians begin to see their status in Christ and what God has made them to be in His Son, and then begin to speak that kind of confession, instead of talking about weaknesses, lack, inability, and sicknesses, they become an irresistible body of Christ. They take their place as New Testament believers, as they march forward in this glorious triumph of faith.

Understanding your relationship to God and your position as a believer re-created in Christ, you must remember that you are authorized to use His name. That name controls Satan and his works, and that name has been legally given to every believer to use.

In my name they shall cast out devils (Mark 16:17).

If we can cast out demons, then we can cast out demon-brought diseases.

Remember: Satan is eternally defeated.

Chapter 20

THE AUTHORITY OF GOD'S WORD

Many times theologians have not been our friends. They have made a philosophy of the truth; they have turned the word into a dogma and a creed when it should have been as though the Master were here speaking to us.

The word speaks to us as Jesus would if He were visibly among us. It takes His place. It has the same authority as He would have if He were to appear before us.

When we pick up the Bible, it would be good to remember that it is the book with God and life in it.

The word is always now. It has been, it is and it will be the voice of God. It is never old. It is always fresh and new. To the heart that is in fellowship with God, the word is God's living voice.

The word of God is like its Author — eternal, unchanging, and living. The word is the mind of God, the will of God.

The word is God speaking. It is a part of God Himself. It abides forever. God and His word are one.

Jesus was the word, and He lives in me. I read the word; I feed on the word; and the word lives in me. When I want more of Him, I feed on His word. If I want to know more of Him, I learn more of His word. I hold His word in my hand. I have it in my heart. I have it on my lips. I live it. It lives in me.

The word is my healing and my strength. It is the bread of life to me. It is the very ability of God in me. The word is the life of Christ. All He is, His word is.

The word is my confession. It is my light and my salvation. It is my rest and my pillow.

The word gives me quietness in the midst of confusion and victory in the midst of defeat. It gives me joy where desolation reigns.

The Word Is Not a Common Book

One of the most dangerous habits that Christians have is that of treating the Bible as though it were an ordinary book.

In one breath, they declare that they believe it to be a revelation from God; yet they turn to others for help when God has promised perfect deliverance.They treat the fact of redemption as though it were a fiction. They read articles about the word.

They sing hymns praising it; yet they live under the dominion of the adversary. They continually confess sickness, want, fear, weakness, and doubts — in the face of this revelation from God of their redemption, of the substitutionary sacrifice of Christ, and of the fact that He is seated now at the right hand of God, having finished a work that perfectly satisfies the demands of justice and meets every need of humankind.

People read about redemption — even sing about it — but then talk about it as though it were a fable.

That is the reason for the great amount of sickness, weakness, fear, and disease in the church (the body of Christ) today. That is why the average Christian manifests no boldness, but fears every threat of Satan.

All of this can be changed immediately. Just purpose to give the word the same place you would give Christ were He to manifest Himself visibly in your presence.

Is He Speaking to Me?

A miner lay dying in his shack in the hills of California. A Christian woman read John 3:16 to him. He opened his eyes and looked at her, asking, "Is that in the Bible?"

"Yes," the lady said.

"Does it mean me?"

"Certainly," she assured him, "it means you."

He lay there for a while, then asked, "Has He said anything else?"

And she read John 1:12: **As many as received him, to them gave he power to become the children of God.** Then she added softly, "He is speaking to you."

The man opened his eyes and whispered again, "I accept Him. I am satisfied." Then he died.

A Christian said, "I wish I knew whether He meant me when He gave us Isaiah 41:10: **Fear not; for I am with you: be not dismayed; for I am your God. I will strengthen you; I will help you; I will uphold you with the right hand of my righteousness.** Did He mean me?

"Jeremiah 33:3 says, **Call to me, and I will answer you, and show you great and mighty things which you know not.** Is He speaking to me? Can I claim this?

"What about Isaiah 45:11: **Ask me of things to come concerning my children, and concerning the work of my hands command you me.** Is this for me?

"In John 15:7 Jesus said: **If you live in me, and my words live in you, you shall ask what you desire, and it shall be done to you.** Was this written for me? Does it mean I can call on Him and He will hear me?"

Yes, these promises are all yours. It is as though you were the only person in the world and He was writing it all for your own special benefit.

> **Up to this time you have asked nothing in my name: ask, and you shall receive, that your joy may be full.**
>
> **John 16:24**

That promise is yours. There is no question about it belonging to you. It is as much yours as a check made out to you and properly endorsed. That is your check. You can get it cashed at the bank. And God's promises recorded in the Bible are as much yours as that check is.

When in need, you can boldly confess: **My God shall supply all your need according to his riches in glory by Christ Jesus** (Phil. 4:19).

When you are sick, you can boldly confess: **by his stripes, I was healed** (1 Peter 2:24).

Faith in God's word is faith in God. If you want to build faith in God, feed on His word. Unbelief in His word is unbelief in God Himself. When you believe God's word, then you will gladly confess His words.

Our attitude toward God's word settles everything.

Meet Satan with the words **It is written** and all of his sicknesses, diseases, pains, and symptoms will have to leave.

Say what God says. Satan can never endure that. He is a defeated foe, and he knows it. He has known it ever since Jesus rose victorious over death and hell. He has always sought to prevent the church from making this discovery. He has always obeyed the command of believers who use God's word against him, and he still does the same. When he finds that we have discovered the secret of using, **It is written**, his surrender is certain.

Confess What God Says

He sent his word, and healed them (Ps. 107:20) is for your individual case. The word will heal you. Confess this scripture in a personal way: "God sends His word and heals me." Then praise Him for your healing.

117

What God will do for one, He will do for everyone who will believe His word.

When you confess God's word, your confession brings healing to you. When you confess your sickness, your confession keeps you sick. Always confess God's word. Even when you may have contradictory feelings, confess the word. Confessing God's word always wins. His word heals today.

Holding fast your confession of healing in the face of natural contradictions verifies that your faith is established in the Bible. God's word is always the victor.

When you declare, **By his stripes, I am healed**, your words bind Satan's hands. He is defeated, and he knows it. The word of God is the greatest weapon on earth to use against Satan.

During the great temptation in the wilderness, Jesus defeated Satan with only one thing: **It is written**. That was the weapon Jesus used every time Satan sought to overthrow Him. **It is written**, Jesus said, then He quoted from the scriptures what God had said. What was the outcome? **The devil left him, and angels came and ministered to him** (Matt. 4:11).

That was ultimate victory. Satan was totally defeated. The only weapon Jesus used was the word of God. It always conquers.

Chapter 21

CONFESSION BRINGS POSSESSION

If you will confess with your mouth the Lord Jesus, and will believe in your heart that God raised him from the dead, you will be saved.

Romans 10:9

This word **saved** is translated from the Greek word *sozo*, which means to be "healed spiritually and healed physically" — healed in body and healed in soul, or saved from sin and saved from sickness. The same word is translated "heal, preserve, save, and make whole."

Express and Experience

Paul adds: **For with the heart we believe unto righteousness, and with the mouth confession is made to salvation** (Rom. 10:10).

Confession is made to salvation. Salvation does not come until after confession is made. One must believe and confess before experiencing the result. This is faith, and **By grace are you saved through faith** (Eph. 2:8).

Always remember: Confession comes first; then Jesus, who is **the High Priest of our confession,** responds by granting the things we have confessed.

There is no such thing as salvation without confession. It is always **confession *to* salvation,** never possession before confession.

Our confession causes **the High Priest of our confession** to grant us what we **believe with our heart** that we have, and this brings us into possession of it. That is faith. God is a faith God. That is to say, He is a God who requires faith. We receive from God only the things we believe we receive.

Whatever things you desire, when you pray, believe that you receive them, and you shall have them.

Mark 11:24

What Is Confession?

Confession is saying with the mouth what one believes in the heart.

119

Confession is agreeing with God in the heart enough to say what God says, to speak God's words, to use God's expressions and declarations, to acknowledge God's word.

Confession is faith's way of expressing itself in our testimony.

Paul declared that he preached the word of faith, then told us that the word of faith must be in our hearts and in our mouths.

The only way to have the word of faith in our mouths is to talk the word of God. This is confession — making our lips agree with God; speaking God's word with our mouths. (Read Romans 10:8.)

Revelation 12:11 tells us that those who overcame the devil did so **by the blood of the Lamb, and by the word of their testimony;** that is, through the scriptures they quoted as they gave their testimony.

He Was No Hypocrite

We were asked to pray for a person who was very sick and weak. He felt no immediate results. We then asked him to repeat what God said: **By his stripes, I am healed**, and to praise the Lord for healing according to His word.

The man considered our request to be outright hypocrisy. He was quick to let us know he did not believe in testifying to something he did not have. He said he was sincere and would never act the part of a hypocrite. The man was measuring his healing by his feelings. That is not faith.

It is not hypocritical to say what God says. Confession of a promise given us in God's word, when confessed from the heart, always brings the possession.

I did not ask this man to say he was not sick. I asked him to say what God had said — to acknowledge God's word: **With his stripes, I am healed.** You are not a liar because you declare what God has spoken.

Finally, God was merciful and added some feeling to his healing. He was like Thomas who said: **Except I shall see in his hands the print of the nails, I will not believe** (John 20:25).

Symptoms Not Reliable

We prayed for a man who had arthritis in his shoulders and arms. As we prayed, he felt a wonderful blessing and was thrilled with what he felt. But later, he felt another pain. That discouraged him. He came to me saying, "Just listen to my joints crack and pop."

Instead of saying, "The word says I am healed, and I know I'll recover," he was more concerned with physical evidence than with the word of God.

I told him of a similar case where we prayed for a lady, and she had believed with perfect confidence. After two days she returned to show us that her joints were completely healed. Her faith had set her free.

To this, the man responded: "I am glad you told me that. It encourages me. I was afraid I would not get healed. But if she got well, then I will be all right."

The word of God had meant nothing to that man. The promise given by Jesus, **They shall lay hands on the sick, and they shall recover** was empty and meaningless to him. He had felt a pain, so God's word must have failed. While he was feeling good, he was sure the word was true; but the pain had annulled the whole thing, so far as he was concerned.

Learn to confess what our Lord says, and He will fulfill His promise to you, because He is the **High Priest of our confession.**

The confessions of **I am the Lord who heals you** and **by his stripes, I am healed** always precede the manifestation of healing, just as the confession of Jesus Christ as Lord and savior always precedes the experience of salvation. (Rom. 10:9-10).

Jesus is the **High Priest of our confession** — our words, what we say with our lips — when it corresponds with His word. He does according to what we say.

We should never confess anything but victory, because Paul says: **In all these things we are more than conquerors** (Rom. 8:37).

Chapter 22

FAITH IN OUR RIGHTS

Praying for Faith

Very often people make the mistake of praying for faith. This you need never do. **Faith comes by hearing the word of God** (Rom. 10:17). That is the unique prescription for receiving faith.

Never pray for faith to be healed. As you learn to know God's word, you will have faith. The word of God develops faith.

A doubter often prays for things already possessed.

Peter says: **His** [God's] **divine power has** [already] **given to us all things that pertain to life** (2 Peter 1:3).

Healing has to do with life.

Things having to do with life have already been given to you. Believe that they are yours. Confess them.

Never Pray for Faith

All the promises of God in Christ are yea, and in him Amen, to the glory of God by us. In other words, Paul is saying: "Every promise of God that Christ died to pay for is *yes*, so go for it! It is yours (2 Cor. 1:20)." Find your promise. Believe it and begin to confess it. It belongs to you.

By his stripes, you were healed. Your healing is already provided, like your spiritual salvation. It is not something you must pray for, but confess and accept.

By reading the Bible, you hear God speak. You hear Him say, **I am the Lord who heals you.** You hear Him say, **By his stripes, you were healed.**

You do not need to pray for faith to believe that God told the truth. You have heard Him speak, and you have believed His word. You may pray for healing, but faith gives birth to healing.

Know your rights, then you will have faith. But you can know your rights only by reading and hearing the word.

It is not difficult to exercise faith for fifty dollars if you know you have that amount in your pocket. Unconsciously, you act your faith by buying anything within that amount of money.

123

You may write a check and never be conscious of having exercised faith in your checkbook, your banker, or the bank.

You know the check will be good because you have read the statement telling you that you have that amount in your account at the bank.

Truth Lives in You

I believe we can become so thoroughly acquainted with God's word that we will no longer consciously exercise faith when in need of healing. We know healing is ours; it has been provided for us. Sickness has been put away, through Christ. We are redeemed from it.

God says: **I am the Lord who heals you.** This becomes a vital truth that constantly lives and functions within us.

We regard it as we do the strength of a bridge which spans a canyon. We do not doubt the ability of the bridge to bear the weight of our automobile. We just drive across it. We have exercised faith, yet we did it unconsciously.

The word becomes so real and vital to us that when we come to face a need which has been provided for in the word of God, we drive on across the impossible, considering nothing but that God is back of that word. It cannot fail. We confess its truth, its ability, and go on. It cannot fail us.

We no longer try to be healed. God says we are healed. We confess it and thank Him for it, knowing it is for us. We no longer try to believe. We are believers if we are saved, and all things are ours (1 Cor. 3:21).

Real faith possesses. Faith's possessions are just as real as physical possessions. Spiritual things are just as real as material things.

Get accustomed to speaking God's language. Acquaint yourself with the words of God and train yourself to speak them because of their abundance in your heart.

Chapter 23

THE LANGUAGE OF FAITH

It is often said that talk is cheap. Many spend their time in idle talk. When I was a child, my father would say to me, "Do less talking and more listening."

A great percent of talking is done by people who should be listening. Wise people always observe more than they express. Their words are few, but weighty.

Marvelous victories have been won, then lost through unnecessary words. Jesus calls it **idle words**, every one of which He says **we shall give account** (Matt. 12:36).

Solomon said, **The one who keeps his or her mouth keeps their life** (Prov. 13:3).

James, who said the tongue is an **unruly evil**, gave some advice well worth heeding when he said, **Be swift to hear** [and] **slow to speak** (James 1:19).

Many fail to receive what they pray for, because they fail to understand how important their confession is regarding that thing.

Some who have been healed by the power of God find their aches and pains, and sometimes the disease itself, returning to their bodies. And they wonder why.

We believe you will understand the "why" of this and that it will never happen to you when you have finished reading this book.

We Unconsciously Confess What We Believe

Faith always talks about the thing prayed for as though it were already received, even before it is seen, heard, or felt.

You see, when you confess sickness, it is because you believe in sickness more than you believe in healing. You confess with your lips what you believe in your heart. **Out of the abundance of the heart the mouth speaks** (Matt. 12:34).

We prayed for a sick man in his home, and God marvelously touched his body. According to God's word, this man would recover. I assured him of this truth.

Then as we left the house, the mother said: "Do continue to pray for him."

By that request, she confessed that she doubted God's words: **They shall recover**. She implied that unless we prayed continuously to God, He would not fulfill what His word promised.

The Bible meant nothing to her.

She even went a step further. She began to brag on the devil and to commend his faithfulness, instead of God's faithfulness.

"As soon as you leave," she said, "the devil is sure to give him a severe test. I know the old enemy will do his best to steal my son's healing. Be sure and pray much for him."

What a confession to be given to the credit of the devil by a "believer." She never confessed any confidence in God or in His unfailing promises.

All of her confession was in praise of the faithfulness of Satan.

I said: "It seems to me that you have more confidence in Satan than you have in God. You seem to be positive that Satan will come and try your son, but you do not seem so sure of God's divine presence and assistance."

Then I asked: "If Satan is faithful, is not God more faithful?"

"Yes," she replied.

I told her, "**The angel of the Lord encamps round about them that fear him, and delivers them**" (Ps. 34:7). And I reminded her of Jesus' promise, **Lo, I am with you alway**, and of how God had promised, **I will never leave you nor forsake you** (Matt. 28:20).

Then I asked: Will you be fearful of Satan's power in the presence of God's angels and of the Lord Himself at your house?"

This, of course, helped her and she was encouraged to believe.

Annulling Faith

Christians often pray according to the scriptures, but when some symptom appears, they disregard the word of God and confess their sickness, annulling their prayer and its effects.

God's blessings are hindered when we let our lips contradict His word.

If a disease threatens your body, do not confess it. Confess the word: **With his stripes, I am healed.**

Say what God says. Confess His word.

Disease gains the upper hand when you agree with the testimony of your natural senses. Your five senses have no place in the realm of faith.

Confessing pains, aches, and diseases is like signing for a package that the post office has delivered. Satan then has the receipt — your confession — from you, showing that you have accepted his package.

Do not accept anything sent by the devil. Even though your five senses may testify that it has come to you, refuse to confess it. Look immediately to the word of God. Remember you were healed.

Doubt Reproduces Doubt

People practice confessing their weaknesses and failures, and their confession adds to their weakness. They confess their lack of faith, and that multiplies their doubt.

They pray for faith, forgetting that by so doing they are only confessing doubt. This increases their doubt because God cannot answer their prayer, seeing that He has said, **Faith comes by hearing** [not by praying], **and hearing by the word of God** (Rom. 10:17).

Sympathy Seekers

You should never talk about your sickness. When you tell people your troubles, it is usually to get their sympathy.

Your sickness came from the devil, your adversary. When you tell of your troubles, you are giving testimony to Satan's ability to get you into trouble.

When you talk about your sickness and disease, you are glorifying the adversary who had the ability to put that disease or sickness on you.

People often welcome pity and sympathy. Pity can never help your pains. Sympathy can never help you get well. Sympathy is suffering *with* another. What you need is not sympathy, but substitution, which is suffering *for* another.

Jesus did not come to be your sympathizer. He became your substitute.

Many prayers for the sick consist of little more than sympathy and pity. These will only feed and nourish the worst enemy you have.

Our position as believers is not to sympathize with the sick and pity them because of their pains, but to assume authority over disease on the basis of Christ's substitution and command those pains and sicknesses to leave in Jesus' name.

God said to Joshua: **Be strong and of good courage; be not afraid, neither be dismayed: for the Lord your God is with you** (Josh. 1:9).

There shall not any person be able to stand before you all the days of your life (Josh. 1:5).

Jesus speaks to you: **Behold, I give to you power over all the power of the enemy — and nothing shall by any means hurt you** (Luke 10:19).

More Than a Conqueror

Learn to confess what God has said in His word. Then you can repeat His words, and no power can succeed against you. By confessing His words, you are always the victor. God knows no defeat, and neither does His word.

With God nothing shall be impossible (Luke 1:37).

Now couple that verse with this: **and nothing shall be impossible to you** (Matt. 17:20).

You begin to see that by using the two unfailing weapons — God's word and Jesus' name — the irresistibility of God becomes your irresistibility. No weapon that Satan may form against these weapons shall prosper. (Is. 54:17.)

Confess: **We are more than conquerors through him that loved us** (Rom. 8:37).

Confess: **I can do all things through Christ which strengthens me** (Phil. 4:13).

You cannot know defeat using God's words. They are eternal. They are all-powerful. They are supernatural.

We confess that God has taken us out of the realm of failure and put us where victory, peace, joy, strength, and health prevail. As we make these bold confessions and act on the word of God, our faith becomes strong.

This will change you. It will change your ministry. It will change your life.

God Is Your Strength

You have prayed for success. You have prayed for power. You have prayed for great miracles of healing. Now you see where your strength lies. **God is your strength** (Ps. 27:1).

Act on what you know, and your wishes and desires will all be realized. It will be like a dream coming true. It will suddenly dawn upon you that much of what you have been praying and begging for, God has already given you, and it has only been waiting for you to claim it by faith and your action.

Suddenly, your redemption becomes a reality, instead of a mere doctrine or creed — something you have analyzed and accepted philosophically.

Your faith is measured by your confession.

People who negatively confess their weaknesses and failures, their pains and symptoms, and what they can *not* do, invariably sink to the level of their confession.

A spiritual law that few realize is that our confession rules us.

When we honor Christ and our hearts fully agree with our confession, then we turn our lives over to Him. That is the end of worry and of fear; it is the beginning of faith.

When we believe that Christ arose from the grave for us, that by His resurrection He conquered the adversary for us — when this becomes the confession of our lips and we believe it with our hearts — then the word of God will be fulfilled in our lives, and through our lives, for the good of others.

If we have accepted Jesus as Savior and confessed Him as Lord, we are a new creation. We are **heirs of God, and joint-heirs with Christ** (Rom. 8:17).

Sickness and disease can no longer dominate us. We have come to know that we are united with deity.

This may not dawn on us all at once; but as we study the Bible and act on it, live in it, and let it live in us, it becomes a living reality. That reality is developed through our confession.

Chapter 24

WHY SOME LOSE THEIR HEALING

In his book, *Jesus the Healer*, E. W. Kenyon writes:

For many years I have been bothered because I could not understand why people, who had received their healing and had all the evidences of perfect deliverance, should have the diseases return. I believe I have made the discovery:

Their faith was not in the word of God, but in "sense evidence." What do I mean by sense evidence? I mean the evidence of their sight, hearing and feeling.

They were like some of the sick people who came to the Master. They had heard that He had healed some of their friends. They said: "If I can get to Him, I will be healed." As they drew near, they saw others healed. The blind could see; the deaf could hear. They cried out for their share of the blessing and were healed.

There are many who come to us for healing because the Father has been gracious in healing many others through our ministry.

Many have no time to be taught the word. They have no interest in the Bible. They have no desire for the word. All they want is healing — deliverance for themselves.

We pray for them, and they are healed. In a little while they return and say, "I cannot understand it. That healing did not last. All the symptoms are back again."Where is the difficulty?

It lies in this: They had no faith in the word of God. They knew nothing about the word, as far as healing was concerned. Their faith was in me, or in some other person, not in God's word. The Bible declares: **By his stripes, I am healed.**

Take this as an illustration: A man came to me with a very bad knee. The doctors had told him that an amputation was necessary. He was instantly healed when prayer was made.

Five or six days later, while walking on the street the old pain returned. He said: "This cannot be. I am healed by His stripes. In Jesus' name, pain, leave my knee."

That man stood on the word of God and the pain left, never to return.

Others accept their sense evidence — what they can see, feel, or hear. They lose their healing because there is no "depth of soil" — as Jesus put it in the parable of the sower.

Real Faith

Our fight is a faith fight. **We wrestle not against flesh and blood, but against principalities, against powers, against the rulers of the darkness of this world, against spiritual wickedness in high places** (Eph. 6:12); but we are **more than conquerors** through Christ our Lord (Rom. 8:37).

Like Peter at the gate of the temple, we say: **In the name of Jesus Christ of Nazareth, rise up.**

Like Paul, when he cast the demon out of the insane woman, we say: **In the name of Jesus, I command you to come out of her.** We should thank the Lord for this authority.

Say this: **Surely he has borne our griefs** (sicknesses and diseases), **and carried our sorrows** (pains).

Have this on your lips: **With his stripes we are healed.**

Confess that, instead of confessing your pain. He bore that pain. Confess your healing, instead of confessing your disease. He bore that disease.

Real faith always holds fast to the confession of the word, while our physical senses hold fast to the confession of our pains and symptoms.

If I accept physical evidence instead of the word of God, I annul the word of God as far as I am concerned.

But I hold fast to what God said: **By his stripes, I am healed.** I maintain that confession in the face of all contradictory symptoms.

Every time you confess weakness and failure, you magnify the adversary above the Father. You destroy your own confidence in God's word.

Study the word until you know what your rights are, then hold fast to your confession.

Many try to make a confession without having a foundation, then the adversary beats them badly.

Jesus said, **It is written**, and Satan was defeated.

You say: "It is written." Then add, **"By his stripes, I am healed; He has borne my sicknesses and carried my diseases."**

They overcame him by the blood of the Lamb, and by the word of their testimony (Rev. 12:11).

Christianity is a confession. Confess the work Christ finished. Confess that He is seated at the Father's right hand. Confess that He perfectly redeemed you. Confess that you are His child.

Confess the authority Christ gave you over Satan. **Behold, I give you power over all the power of the enemy: and nothing shall by any means hurt you** (Luke 10:19).

Confess that. Confess your supremacy over the devil.

Believe that you are more than a conqueror over Satan. You are his master. He knows that. He cannot rule you any longer. Believe God's word. Be bold in its truth. Confess only what God says. Keep that confession — do not change it every other day. Let God's word *live in you* and you *live in it.*

Have Faith in the Word, Not in the Pain

Someone said "I felt perfectly well for several days after you prayed for me. Then, suddenly, the symptoms returned and I have been in pain and very sick ever since. What is the trouble?"

Here is the answer: Evidently, you received healing through the faith of someone else. The adversary took advantage of your lack of faith and brought back the symptoms. He camouflaged the whole thing, and you were filled with doubt and fear instead of faith.

Instead of meeting the adversary with the word and in the name of Jesus commanding that his power be broken, you yielded, confessed the pain, signed the receipt, and accepted the sickness back again.

Why did you yield? Because you had never studied God's word and you had no foundation in His word. You were like the man who built his house upon the sand. The storm came and destroyed it. (Matt. 7:26-27.)

Get to know, Jesus personally through His word. When you know that **by his stripes, you were healed** as well as you know that two plus two are four, the enemy will have no power over you. You will simply laugh at him and say, "Satan, you know you were defeated. In Jesus' name, I command you to leave my body," and he will obey.

Many, whose healing comes through the faith of others, lose their healing simply because they have no knowledge of their rights as set forth in the word of God.

David says: **Forget not all his benefits: who forgives all your iniquities; who heals all your diseases** (Ps. 103:2-3).

Physical healing is one of the **benefits** of Christ. Your confession about that is your faith talking.

Sympathy or Healing

You cannot talk sickness and disease and walk in health. You cannot talk about disease and pains, complaining about your troubles and obtaining everybody's sympathy, and be healed.

By telling others about your troubles, sorrows, pains, and aches, you invite disease and deny your rights to divine health. You tell people your troubles in order to get their sympathy.

Peter said: **Cast all your care upon him; for he cares for** (is concerned about) **you** (1 Peter 5:7).

If people will extend sympathy to you by hearing of your difficulties, how much more will your heavenly Father show compassion to you when you tell Him of your needs.

Learn to talk faith, then you will be a victor in every battle. First John 5:4 should be known to every believer, and you should confess it boldly: **Whatever is born of God overcomes the world: and this is the victory that overcomes the world, even our faith.**

Talk faith talk. Give up Satan's confession. Stop talking defeat. Stop talking sickness.

Sickness is of the devil. Weakness is of the devil. Disease is of the devil. Troubles are from the devil. As long as you are praising Satan's works, you cannot expect to maintain victory.

Your lips can be filled with faith words. **The word is near to you, even in your mouth and in your heart: that is, the word of faith, which we preach** (Rom. 10:8).

When you have faith, you no longer moan and groan; you praise and rejoice. *Faith talks positively. Faith sings joyfully. Faith prays confidently.*

Chapter 25

THE THREE WITNESSES

In every case there are three witnesses:

1. *The word of God.* The word declares: **With his stripes, we are healed.**

2. *The pain.* The pain declares that the sickness and disease are not healed, that the symptoms are still present, that the word is not true.

3. *The sick person.* The sick one declares: **By his stripes, I am healed,** placing his or her testimony alongside the word of God, refusing to take back their testimony. They declare in the face of pain — in the face of sense evidence — that they are healed. They hold fast that confession of their faith, and God makes it good. God always stands by those who stand by His word. He says: **My word shall not return to me void** (Is. 55:11).

But often, when we open the word and prove that **with his stripes, we are healed,** people say: Yes, I can see that, but the pain is still there. It has not left me. They have accepted the testimony of their senses rather than the testimony of the word.

Here is a woman who is weak. She cannot walk. I bring her the word that says: **The Lord is the strength of my life, of whom shall I be afraid?**

She says, "Yes, I see that scripture, but I cannot walk."

She denies the word of God. The testimony of her lips, joined with the testimony of her senses, annuls the word of God; and she remains ill.

On the other hand, had she steadfastly maintained her testimony that the word was true, in the face of contradictory sense evidence, she would have been healed.

A young man with a hard growth under his heel came to us for prayer. He was compelled to walk on his toes. His foot was painful. I told him, after praying, to walk on that heel in Jesus' name, and the hard growth would leave. He quickly obeyed, and the growth vanished.

A few days later, when he was about to remove his shoe to prove his healing to a skeptic, the pain struck him a terrific blow, and it felt as though the growth had returned.

Instead of accepting the testimony of his senses, he accepted God's word. Immediately, he said: "Pain, I rebuke you in the name of Jesus. Leave my foot. I was healed, through the stripes of Jesus."

The pain left, to return no more. He proved to the skeptic that he was healed. He confessed the truth, and the truth set him free.

One who was ministered to for stomach ulcers had been vomiting as many as five and six times a day. After being prayed for, a test came. After vomiting, she would say, "Thank You, Jesus, for healing me. Your word says I am healed."

The enemy was defeated, and she was completely restored. Faith always wins.

The word declares that you are healed. What the word says is true. You declare that you are healed because God said so. You maintain your confession of healing in the face of every symptom contrary to the word, and God always makes it true.

Our Senses and the Word

Never confess your feelings. They weaken your faith. There will always be a conflict between your feelings and the word of faith.

The word demands that we walk by faith. Our senses demand that we walk by sight. The word demands obedience to that word, while our senses lead an open rebellion against the word.

Walking by faith is walking by the word. To walk in the flesh is to walk according to the senses.

We look not at the things which are seen, but at the things which are not seen (2 Cor. 4:18).

Renewing of the Mind

Our natural mind cannot comprehend such a battle, so Paul commands us to **cast down imaginations, and to bring into captivity every thought** (2 Cor. 10:5).

The unrenewed mind rejects what God says. **The carnal mind is enmity against God: for it is not subject to the law of God, neither indeed can be** (Rom. 8:7). It cannot understand this message, so it refuses to listen to it.

What we need is a **renewing of the mind** (Rom. 12:2) so that we can grasp these vital truths. We receive this **renewing** through studying the Bible.

Not only must we speak right, but we must also think right: **Whatever things are true** [the word is true], **just, pure, lovely, of good report;** *think on these things* (Phil. 4:8).

As you think in your heart, so are you (Prov. 23:7).

In 2 Corinthians 10:5, we are taught to bring **every thought into captivity**. We cast down reasoning and give the word of God its place in our hearts and in our minds. **We have the mind of Christ** (1 Cor. 2:16).

God's spiritual and physical transformations are to come to us through **the renewing of the mind**.

Paul says, **Present your bodies a living sacrifice** (Rom. 12:1). The body is the laboratory of the five senses; no wonder it needs to be presented as a sacrifice. Paul goes on to say: **Be transformed by the renewing of your mind, that you may prove what is that good, and acceptable, and perfect will of God** (Rom. 12:2).

When the mind is renewed, it can see the spiritual value of the right confession.

Confess Your Healing Today

Paul says; **Behold, now is the accepted time; behold, now is the day of salvation** [or deliverance] (2 Cor. 6:2).

Webster says salvation means "deliverance from sin and its penalty." Since 2 Corinthians 6:2 is true regarding sin, it must be true regarding sickness, which is a part of the penalty of sin.

Arise out of your doubts, weaknesses, and fears. Do not talk about them. Take deliverance from your disability. Have a strong body with which to glorify God.

Kneel and pray. Tell the Father that you are His child. Tell Him that you give good things to your children. Tell Him that you are sure He is more willing to give good things to His children.

Speak to your disease or sickness, calling it by name. Command it in Jesus' name to leave your body. Command your weakness to leave, confessing that **the Lord is the strength of your life** (Ps. 27:1). Sin and sickness were nailed to the cross, so you are free from their curse forever. You are healed.

The Lord has redeemed you from the curse of the law (Gal. 3:13).

The Lord has redeemed [you], **and ransomed** [you] **from the hand of him** [Satan] **that was stronger than** [you] (Jer. 31:11).

For the right of redemption is yours to buy (Jer. 32:7).

Behold, you have made the heaven and the earth by your great power and stretched out arm, and there is nothing too hard for you (Jer. 32:17).

EXPLANATORY NOTE

This material on "**confession**" has been inspired by the works of Dr. E.W. Kenyon. The material abridged has been used by written permission, taken principally from his four books:

IN HIS PRESENCE
JESUS THE HEALER
TWO KINDS OF FAITH
TWO KINDS OF KNOWLEDGE

Some of the statements have been re-arranged, but the essence is unchanged because of his unique gift for communicating truth with unambiguous clarity. I treasure Dr. Kenyon's books above all others in my library, except my Bible. No author has matched his perspicuous talent for expressing redemptive truths so that believers can appropriate them.

Chapter 26

INTRODUCTION

(To the Next Four Chapters)

By Dr. Daisy Washburn Osborn

The first teaching I ever heard concerning divine healing was entitled, *Where Does Sickness Come From?* I had never really thought about where sickness came from. I can never tell you what this message did for us and the effect it had upon our lives.

In this message, the evangelist clearly showed us, by the word of God, that Satan is the author of sickness, disease, and pain, and that God is the Author of life and health.

I had never heard that Satan was the cause of infirmities and diseases, but had assumed, as I had been taught, that God placed them on people to discipline or refine them or to bring glory to Himself.

When I heard that sickness was from the devil, I immediately determined to resist sickness as I would resist the devil. I hated sickness and disease as I hated Satan and his power, and certainly never wanted his diseases in my body.

The evangelist went on to show us our authority over the devil and over his works in the name of Jesus Christ. When the teaching was concluded, I felt like a conqueror. My life was changed, and it has been different ever since.

A noted Christian leader once said, "No great spiritual awakening has ever come to any nation until, first, the church has learned to discern devils and to cast them out."

It is for this purpose that I have prevailed upon my husband to write the following four chapters, so that you may have a clear understanding of the work of demon spirits in disease today, and shall be able to resist them, to discern them, and to cast them out in Jesus' name.

Now, as you read, do so with an open heart. Compare the contents of these chapters closely with the scriptures; and when you discover the facts to be true, treasure them in your heart and begin to act on them.

Rev. F. F. Bosworth once said, "Every Christian can become a devil-master at once by receiving a clear understanding of the work of demons, and of their legal defeat at Calvary."

My husband and I have found this to be true wherever we have taught these Bible truths. You will never fear the devil again once you understand how totally powerless he is. Every believer has authority over Satan. Learn about yours and exercise it by faith in the word of God.

Chapter 27

SCRIPTURE READING

After these things the Lord appointed other seventy also, and sent them two and two before his face into every city and place, where he himself would come.

Therefore he said to them, into whatever city you enter, heal the sick that are there. And the seventy returned again with joy, saying, Lord, even the devils are subject to us through your name.

And he said to them, I beheld Satan as lightning fall from heaven. Behold, I give you power to tread on serpents and scorpions [two scriptural emblems of devils], and over all the power of the enemy: and nothing shall by any means hurt you.

Notwithstanding in this rejoice not, that the spirits are subject to you; but rather rejoice, because your names are written in heaven.

Luke 10:1-2; 8-9; 17-20

These verses make it clear that the important thing is not to cast out demons in Jesus' name, but for the lost to be saved. The main objective of our ministry is not to cast out devils, but to preach the gospel to the lost.

But in order to successfully preach the gospel with power and demonstration of the Spirit, it is vital that we have authority over satanic evil, and that we exercise this authority. Two great powers are engaged in a life and death struggle over human beings. Jesus described them when He said:

The thief [speaking of Satan] comes to steal, and to kill and to destroy.

I am come that they might have life, and that they might have it more abundantly.

John 10:10

Peter said:

Your adversary the devil, as a roaring lion, walks about, seeking whom he may devour.

1 Peter 5:8

But John said:

The Son of God was manifested, that he might destroy the works of the devil.

1 John 3:8

141

Chapter 28

WHAT ARE DEMON SPIRITS?

Demons are wicked, hateful, and destructive. Demon spirits are personalities, just like human spirits are personalities. Demons are spirits without bodies in which to dwell. We are spirits with bodies. Our spirits are from God. Demon spirits are from Satan.

Difference Between Body and Spirit

I *have* a body, but I *am* a spirit. My spirit dwells in my body. I express myself (my spirit) with the faculties of my body. You can see my body, but you cannot see me because *the real me is a spirit living inside my body.*

My body is simply the house my spirit lives in. Someday my body will die and return to the dust, but I (my spirit) shall never die. I shall return to God from where I came.

I (my spirit) am a personality. I express myself with my body. If my body were taken away, I (my spirit) could not express myself.

Sever my tongue and my spirit could not talk. Destroy my ears and I could not hear. Blind my eyes and I could not see. Even though my eyes would be blind, my ears deaf, and my tongue removed, my spirit would still be there, but could not see, hear, or speak.

Amputate my legs and arms, destroy my sense of smell and my vocal cords, and still you could not have destroyed my spirit. But my spirit could no longer express itself. My spirit would still have a body, but its faculties of expression would have been destroyed.

Now you can understand what I mean when we talk about the difference between my spirit and my body, or the difference between me and my body.

Demons Desire Expression

Demons are evil spirits without bodies with which to express themselves in this world. They long to find expression but cannot do so until they are in possession of a body.

143

Now you can understand why the evil spirit which was cast out of the man, had no rest and could not be satisfied. It was a spirit of Satan sent forth to destroy and to kill. When it could not find expression in a body, it was tormented until, with the aid of seven other spirits more wicked than itself, it was able to re-enter the man and once again find expression for its evil and destruction. (Matt. 12:43.)

A demon is a personality — a spirit, just like you and me. As you yearn to do good, to speak kind words, to hear music, to see the flowers, to express yourself in conversation, and to respond to impulses with some expression, demon spirits yearn to express themselves.

But since they have no bodies of their own, they must wander through the land (Matt. 12:43), seeking a body in which they can enter and find expression to carry out their mission of evil.

Humanity — Satan's Tool for Destruction

Demons delight to use people to do their dirty work. Their greatest power to defile, to destroy, and to abuse people is through another human being.

God must also use human instruments anointed by the Holy Spirit, to bless, to inspire, to encourage, and to lift those who need His divine help.

The message of good news must be reported by human lips.

God uses human instruments to minister to the human family; likewise, Satan uses human instruments to destroy the human family.

Satan uses some man or woman to defile an innocent boy or girl, then sends that boy or girl out as his missionary into the public schools and colleges to defile the minds of others.

The virtues of life are abused and destroyed by sinful living as young people are scarred and marked by Satan's influence.

Who Is Satan?

Satan is the god of this world. (2 Cor. 4:4). He is the prince of nations. He is the author of all our miseries and sorrows, of our diseases and pains, of death itself. He is the king and ruler of all demon spirits. He rules the dark hosts of hell.

His chief desire and design is to destroy human life and, therefore, to bring sorrow to the heart of God, our heavenly Father.

We can better understand who Satan is by the names given to him in the Bible:

In Matthew 13:19, he is called **the wicked one**. In verse 39 he is called **the enemy**, and **the devil. Devil** means "accuser" "defamer," or "slanderer."

144

In Revelation 12:10, he is called the **accuser of believers.**

In 1 Peter 5:8, he is called **the adversary** and is compared to **a roaring lion, seeking whom he may devour.**

In Revelation 20:2, he is described by a group of names almost too hideous to contemplate: **the dragon, that old serpent which is the devil,** and **Satan.**

In John 8:44, he is called by Jesus **a murderer, a liar,** and **the father of it** (lies).

In Matthew 4:3, he is called **the tempter.**

In Matthew 12:24, **the prince of the devils.**

In Ephesians 2:2, **the prince of the power of the air.**

In John 14:30, **the prince of this world.**

In 2 Corinthians 11:3, **the corrupter of minds.**

Demons' Most Useful Agents

Since a human body has the broadest means of expression, having been the only creation made in the likeness of God, demons seek as their highest prize to enter human beings.

But when they cannot find this most prized possession, then a body of less expression will do. But one thing is certain, they cannot rest without being in possession of some body through which they can find expression.

Perhaps now you can understand why, when Jesus went to cast out the legion of demons from the maniac, the demons begged, saying, **Send us into the swine** (Mark 5:12).

> **And being cast out of the man, the demons entered the whole herd of swine and they all ran into the water and were drowned.**
>
> **Mark 5:13**

Different Types of Demon Spirits

Since demon spirits are actual personalities, they manifest their own personalities in the persons whom they possess.

There are various classes, or types, of demon spirits just like there are different types of people. The Bible record shows many different types of demon spirits at work, a few of which we shall discuss later.

The Problem of Fear

Christians need to know what the Bible clearly teaches about demons. People fear them because they do not understand their position and have never heard about their legal defeat by Christ our Lord.

Until Daisy and I understood about demons and their work, about Satan and his defeat, we feared to speak or to teach about them. But now that we understand their work, we would not think of fearing them — knowing that, instead, they fear us.

Some say there are no such things as demons today, that the title is merely a figure of speech; but this is not true. The Bible is as clear and definite in its teachings about demons as it is about angels. Both are actual and real today. Both should be understood.

I will give you a few accounts of how demons have challenged us in our own ministry, exactly as they did in Bible days, which is proof of their existence and of their work today.

Chapter 29

THE MANIFESTATIONS OF DEMONS

1. Demons Talk

In the Bible, we have the record of demons talking. They talk through a person's faculties which they have possessed, in the same way that your spirit (the real you) talks through your own tongue and vocal cords.

> For he had healed many; so that they pressed upon him to touch him, as many as had plagues. And unclean spirits, when they saw him, fell down before him, and cried, saying, You are the Son of God.
>
> Mark 3:10-11

> Now when the sun was setting, all they that had any sick with various diseases brought them to him; and he laid his hands on every one of them, and healed them. And devils also came out of many, crying out, and saying, You are Christ, the Son of God.
>
> Luke 4:40-41

> He [Christ] taught them as one that had authority, and not as the scribes. And there was in their synagogue a man with an unclean spirit, and he cried out, saying, Let us alone; what have we to do with you, Jesus of Nazareth? Are you come to destroy us? I know who you are, the Holy One of God. And Jesus rebuked him, saying, Hold your peace, and come out of him.
>
> Mark 1:22-25

These and many other scriptures show us how demon spirits, which had possessed people, spoke and talked to those who had come to cast them out.

In a certain city, a man brought his wife to be healed and delivered from the power of the devil which had possessed her.

We were told that the woman could not be brought into the meeting and was, therefore, being kept in a side room of the building where we were conducting the crusade.

As we walked into the room, I saw a very large, tall woman sitting in a chair, with her face to the wall. She weighed at least 220 pounds and was very strong.

As we entered the room, she turned around quickly and stared right into my eyes with a fearful, sullen look and said, as she began to rise from her chair, *"Why, I know you. They told me this morning that I would be met by a true servant of the most high God."*

The family was amazed because they had not breathed a word about taking her to a gospel crusade, or to a man who would pray for her, because she hated all religious gatherings.

The demons were fearful and, therefore, tried to be religious. (Read the account in Acts 16 of the demon-possessed woman following Paul and Silas and crying out, **These men are the servants of the most high God.**)

When the demons spoke to me like that, the Spirit of the Lord moved in me with indignation at the sullen acknowledgment of the demons and I said, "Yes, you demons told the truth. You are met by a true servant of the most high God, and I adjure you in the name of Jesus Christ to come out of the woman now and leave her so that she can be sane and normal again. Come out of her now, I command you."

The demons obeyed. The woman was set free and was soon embracing her happy husband, while tears of gratitude poured from her eyes.

2. Demons Are Intelligent

Jesus met two demon-possessed men coming from among the tombs. When He was about to cast them out, they cried out, **What have we to do with you, Jesus, Son of God? are you come to torment us before the time?** (Matt. 8:29).

What did the demons mean by saying, **are you come to torment us before the time?** Of what time were they speaking?

Demons know that hell was prepared for the devil and his angels. They know the day will come when the devil will be **cast into the lake of fire and brimstone, where the beast and false prophet are, and shall be tormented day and night for ever and ever** (Rev. 20:10), **together with the fearful, and unbelieving, and the abominable, and murderers, and whoremongers, and sorcerers, and idolaters, and all liars** (Rev. 21:8), **and with whoever was not found written in the book of life** (Rev. 20:15).

Demons know that the day is coming when they shall be tormented, day and night forever and forever. They know that then, they will no longer be able to torment humanity, because **their time** will have come.

Therefore, knowing this, they trembled before Jesus and cried out, **Are you come to torment us before the time?**

Demons fear. They tremble before God's anointed servants today, because they know that we have been given power over them in Jesus' name, and that they must obey us.

That is why demon-possessed people often become violent when they are being brought to a gospel meeting. Though the possessed person may know nothing about where he or she is being taken, the demons are intelligent and they know they are being taken into the presence of God's word, to face God's servant who has power and authority over them.

Now you can understand why so many totally deaf people are healed while sitting or standing in our crusades as the word of God is being preached.

Even though the deaf person does not hear the sermon, the deaf spirit knows that its defeat is certain.

Fearing to stand in the presence of the word of God and of His anointed servant, the evil spirit leaves the body it possessed, and the deaf person can then hear. The same thing is true of any other kind of disease.

Some people were bringing a demon-possessed woman to one of our crusades to be prayed for. When they arrived, Daisy, my wife, happened to be standing in the crowded entrance, speaking to someone.

The demon-possessed woman began acting very strange toward those who had brought her. The demons, of course, knew that someone with knowledge of Satan's defeat was near.

This demon-possessed woman quickly looked all about her, then located Daisy. She stared at her, and her eyes became wild and fierce. She raised her hand and pointed to my wife with these words: *"I know who you are, and I don't want to have a thing to do with you."* Then she cursed aloud as she was led into the meeting.

Later that evening, Daisy and I took the lady into a room and prayed for her, and she was wonderfully delivered from the demons.

3. Demons Resist Surrender

The eighth chapter of Matthew, the fifth chapter of Mark, and the eighth chapter of Luke set forth the story of Jesus casting out the legion of demons from the maniac.

The context of these scriptures reveal the following:

First: The demons actually professed to worship Christ, evidently seeking to prevent the Lord from being too stern with them. (Mark 5:6.)

Second: Jesus commanded them to come out of the man. (Luke 8:29; Mark 5:8.)

Third: The demons begged Him that He would not torment them; but when Jesus spoke to them, the demons became fearful. (Luke 8:28.)

Fourth: Christ demanded of them, **What is your name?** (Luke 8:30).

Fifth: The demons responded, **My name is Legion: for we are many** (Mark 5:9).

Sixth: When Jesus insisted that they depart, the demons, shocked at being expelled from their habitation in the man's body, **begged him much that he would not send them away out of the country** (Mark 5:10).

Then the legion of demons, which had possessed the maniac, tried to bargain further. If they were to be forced out of their human possession, the next best place to settle would be the herd of swine which was feeding nearby.

All of the devils begged him, saying, Send us into the swine, that we may enter into them (Mark 5:12).

Seventh: **Immediately Jesus gave them permission. And the unclean spirits went out, and entered into the swine: and the herd ran violently down a steep place into the sea (they were about two thousand), and were choked in the sea** (Mark 5:13).

This remarkable story shows how demons resent surrendering their place of possession, yet how they must yield to the authority of God's servants; and to us Christ has said: **I give you power and authority over all devils;** and, **in my name you shall cast out devils** (Mark 16:17; Luke 9:1; 10:19).

The Case of Insanity

An insane lady, possessed of devils, was brought to us for prayer. I spoke kindly, saying, "Bow your head, please."

This lady replied with angered eyes, "We don't bow our heads."

This surprised me, and I knew I was face to face with demons who were daring to challenge the authority Christ had given to me. I said in a command, "Yes, you will bow your head and be silent while I pray."

The demons spoke again, defying me, "We don't pray and we don't bow our heads."

The Holy Spirit, which has given us power for such occasions (Acts 1:8), moved within me and I said boldly, "You hold your peace and obey me, because I speak in Jesus' name, according to God's word."

The demons then, fearing, because they knew they had met one with power over them, proposed to bargain with these words: "We'll hold our peace today, but we'll talk tomorrow."

Then I commanded, "In Jesus' name, come out of her now." The demons obeyed, her countenance was changed, and she was gloriously delivered.

Demons resist surrender, but they must obey.

4. Demons May Call for Reinforcements

Jesus taught a most revealing lesson about demons in the twelfth chapter of Matthew:

> When the unclean spirit leaves a person, he walks through dry places, seeking rest, and finds none. Then he says, I will return to my house from which I came out; and when he is come, he finds it empty, swept, and garnished. Then he goes and takes with himself seven other spirits more wicked than himself, and they enter in and dwell there: and the last state of that person is worse than the first.
>
> **Matthew 12:43-45**

We learn from this, that it is possible for demons, which have been cast out, to call other demons for reinforcement and to re-enter the person out of whom they have been cast, when the person delivered fails to consecrate completely to Christ.

In the above case, the demon was cast out, but then the person's heart had not been filled with good things. Therefore, the demon called on other spirits, more wicked than himself; they entered and settled there **and the last state of that person was worse than the first**.

Jesus said to the crippled man who had been healed, **Sin no more, lest a worse thing come to you** (John 5:14).

5. Demons May Occupy Alone or United

We have shown that where one demon cannot gain possession of a person, he may call on others to help him. While one may fail, in united strength they might succeed in cases where wholehearted devotion to Christ does not exist.

But let the Christian believer be assured that though Satan may send legions of demons to attack you, they shall all fall back in defeat because you have power and authority over all devils; and the Bible says: **When the enemy shall come in like a flood, the spirit of the Lord shall lift up a standard against him** (Is. 59:19).

The daughter of a certain woman was possessed of a devil. The evil spirit left the girl when faith was exercised. (Matt. 15:21-28.)

Mary Magdalene was possessed of seven devils, but they all came out when Jesus commanded them to. (Mark 16:9; Luke 8:2.)

The maniac among the tombs was possessed of a legion of demons, but every one of them obeyed the command of the Lord and went out. (Mark 5:1-19.)

Whether it is one demon, seven demons, or a legion of spirits, they all must obey the command of the believer, given in Jesus' name.

The Old Man With Strange Spirits

An old man was brought to us to be prayed for. His people thought he had arthritis and that he was feeble-minded. When he walked up to me, I shall never forget how I felt. I knew that the man was demon-possessed, but it was a strange personality.

151

Before I knew what I was saying, I placed my hand on his forehead and commanded, "You strange spirits, come out of this man and leave him."

At first, the relatives were surprised that I implied that devils were possessing the old man.

No sooner had I commanded the strange spirits to leave the man than a voice spoke back: "We won't come out. We won't come out."

I became indignant at the devils who would dare to disobey me when they knew they must do as I said. I commanded again, "Obey me and come out now, I order you in Jesus' name.

Immediately, the voice responded in fearful tones: "All right, we will come out. Yes, we will come out."

Then the old man smiled. His eyes became clear. He raised one hand, looking straight at me, and said softly, "Oh, praise the Lord, I'm healed. I know I'm healed."

He was completely changed in a second, his arthritis was gone, and the family wept for joy.

6. Demons Recognize and Obey Those Who Have Power Over Them

When Jesus was met by those who were demon-possessed, the demons would often cry out: **We know who you are. You are the Son of God.**

Demons have never changed. The lady I mentioned previously said to Daisy, "I know who you are, and I want nothing to do with you." The old woman said to me, "I know you. They told me this morning that I would be met by a true servant of the most high God."

Instances such as these happened in Paul's ministry:

> **Then certain of the vagabond Jews, exorcists, took upon them to call over them which had evil spirits the name of the Lord Jesus, saying, We adjure you by Jesus whom Paul preaches. And the evil spirit answered and said, Jesus I know, and Paul I know; but who are you? And the man in whom the evil spirit was leaped on them and overcame them, and prevailed against them, so that they fled out of the house naked and wounded.**
>
> **Acts 19:13-16**

Demons know who have power over them. They knew Jesus and they knew Paul; but as for those seven sons of Sceva who tried to cast them out just for the attention they would receive, the demons mocked them and completely overpowered them.

God anointed Jesus of Nazareth with the Holy Ghost (Acts 10:38). **It was the Holy Ghost who said, Separate me Barnabas and Saul for the work to which I have called them** (Acts 13:2).

The two persons whom the devils acknowledged were both anointed with the Holy Ghost, the power of God. The devil knows such and obeys them.

But this case is a clear warning never to play with the devil. Every believer has been given power and authority over all devils and should never fear nor hesitate to execute this authority.

Jesus said, **These signs shall follow them that believe; In my name they shall cast out devils.**

Mary Magdalene was possessed of *seven devils*; yet one man, anointed of God, cast out *all seven devils*.

On the contrary, there were *seven men*, none of them God's anointed servants, and *all seven men* could not cast out even *one* devil; but the *one* devil overcame *all seven men* so that they fled naked and wounded. What a comparison.

It proves that all of our natural strength and wisdom is helpless before the devil; yet, all the devils in hell are helpless before one believer who is anointed of God.

It also proves that demons recognize and obey those who have power over them.

7. Demons Are the Cause of Disease

This fact, shown clearly in the scriptures, will, when fully understood, serve as a great source of strength to your faith in God for divine healing.

A minister, who was present on a certain night when I preached on the relation of demons to disease, said, "Dr. Osborn, the message tonight has helped me more than any I have ever heard to have faith in God for the healing of all diseases. Knowing that disease is Satan's attack on our bodies, rather than God's blessing, I am ready to resist Satan's work, rebuke him, and take dominion over him."

This minister's life was changed. My life and ministry were transformed the night when Daisy and I heard that minister in Portland, Oregon, preach about the work of demons in disease.

The Source of Disease

Here is what the evangelist had explained:

Every disease has a life — a germ causes it to grow. That evil life in the germ did not come from God because it kills and destroys human life. It is from Satan. It is that evil life, or **spirit of infirmity**, that gives life to the disease, or growth, just as your spirit gives life to your body.

Just as your body, when the spirit leaves it, dies (James 2:26) and returns to the dust, so your disease, when the **spirit of infirmity** is cast out, dies and disappears.

We all matured from a tiny germ. The life of that germ came from God. The body, living by the germ or spirit of life which God caused to exist, developed until it became a complete human body.

So long as that life, or spirit, remains in the body, the body continues to live. But as soon as the spirit leaves the body, the body is dead; it decays and returns to the dust.

Many human sicknesses and diseases begin from a tiny germ, an evil satanic life, sent to live in and possess the human body and to destroy it. As long as that life, the **spirit of infirmity**, exists in the body, the growth or disease lives and continues its destructive work.

But as soon as the evil spirit, the evil life, or **spirit of infirmity**, has been cast out of the body in Jesus' name, that disease or growth is dead. It will decay and pass from the body. This is the process of healing.

The life of the disease or growth is rebuked and cast out, then the effects of the disease or growth disappear in a short time.

When one is healed by a miracle, of course, the complete work is instantly done by the power of God.

For example, a cancer is a living thing. Its life is satanic. Doctors all agree that if one could remove the life from the cancer, the effects of that cancer would disappear from the body.

But there are two lives warring against each other; the evil life of the cancer and the divine life from God which is in your body.

Any method of destroying the life of the cancer jeopardizes the life of the body in which the cancer lives.

What is the answer? Only faith in the supernatural power and authority of God.

Jesus said, **In my name they shall cast out devils**.

In the name of Jesus Christ, we as believers have the authority to expel the spirit, or life, of the cancer. It is satanic.

When the life of the cancer, which is from Satan, has departed, the cancer is dead, and its effects disappear.

When we heard that evangelist explain all of this and saw the people instantly healed, then for the first time in my life, many scriptures began to have meaning in my mind. The ministry of healing became a living reality from that moment.

We concluded: Then sickness is of the devil, and we have power over the devil in Jesus' name. We will call the sick, rebuke the devils that have bound and possessed their bodies with disease, and cast out the evil **spirits of infirmity**. The diseases will die, and the sick will recover.

I said to Daisy, "Let's announce a special healing meeting for Sunday night in our church."

We did, and the sick were brought from near and far.

We laid hands on them as Jesus commissioned us to do. We rebuked and cast out the spirits of the diseases in Jesus' name. We knew the work was done. The sick recovered, just as Jesus said they would.

People began telling everywhere: "The Osborns prayed for me and I am healed." "I had a tumor and now it is gone." "The cancer I had, disappeared a few hours after prayer." "The ulcers in my stomach are healed. They are gone."

Healing the Sick and Casting out Devils

Now you can understand this scripture: **They brought to him** (Jesus) **many that were possessed with devils** (notice, this was the only class of people specified who were brought to the Lord): **and he cast out the spirits with his word, and healed all that were sick** (Matt. 8:16).

This verse implies that the sicknesses which Jesus healed were caused by devils. He cast out the devils and healed the sick.

Peter said the same thing when he wrote, **God anointed Jesus of Nazareth with the Holy Ghost who went about healing all that were oppressed of the devil** (Acts 10:38).

The Woman Bowed Over

In Luke, chapter 13, Jesus was **teaching in the synagogue, and there was a woman who was bowed together and could not straighten up.**

The Bible says she had a **spirit of infirmity** (Luke 13:11).

What kind of a spirit?

Was it a blessing from God?

Jesus said, *Satan* **has bound her** (Luke 13:16).

Had doctors been asked to diagnose that woman's case, not a specialist in the world would say, "A spirit of Satan has bound her."

Doctors would call it arthritis of the spine, displaced vertebrae, or some other medical term. They would be correct as far as medical science is concerned.

But the real source of the trouble was: **a spirit of infirmity from Satan had bound her.** Cast out the spirit. Rebuke Satan's oppression, and she is healed. That is what Jesus did.

Spinal afflictions are still caused by Satan.

The Blind and Dumb Man

Then was brought to him one possessed with a devil, blind, and dumb (Matt. 12:22). When the devil was cast out, the blind could see and the dumb could speak.

A blind spirit caused the blindness in that man. Blindness is still caused by Satan.

The Dumb Man

They brought to him a dumb man possessed with a devil. And when the devil was cast out, the dumb spoke.

Matthew 9:32-33

In this case, dumbness was caused by a dumb spirit. And today, the source of dumbness is still Satan.

The Deaf and Dumb Boy

He rebuked the foul spirit, saying to him, You dumb and deaf spirit, I charge you, come out of him, and enter no more into him.

Mark 9:25

Then, and now, those deaf and dumb are held by a deaf and dumb spirit.

The Unclean Man

There was in their synagogue a man with an unclean spirit, and he [the demon] **cried out. And Jesus rebuked him** [the foul spirit], **saying, Hold your peace, and come out of him** (Mark 1:23,25; Luke 4:35).

Here was an unruly man in the synagogue, and his condition was caused by a foul unclean spirit. The cause of a rebellious, unclean character is still the devil.

The Fever

Peter's wife's mother was sick of a fever. And he [Jesus] **stood over her and rebuked the fever; and it left her** (Mark 1:30-31; Luke 4:39). You cannot rebuke something that cannot understand your words. You can rebuke only a personality.

Jesus recognized Satan at work in this body, causing the fever. He rebuked it, and it left. Fever is still of the devil; and when rebuked in Jesus' name, it will still leave.

Medical Terms and Bible Terms

Doctors may call it arthritis, but a binding spirit of the devil is the real cause.

The scientific term may be undeveloped vocal cords and dead nerves in the ear, but the real trouble is a deaf and dumb spirit that should be cast out in Jesus' name.

The specialist may say it is glaucoma or cataracts, but Jesus said it is a blind spirit.

The Case From New York

A woman, who was demon-possessed, was brought to one of our meetings. Satan was determined to take her life. Her throat would constrict so that she could not swallow. Strange voices would speak from her throat and say terrible things. She was resentful and tormented continually because the voices told her someone was following her and watching her.

When we prayed for her and cast out the devils, she reeled to and fro for a few moments like a drunk person; then, all at once she became normal.

Her eyes, which had glared with hatred, became gentle and kind; her lips, which had been set over gritted teeth, formed a kind, relaxed smile.

Tears trickled down her cheeks as she said calmly, "Oh, I feel free. I feel so happy. I am healed. I am well. Oh, I feel like I have a new throat. Oh, thank God."

She was well as soon as the devil left her, and her throat was healed.

The Blind Lady

A totally blind lady was brought to us for prayer. The doctors had said her optical nerves were dead. For about fifteen years she had groped in total blindness with a seeing-eye dog.

I rebuked the blind demon which had bound her. It left when I commanded it to go in Jesus' name, and the lady screamed with joy, "Oh, now I see. I am healed."

The Insane Girl

A beautiful girl was brought to us for prayer, whom the doctors said had lost her mind because of constant pressure and anxiety about her college studies.

When the demon of insanity was cast out in Jesus' name, we believed it left her, though nothing instantly changed to indicate that she was healed. But in a few days, she was normal and was soon working in a factory.

A Miracle in Kingston, Jamaica

In Jamaica, a woman was hauled to our crusade in an old wheelbarrow by three women. She had suffered, the doctors said, a complete stroke of paralysis.

She had lain lifeless for four days and nights without swallowing a drop of water or a bite of food. Her eyes were rolled back in her head and her body appeared to be dead, except for the pulse beat of her heart.

I rebuked the demon that had paralyzed her and commanded it to turn her loose and to come out of her.

Then I called with a loud voice, "Open your eyes and be made whole." She was instantly healed.

In a few minutes she was on her feet. She walked home, sound and well.

Hundreds of people in Kingston, Jamaica, know about the miraculous healing of this woman, Veda McKenzie. The cause of her illness was a demon sent from Satan to kill and to destroy her, but God delivered her.

We could record hundreds of such cases which have occurred in our own ministry; but I believe we have related enough to prove, when coupled with the scriptural evidence given, that sickness is still of Satan, caused by **spirits of infirmity**. When these spirits are cast out in Jesus' name, the sick still recover.

Food for Thought

If sickness is of God, then doctors would be of the devil because they are trying to get rid of sickness.

If sickness is of God, all hospitals would be houses of rebellion rather than houses of mercy, because in seeking to get rid of disease, they would be rebelling against God and His alleged sickness program.

If sickness is of God, every nurse would be defying God with each effort to relieve suffering.

If sickness is of God, we should be against hospitals, nurses, doctors, and medicine, because they are all seeking to relieve and restore those who are suffering with sickness.

But since sickness is of Satan, then doctors, medicines, hospitals, and medical science must be from God.

Since sickness is of Satan, every manner of relieving the suffering must be ordained of God.

Those who believe that God wants His children to suffer should never call a doctor, nor recommend medical treatment to members of their churches; in doing so, they would be seeking to violate God's divine will in their lives.

Many who believe sickness is from God are ready to recommend the doctor whom they feel is best qualified to relieve suffering through medical means, whether God wants His child to suffer or not.

Those who believe that sickness is a blessing should never accept medical treatment to get rid of their disease, but should rather pray that all of their family and fellow church members would receive a similar blessing.

Those who believe sickness is from God are often anxious for the doctor to operate and remove the blessing, whether God wants them to have it or not.

Those who believe that sickness is God's chastisement for His disobedient children should never recommend hospitalization, but should rather tell the sick one to receive the divine punishment until God sees fit to stop the chastisement, at which time the sickness would disappear.

But I notice that *those who believe sickness is a blessing from God* are generally the first to recommend going to the hospital for surgery or treatment in an attempt to get rid of the sickness, whether it was God's chastisement or not.

Those who believe that sickness is from God should be against every means of relieving the suffering. It is not consistent to teach that disease is of God, then to recommend medical treatment to get rid of the disease.

If God wants us to suffer for His glory, then we should rather suffer than to be well.

If it is God's will that we be sick, then we should do nothing to interfere with God's divine will, and patiently bear the sickness until it has run its course.

But since sickness is of Satan, then every means of relief must be a blessing — whether it be the **prayer of faith**, or the **gift of healing** for those who serve God faithfully and who believe and trust His divine promises.

Chapter 30

SYNOPSIS

When Trouble Began

In the beginning man and woman were created well and strong, healthy, happy, and in fellowship with God.

But Satan, the deceiver, caused Adam and Eve to disobey God and to doubt His word. They sinned against God and yielded themselves to the authority of Satan to be his slaves forever.

Because of this, they were driven from the garden of Eden, to be forever separated from God's presence.

It was then that disease, pain, and sickness began destroying the health of God's creation, and has done so ever since until Christ, the Son of God, came and bore our sins and our sicknesses and carried them away. He paid the penalty for our disobedience by being beaten and crucified. He endured our sentence of death for us.

Now that Jesus Christ has paid our debt and suffered our penalty, in our place, God has declared us free. Through His blood, we have received remission for sins, and by His stripes we were healed. (Matt. 26:28; 1 Peter 2:24.)

Our Liberation

Our salvation, our deliverance, and our redemption from all the works of Satan have been accomplished by Christ for us. When He uttered those words, **It is finished**, it was like hoisting the flag of the victor over a liberated land where the battle had been fought, where the enemy had been conquered and forced to surrender.

Christ, the **captain of our salvation and the author and finisher of our faith** (Heb. 2:10; 12:2), came to this world, defeated our enemy, Satan, stripped him of his authority, carried away our pains and our defeats, and arose from the grave, triumphant over the devil. He declared those triumphant words: **It is finished**.

Our salvation, our healing, and our deliverance are finished. The flag of victory is unfurled. The blood-stained banner of love and peace has been hoisted and flies as a symbol of Christ's total triumph and complete victory over all the works of the devil which He came to destroy.

Now we are liberated from the hand of the oppressor.

Body, mind and spirit, we are free. Our land is liberated. **You are bought with a price: therefore glorify God in your body, and in your spirit, which are God's** (1 Cor. 6:20).

Christ, the captain of our salvation, has fought our battle for us and has liberated us from the power and dominion of the enemy.

Now you can say, "I am saved through His blood, and I am healed through His stripes," because redemption is yours forever.

Guerrilla Opposition — Illegal Warfare

But why, then, are so many Christians still sick and diseased?

Because, though our property has been liberated from the enemy, though Satan's reign has been destroyed by Christ, though Satan's power over our lives has been taken from him, there remains a host of demons who continue to resist our freedom and resent our victory.

Demon spirits have no legal right to continue oppressing and afflicting believers with disease and infirmity, but they know that thousands of people do not know that Satan has made a surrender and has been defeated.

Thousands of people do not know that Satan's forces have no rights over them at all. So demons continue their illegal opposition to their heritage in Christ and they defeat many.

As long as people do not know about Satan's legal defeat, he can operate unhindered. But our business is to read and to know God's word and to discover the record of Satan's complete defeat. Then we can resist the devil, steadfast in the faith, and he will flee from us. (James 4:7; 1 Peter 5:9.)

Recognizing the Enemy

Satan is your adversary. Demons are your enemies. They resent your legal rights over them and are jealous of your heritage. They will always seek to hinder your progress and cheat you out of every inch of your promised land. But, like Joshua and the children of Israel, you must go in and possess your land, without fear.

You must recognize your enemy, spot him, study his tactics of warfare, and be skilled in ability and faith to drive him out. This can be done by reading and knowing God's word.

The weapons of our warfare are not carnal, but mighty through God to pull down the strong holds of Satan.

2 Corinthians 10:4

For we wrestle not against flesh and blood, but against principalities, against powers, against the rulers of the darkness of this world, against spiritual wickedness in high places.

Ephesians 6:12

Everything evil, destructive, discouraging, malicious, and binding is of Satan. Everything good, blessed, lovely, kind, and pure is of God.

Every good gift and every perfect gift is from above, and comes down from the Father.

James 1:17

God has given us all things that pertain to life.

2 Peter 1:3

The Son of man is not come to destroy our lives, but to save them.

Luke 9:56

We have concluded that Satan is bad and God is good. Good things are from God and bad things are from Satan.

Satan, your adversary, is always present to challenge your faith, your integrity, and your covenant rights. Satan always leads an open rebellion against God and His family.

But Jesus Christ **was manifested, that he might destroy the works of the devil** (1 John 3:8). The works of the devil are, and always have been, **to steal, and to kill, and to destroy** (John 10:10) the spirits, minds, and bodies of God's creation, in whole or in part.

Christ came to destroy all of these wicked works of Satan. He has overcome them and has given us power and authority over all devils.

How Satan resents this!

How jealous he is! He opposes us. He despises us. But we have been warned to be on the alert. We have been given a full armor with which to resist him.

Jesus, before going back to the Father, conferred upon every believer the right to use His name against the devil.

The sword of the Spirit, which is the word of God, is ours to use against Satan.

Our feet are shod with the gospel.

The helmet of salvation is on our head, and the shield of faith is our defense with which we shall be able to quench all the fiery darts of the wicked. (Eph. 6:13-18.)

Jesus, our captain, says: **Behold, I give you power over all the power of the enemy** (Luke 10:19).

He gave them power and authority over all devils.

Luke 9:1

In my name they shall cast out devils.

Mark 16:17

They shall lay hands on the sick, and they shall recover.

Mark 16:18

We need never fear nor tremble; but only be strong, bold in faith. With the **whole armor** of God, we are to resist Satan; in the name of Jesus, we are to cast out devils; and with the sword of the Spirit, which is the word of God, we can defeat every opposing force.

Chapter 31

SICKNESS — A BLESSING OR A CURSE?

Many say, "Perhaps God has seen fit to lay this disease on my body. Maybe it is His will for me to be sick. Perhaps it is His blessing in disguise. It may be one of the mysterious ways in which He works out good things in my life."

The following thoughts will help you to understand that these things are not true:

1. God Calls Sickness Captivity

The Lord turned the captivity of Job, when he prayed for his friends.

Job 42:10

The Bible says: **So Satan went forth from the presence of the Lord, and smote Job with sore boils from the sole of his foot to his crown** (Job 2:7).

When God healed Job, the scriptures record the great healing of this man of God as **deliverance from captivity.**

Captivity could not be the will of God. Jesus came in the Spirit of the Lord to **preach deliverance to the captives** (Luke 4:18).

So we see that God called sickness *captivity*, and every **captive** of sickness has now been granted complete **deliverance.**

2. Jesus Calls Sickness Bondage

Ought not this woman, whom Satan has bound, be loosed from this bond?

Luke 13:16

Jesus, seeing this woman bowed over, said to her, **Woman, you are loosed from your infirmity** (Luke 13:12). He said that Satan had bound her. He never once inferred that His loving Father, in an effort to perfect some hidden quality in her life, had bound her. God does not bind people — He looses them.

Jesus never said that this woman was bowed over to keep her humble, or that it was a mysterious way God had of working out His will in her life. Jesus said that **Satan had bound her.**

165

Bondage could not be the will of God. Jesus came to **set at liberty them that are bruised** (Luke 4:18).

It was prophesied of His ministry that it would **loose the band, undo the heavy burdens, and break every yoke** (Is. 58:6).

So we see that Jesus called sickness *bondage*, and every bound person is commanded to be loosed, to be set free.

Jesus came as **the way, the truth, and the life** (John 14:6). He said, **You shall know the truth and the truth shall make you free** (John 8:32).

3. The Holy Spirit Calls Sickness Oppression

Acts 10:38 says, **Jesus went about doing good, and healing all that were oppressed of the devil** — not, "all who were blessed of the Father."

This is the language of the Holy Spirit because, while Peter was speaking these words, everyone who listened to him was filled with the Holy Spirit. The Holy Spirit, speaking through Peter, at the house of Cornelius, said that sickness is *oppression*.

God does not intend for you to be oppressed with any form of sickness or any other kind of oppression. Jesus, according to the words of the prophet, came **to let the oppressed go free** (Is. 58:6).

Liberty, freedom, deliverance, broken yokes, released burdens, and liberated captives are the great results of New Testament ministry.

God calls sickness *captivity*; Jesus calls it *bondage*; and the Holy Spirit calls it *oppression*. Align your attitude with that of the word of God and **be made whole.**

> **If the Son therefore shall make you free, you shall be free indeed.**
> **John 8:36**

> **You shall know the truth, and the truth shall make you free.**
> **John 8:32**

> **Stand fast therefore in the liberty by which Christ has made us free.**
> **Galatians 5:1**

Chapter 32

THE BELIEVER'S AUTHORITY

He called the twelve disciples together, and gave them power and authority over all devils, and to cure diseases. And he sent them to preach the kingdom of God, and to heal the sick. And they departed, and went through the towns, preaching the gospel, and healing every where.

Luke 9:1-6

He ordained twelve, that they should be with him, and that he might send them forth to preach, And to have power to heal sicknesses, and to cast out devils.

Mark 3:14-15

The Ministry of Authority

The words of Jesus are astonishing when accepted as spoken. They were clear and they were powerful.

They were astonished at his doctrine: for his word was with power.

Luke 4:32

What a challenge it is to accept the words of our Lord just as He spoke them and to follow the ministry as He gave command.

Power Given to the Believer

We consistently tell people not to look to us, promising them disappointment if they expect us to help them. We tell them we have nothing.

We say, "Do not look to us, for we have nothing."

But Peter said the opposite. He said, **Look on us. Such as I have, I give to you** (Acts 3:4,6). Could this difference in attitude account for the difference in results?

After Peter told the lame man to rise and to walk in Jesus' name, he explained in Acts 3:12,13 that it was the power of the risen Christ that did the miracle. But that power was in Peter, and it is promised to **every believer** according to Acts 2:39.

167

Look on Us

People today think it was all right for Peter to say, **Look on us,** but if we say the same, it would be sacrilegious.

The fact is that believers today have the same power and authority that Peter had. Every believer today may do the same things that believers did then by acting on Jesus' words now as they acted on them then.

Being filled with this power we, too, may say, *Such as I have, I give to you* and see the sick and lame recover.

Has Elijah Risen From the Dead?

Herod heard about the miracles and was convicted because he had beheaded John the Baptist. **He was perplexed, because it was said of some, that John was risen from the dead; And of some, that Elias [Elijah] had appeared; and of others, that one of the old prophets was risen again** (Luke 9:7-8).

Not a Risen Prophet, Just Fishermen

But it was not Moses who did those things. Elijah was not risen from the dead. It was *ordinary people* who had become followers of Jesus Christ.

Many today are like Herod was then. They think of great men and women of God, or of special saints of the past, and they muse: "Were one of these to raise from the dead, we could then see great things."

God used other people in other generations but this is your day. Now He wants to use you. You are the believer of today.

These signs shall follow them that believe.

That includes you.

These miracles, which were disturbing Herod, were not taking place at the hand of a risen prophet. They were being done by those who lived in the day in which Herod lived — *ordinary people* who had been given the same power that Elijah or Moses or Daniel had.

If Paul Lived Today

Christians sometimes fancy: "If only Elijah were here"; or, "If Paul lived today"; or, "If we could have Moses or some other prophet in our midst today, they had great power with God."

But this sort of spiritual speculation will not solve the problems of today. You and I must look about us and see our position today. The believer today has the same power and authority that the believer had then, if we will use it.

(Joshua could compel the sun to stand still; so can we.)

David could tear apart a lion as he would have done a kid; so can we.

Three Hebrew children escaped the heated furnace without a hair of their heads being singed and John came out of boiling oil without suffering harm; so can we, in similar circumstances, if we believe.

Strength in Weakness

You may say, "I am so small and weak." But God is strong even in weak people.

Moses said that. (Ex. 3:11; 4:1,10.)

Isaiah said that. (Is. 6:5.)

Jeremiah said that. (Jer. 1:6.)

You see, this allows God to choose **the foolish things of the world to confound the wise, and the weak things of the world to confound the things which are mighty** (1 Cor. 1:27).

This provides the circumstances in which you may confess, **I can of my own self do nothing** (John 5:30).

Jesus said, **Without me you can do nothing** (John 15:5).

When I am weak, then am I strong (2 Cor. 12:10).

Let the weak say, I am strong (Joel 3:10).

My (God's) **strength is made perfect in weakness** (2 Cor. 12:9).

Out of weakness the old prophets were made strong (Heb. 11:34).

The weaker you feel, the stronger you are in God.

This fact, as proven by so many scriptures, does not agree with the testimony of our five natural senses. But **we walk by faith, not by sight** (2 Cor. 5:7) and **faith is the substance of things hoped for, the evidence of things not seen** (Heb. 11:1).

Faith deals with the unseen and the unfelt things, so we declare ourselves strong in Him, even though we may feel weak in ourselves.

The Natural Person and God's Word

God's word declares that when we feel weak, we are strong.

The natural mind will never grasp this fact, nor will the natural person ever be able to comprehend it. **The carnal mind is enmity against God: for it is not subject to the law of God, neither indeed can be** (Rom. 8:7).

> **The natural person receives not the things of the Spirit of God: for they are foolishness to him: neither can he know them, because they (the things of the Spirit) are spiritually discerned.**
>
> **1 Corinthians 2:14**

Faith Is Not Feeling

We may never feel that we can do the things that Jesus said we can do, such as heal the sick, cast out devils, cleanse the lepers, and raise the dead, because we may feel so powerless in ourselves.

No person who is willing to act according to feelings, or who judges things from their outward appearance, will ever know the blessing of God's strength being perfected in human weakness.

When we feel weak in our flesh and confess our weakness, we glorify the adversary, who delights to tear down our strength and prevent God's miracle power in our lives.

On the other hand, when we feel weak, if we testify according to what God has said and we are persistent in declaring, **When I am weak, then am I strong,** our confession of the word will defeat our sense of weakness, and we will be strong and do exploits. We will glorify God, who alone is able to transform our weakness into strength, bringing victory out of defeat.

The Secret That Will Bring Another Great Revival

If Christians can be convinced that they can do what God says they can do, and that they are what God says they are, another great day of triumphant victory, like those witnessed by the early church, will inevitably be the result.

Recall Jesus' great prayer for us in the seventeenth chapter of John: **As you have sent me into the world, even so I have also sent them into the world** (John 17:18).

Now we are ordained to represent Christ in this life. (John 15:16.) We are to work the works of Jesus. We are to manifest His faith and His love. We are to speak the words of the Father which Christ gave us to speak. (John 17:7,14.)

We are ordained to represent Christ in this world, exactly as He came and represented the Father to the world.

Jesus revealed to us just what the Father's dream of a son or a daughter was. Jesus was the perfect Son. Now, Paul says, **Because you are sons and daughters, God has sent the Spirit of his Son** (Jesus) **into your hearts. Wherefore you are no more a servant, but a son or a daughter** (Gal. 4:6-7).

The part of a son or daughter of God is now ours to share.

Let us take our place as authorized **ambassadors for Christ, acting in Christ's stead** (2 Cor. 5:20). What a privilege to be a child of God, **and if a child, then an heir of God through Christ** (Gal. 4:7).

When you take such a stand, you will be accused as Jesus was of making yourself *equal with God.* I recall preaching on this subject, and a dear man retorted, "You make yourself equal with Christ." I answered,

"No, I do not make myself equal with Christ. He makes me equal with Himself and I let Him do so."

Of course, in speaking of this position with its authority and power, we are very careful to keep in mind that even Jesus said, **I can of my own self do nothing** (John 5:19,30), and again, **without me you can do nothing** (John 15:5).

The Father is greater than the firstborn Son (Rom. 8:29; 1 Cor. 15:22-28); and the firstborn Son, (Rom. 8:29; Heb. 1:6) is greater than His brothers and sisters (Heb. 2:7-11); so Paul says, **The head of every** (believing) **person is Christ, and the head of Christ is God** (1 Cor. 11:3).

But that does not change the fact that just as Jesus, our elder brother, was the visible representative and agent on earth of His Father who was in heaven, so we are expected to be the visible representatives and agents on earth of our elder brother, who returned to and is now in heaven. (John 3:13.)

The Authority of Jesus' Name

Wherefore God has also highly exalted him, and given him a name which is above every name: that at the name of Jesus every knee should bow, of things in heaven (angels), **and things in earth** (people), **and things under the earth** (demons).

Philippians 2:9-10

Beings in all three worlds are compelled to bow before that all-prevailing, all-powerful name; and Jesus said that in His name we could do the works that He had done. His words are: **The ones that believe on me, the works that I do shall they do also; and greater works than these shall they do; because I go to my Father** (John 14:12).

What power we have when we believe this and act with this authority.

Paul says, **We are ambassadors for Christ** (2 Cor. 5:20).

Ambassadors never doubt that the country which they represent will back up their word. They know it will. The very title of their office implies that.

We are to act representatively **in Christ's stead** (2 Cor. 5:20), and God the Father never failed to make good the words of Jesus Christ.

Children — Not Servants

If I am to act in Christ's place, then I expect my Father to deal with me as He did with Jesus Christ. According to Galatians, chapter 4, He has adopted me and made me His child, even a joint-heir with Jesus.

171

Joint-Heir — Combined Inheritance

If two persons become joint-heirs to $1,000, it does not mean that they each receive $500. They both become heirs of the same $1,000. They have a combined inheritance.

Paul says, **Wherefore you are no more a servant, but a son or daughter, and if a son or daughter, then an heir with God through Christ** (Gal. 4:7).

In Romans, he makes it still plainer and more powerful: **And if children, then heirs; heirs of God, and joint-heirs with Christ** (Rom. 8:17).

No wonder Jesus tried to give this truth to the disciples, who were so dull of hearing, when He said, **Believe on me** (and) **the works that I do, you shall do also; and greater works than these shall you do; because I go to my Father** (John 14:12).

We have become joint-heirs of the same power that Jesus possessed. We are heirs of God, as Jesus was an heir of God. It is through Him that we have this privilege. It is by faith that we may claim this heritage. It is ours to claim because we have a legal right to it.

We should assume our place as a child of God, as an heir of God; and with this equal power with Christ, according to John 14:12, take our place, acting representatively in Jesus' stead, bringing to the world the blessings promised by our heavenly Father.

Defeat Magnified

Much has been said and preached concerning what Christians need and what Christians ought to have; about what they used to possess and the things they cannot do; of their defeats, their failures, and their shortcomings. Very little has been told Christians about what they can do, of the power that they do have, and of the secrets of faith that will win.

Great emphasis has been placed upon the ministry of the preacher who can expose the failures, weaknesses, disabilities, and faults of Christians, though a remedy for their condition may never be given. To diagnose the case, but never prescribe the remedy, is futile.

Common sense would tell us that greater stress should be placed upon the message that encourages believers to attempt the impossible, instead of causing them to feel that they are destined to failure.

I know that Peter began to sink when he got his eyes off the Lord; but why magnify his failure? I would rather commend him for walking on the water, even for only a short distance. I would try to convince him that he could do it again, perhaps adding that the next time he would not sink at all.

The Power of Bible Courage

I have read many books about divine healing, miracles, and supernatural ministries through the power of God. So many times a writer can leave the reader with the impression that, while miracles are possible, only a very few special chosen ones would really have that kind of faith.

But when the book, *Two Kinds of Faith,* by E. W. Kenyon was placed in our hands, we noticed that the author sought to convince us that we could do anything and everything God said we could do. This message carried with it the spirit of a conqueror. It made us know that we could succeed.

We accepted the challenge of the author. By acting on the word of God, as he suggested, and having this encouragement that we could do exploits, that we could be conquerors, our lives and ministries were revolutionized. We began to succeed from the day we read that book.

You Can Be a Conqueror

Christian, you can do everything God or His Son Jesus said that you can do. Jesus said, they **shall lay hands on the sick, and they shall recover.** That is exactly what will happen when you lay your hands on the sick, expecting God to keep His word.

Jesus said, **In my name they shall cast out devils.** He gave you power and authority over all devils. The Bible says He did. Therefore, when you command a demon to come out of one who is possessed, the demon must obey you, because you believe and expect God to keep His word.

If Jesus meant anything, He meant what He said. If the word of God means anything, it means what it says. God will do what He said He would do, and we can do what God says we can do.

I Can Do All Things

You will never grow spiritually by confessing what you cannot do. Learn to make your testimony declare what you can do, according to what God said in His word, and you will begin to grow spiritually.

Paul says: **I can do all things through Christ which strengthens me** (Phil. 4:13).

Paul never spoke of what he could not do, but of what he could do. Believe that you can do everything God says you can do. Believe that you are what God says you are.

We are more than conquerors through him that loved us (Rom. 8:37). We are victors. We are overcomers.

We always triumph when we believe God's word. (2 Cor. 2:14.)

If God was with Moses, He will be with us. When He promised to be with Joshua even as He had been with Moses (Josh. 1:5), He meant that He would be with us just as He had been with Moses.

Ordinary People Like You and Me

Moses, Daniel, David, Elijah, Peter, and Paul were made of the same material we are made of. They were ordinary people like you and me.

Elijah was a man subject to the same passions as we are (James 5:17).

Men and women who have been examples of God in other generations were *ordinary people* like you and me. They yielded their lives to God, believed His words, and acted on them. This is precisely what you can do; and when you do, you will realize the same results.

This Is Our Day

God wants us to face *our* world and to meet her need today as Peter did in his day. This is *our* day of ministry.

Roll up your sleeves and go set the captives free. Open the blind eyes, unstop the deaf ears, and break the bands of Satan and his sicknesses. The world is depending on you. You have this power in you. It is given to you by God. Act on it today. Begin today, acting in Jesus' name — in His stead.

Others Have Gone — We Remain

In the spring of 1947, while pastoring a church at McMinnville, Oregon, we heard of Dr. Charles Price's death. We had never seen him; yet when we heard that he had died, I wept bitterly. God began to talk to me.

The Spirit called to my mind the names of spiritual leaders of the past, not one of whom we had ever met or heard preach. Now they were gone forever from this world's scene of action. We would never meet them in this life. The world would never again feel the impact of their ministries. We would only hear of their dynamic faith.

I said, "Lord, they are gone. Millions are still dying. Multitudes are sick and suffering. To whom will they go for help? Who will reach our large cities and fill our large auditoriums with your power, healing the sick and casting out devils? What will this world do now?"

My Commission

God answered me and said, "*My son, as I was with Moses, so will I be with you. You go and cast out devils. You heal the sick. You cleanse the lepers.*

You raise the dead. I give you power over all the power of the enemy. Do not be afraid. Be strong. Be courageous. I am with you as I was with them. No demon shall be able to stand before you all the days of your life if you can get people to believe my word. I used those men and women then, but now I desire to use you."

Miracles and Healing

Daisy and I took God at His word. It had never occurred to me that God might want to use us like that. Since then, we have taken the gospel to seventy nations and have probably reached and led to Jesus Christ more UNreached souls and may have witnessed more great healing miracles than any couple who has yet lived.

Multitudes have received Jesus Christ as Savior and Lord, and tens of thousands of amazing miracles have been done by God's power as we have obeyed Christ and preached the gospel.

We made the discovery that Jesus meant what He said. As we have witnessed the deaf hear, the blind see, the dumb speak, and the lame walk, it has strengthened us to know Jesus' words: **Lo, I am with you alway, even to the end of the world** (Matt. 28:20).

God is wanting to use you, too. If you will obey His word and act on it, all things are possible to you.

Luke 1:37 says, **For with God nothing shall be impossible**. Now, add to that promise Matthew 17:20, **Nothing shall be impossible to you.**

When God called Moses, He needed an obedient person whom He could use. When He called Joshua, or David, or Rahab, or Esther, or Ruth, or John the Baptist, or Mary, He needed someone obedient to His call. When Peter was anointed at Pentecost, God needed a vessel. People have always used methods, but God uses people.

God Will Use You

God needs people for today. He chooses ordinary people like you and me. Be God's instrument for today. **Who knows whether you are come to the kingdom for such a time as this?** (Esther 4:14).

Chapter 33

HEALING IN THE LORD'S SUPPER

Are you one of the millions who has been sick or physically infirm for a long period of time?

If so, are you earnestly seeking deliverance from that sickness? Do you want to be well? Do you want a reason to be healed?

The attitude with which you read this message has everything to do with the benefit you will receive from it.

God's Attitude Toward Sickness

God places no premium on sickness, and He does not want you to suffer sickness for His glory. Sickness does not glorify the Father any more than sin does.

Paul told the church at Corinth that **many were weak and sickly** among them because they were **not discerning the Lord's body** (1 Cor. 11:29-30). That properly answers the question of so much sickness in the church today.

It is not that God is purifying or glorifying His church through affliction. It is not that God is testing His children's faith. *Sickness is due to the failure of being taught about the **body** of Christ as we have been taught about the **blood** of Christ.*

Why are so many Christians in the church sick or infirm, suffering from the very diseases and sicknesses that Jesus Christ, our substitute, has already borne for us? (Matt. 8:17.)

The answer is simple when our attitude is right: We must discern the Lord's body properly.

An Old Testament and a
New Testament Church Contrasted

As a contrast to the church at Corinth, in which (although their number was small) there were many weak and sickly members, there was a much larger church (Acts 7:38; Ex. 12:37), about three million in number, which existed under much more trying circumstances, yet among which **there was not one feeble person among their tribes** (Ps. 105:37). It was the children of Israel while going from Egypt to Canaan.

Here are two bodies of people: one in the Old Testament, the other in the New Testament. One under law, the other under grace. One under a covenant based on the *blood of animals*, the other under the covenant sealed by the *blood of the Son of God*.

Yet, there was not ONE **sick or feeble person** among those three million people who lived under that old covenant established by the *blood of animals*; while there were MANY **weak and sickly ones** among the relatively small number of Corinthians who lived under the new covenant established by the *blood of Jesus Christ*. Surely something was lacking at Corinth, and something is still lacking where such conditions exist.

Health Provided in Israel's Deliverance

Let us take a trip down to Egypt, where during four hundred years the children of Israel had lived. Egypt had made slaves of God's people. Many difficult years passed while the children of Israel served as slaves in a heathen nation. They spent long hours crying out to God for deliverance.

But one day God **heard their groanings, and God remembered his covenant with Abraham, with Isaac, and with Jacob. And God looked upon the children of Israel, and God had respect toward them** (Ex. 2:24-25).

God chose a man named Moses, to whom He said: **I have surely seen the affliction of my people which are in Egypt, and have heard their cry by reason of their taskmasters; for I know their sorrows; And I am come down to deliver them out of the hand of the Egyptians. Come now therefore, and I will send you to Pharoah, that you may bring my people the children of Israel out of Egypt** (Ex. 3:7,8,10).

God still hears the prayers of those in bondage and speaks these same words to everyone who needs deliverance.

Moses obeyed this call to deliver God's people. After many signs and wonders had been shown by him in Egypt, the final step came and God said to him: **Speak to all the congregation of Israel, saying, take to them every man a lamb and kill it, and take the blood, and strike it on the two side posts and on the upper door post of the houses, and eat the flesh** (of the lamb); **it is the Lord's passover** (Ex. 12:3-11).

They Applied the Blood — They Ate the Flesh

There were two things to do: *apply the blood* of the lamb and *eat the flesh* of the lamb. Many have forgotten this eating of the lamb's body, which is as significant and important as the partaking of its blood.

The **destroyer** (Ex. 12:23) would pass through Egypt and slay the firstborn in every family — a type or example of spiritual death which comes to every person outside of God's covenant protection. (Ezek. 18:4; Rom. 6:23.)

Two steps were to be taken by each Israelite in order to be saved from this **destroyer**.

First: A lamb was to be slain and its blood was to be applied to the doorposts of each Israelite's house identifying it with God's covenant of protection. God said: **The blood shall be for you a token upon the houses where you are: and when I see the blood, I will pass over you and the plague shall not come upon you to destroy you** (Ex. 12:13).

This represented, in type, our identification by faith with the blood of Jesus, our Lamb. (John 1:29.) **Being now justified by his blood, we shall be saved from the wrath to come** (Rom. 5:9).

Second: Each Israelite was to eat the lamb's flesh, appropriating physical strength for his or her journey. Eating the lamb's flesh had nothing to do with the passing of the **destroyer**. The blood was the sign or token which signaled that the **destroyer** had no authority to touch that house.

Israel was beginning a journey, which was a type of our Christian journey through life. God planned that His children be well and strong for this journey, and that is still His plan.

The Lamb's Body Became Their Body

What happened when the Israelites ate the flesh of the lamb? God has installed in the human body a processing plant which we call a stomach. The food we eat is digested there and sent out into our bloodstream. Its chemical essence becomes flesh of our flesh, bone of our bone, skin of our skin, body of our body. It becomes part of us.

The flesh (or body) of the lamb slain in Egypt, when eaten, became a part of each Israelite. It became flesh of their flesh, bone of their bones, skin of their skin, body of their bodies. It was a type of the *body* of Jesus Christ, the Son of God, who was to be slain for the whole world. (Compare John 6:53.) Paul later said that Jesus' life would **be made manifest in our mortal flesh** (2 Cor. 4:11).

Paul said that we, by faith, have become **members of his *body*, of his *flesh*, and of his *bones*** (Eph. 5:30).

We partake of that same *body* of Christ, in type, each time we partake of the *bread* in the Communion service. (1 Cor. 10:16.) Faith recognizes that fact and claims the promised benefits because Christ's body was beaten for us, in the death by which was borne all of our physical infirmities, pains, diseases and weaknesses. The results: **By his stripes we are healed** (Is. 53:4; Matt. 8:17).

The Israelites ate the lamb's *body* and began their journey the next day. As they journeyed, their sicknesses vanished and their infirmities disappeared. They were *physically* strong and whole.

There was not one feeble person among their tribes (Ps. 105:37).

No one was sick, no one was feeble, no one was weak; but every person among them was strong, well, and healthy.

They had eaten the lamb's body which had become a part of their own bodies. Think of three million people, and there was **not one feeble person** among them.

God's Covenant To Heal

When they obeyed Moses' orders, accepting his message concerning the *lamb*, God covenanted (or contracted) with them, saying, **I am the Lord who heals you** (Ex. 15:26).

God declared that He would allow no disease to come upon them as long as they were obedient to Him. That is still His promise. He further promised: **The number of your days I will fulfill** (Ex. 23:26).

That is still His promise, in spite of the fact that many in the church at Corinth died prematurely, and that many more in our day are dying prematurely. All of God's promises are ready for us to claim by faith. When we do so, they become ours personally.

Remember that Israel not only **applied the lamb's blood to the doorposts**, which was a type of salvation from sin, but they also **ate the lamb's body**, which was a type of healing from sickness. Why do I say that?

Sin and sickness are Satan's twin evils, designed to tear down, to kill, and to destroy the human race — God's creation.

Salvation from sin and *healing* from sickness are God's twin mercies provided to replace these spiritual and physical evils with the abundant and miracle life of Jesus Christ in the believer's spirit and body.

When Jesus Christ became our substitute, bearing our sins and our sicknesses, He did it in order that we might be delivered from them and their power. **He shed His blood for the remission of our sins** (Matt. 26:28), and He put away **our sicknesses and our infirmities** (Matt. 8:17) so that we need never suffer them again.

Deliverance From Sin and Sickness Alike

God was not only the *deliverer from the destroyer* for the Israelites, but also the *healer of their diseases*, and, in Malachi 3:6, He said, **I am the Lord, I change not.**

Every Israelite who put the lamb's blood on the doorpost was protected from the **destroyer** who brought death. Every Israelite who ate the Lamb's body was freed from sickness and made well, strong, and healthy. That has been the plan of God for His obedient children throughout all the scriptures. His plan for us is redemption, restoration, salvation. We are bought back and restored. It is as though we had never sinned. No more sin. No more sickness. No more separation from God.

In his praise to God, David said, **Bless the Lord, O my soul, and forget not all his benefits: Who forgives all your iniquities** (there is the sin question) **who heals all your diseases** (there is the sickness question) (Ps. 103:2-3). Provision has been made for deliverance from both sin and sickness.

Isaiah said of the Christ who was to come: **He was wounded for our transgressions, he was bruised for our iniquities** (there is the sin question) **and with his stripes we are healed** (there is the sickness question) (Is. 53:5). Again, we see provision for deliverance from both sin and sickness.

When Jesus began to preach the gospel of the kingdom, He proved to be the healer of sickness as well as the forgiver of sins.

The same Christ who said, **Arise, and take up your bed, and go your way into your house** (there is the sickness question), also said, **Son, your sins be forgiven you** (there is the sin question) (Mark 2:5-11). To the man sick with palsy, Jesus provided forgiveness for his sins and healing for his sickness.

Jesus the Healer and the Savior

Three years of Jesus' life were occupied in healing the sick and forgiving the sinful. Then came the crucial time during which He was to become our substitute. He would become **sinful with our sins** (2 Cor. 5:21) and He would become **sick with our sicknesses** (Is. 53:5).

Both sin and sickness had to be put away; but, first, the penalty for both had to be paid.

Jesus Christ, sinless and sickless, was the only one who could do this, and He did it because of His great love. He did it for us. (Is. 53.)

Before Jesus went to the cross, He tried to show His disciples what would be the effects of the suffering which He would undergo. So Paul relates it all:

> The Lord Jesus the same night in which he was betrayed took *bread*: and when he had given thanks, he brake it, and said, Take, eat: this is *my body*, which is broken for you: this do in remembrance of me. After the same manner also he took the cup, when he had

supped, saying, **This cup is the new testament in my** *blood*: **this do, as often as you drink it, in remembrance of me.**

1 Corinthians 11:23-25

It is doubtful that the disciples, who sat at the table and heard Him speak these words, understood much of what He was saying. Little did they expect what was coming — but it came, and it was all for our deliverance, yours and mine.

The Sufferings of Christ

At the hands of cruel men, Jesus our Lamb was beaten. He was spit on, bruised, tortured. On His body, deep furrows were plowed by the Roman lash as it tore pieces of flesh from His back. These were **the stripes by which,** Isaiah and Peter say, **we were healed** — and they were laid on His body.

His body was brutally beaten for us. This was not the sacrifice made for our *sins*, but the bearing of our *sicknesses*, so that provision could be made for the healing of our bodies. **The stripes by which we were healed** were laid on His body. Matthew says, **Himself took our infirmities, and bore our sicknesses** (Matt. 8:17).

After they had striped and bruised His body — the stripes by which we were healed — then they nailed Him to the cross and pierced His side. His blood ran down on the ground — blood that was **shed for many for the remission of sins** (Matt. 26:28), not for the healing of sickness.

Jesus our Lamb suffered in two ways: He shed His blood on the cross for our salvation from sin, and He bore the stripes on His body for our healing from sickness.

Jesus suffered intense *spiritual* agony at Calvary, for during that time even His Father turned away from Him. He bore our sins, being made sin for us. (2 Cor. 5:21.)

But in His excruciating *physical* agony at the Praetorium, where Jesus suffered in His body from the terrible Roman lash, He bore our sicknesses. He was made sick for us, and. **by his stripes, we were healed.**

Paul's Revelation

When it was ended, Jesus returned to the Father's right hand and sat down, all things being *finished*. He had completely delivered humankind both spiritually and physically from all satanic bondage. The Holy Spirit later revealed to Paul the significance of it all, and you will find it interpreted in Paul's writings.

Paul tells us in 1 Corinthians, chapter 11, about the sacrament of the Lord's Supper, which every church observes. He speaks of the two emblems by which we remember the suffering of Jesus Christ, our Lamb: the bread and the wine — types of His body being striped and lacerated for our physical healing, and of His blood being shed for our spiritual healing.

Then Paul tells us: **As often as you eat this bread, and drink this cup, you show the Lord's death until he comes** (1 Cor. 11:26).

In chapter 10 of 1 Corinthians, verse 16, Paul interprets these two emblems: **The cup of blessing which we bless, is it not the communion of the blood of Christ? The bread which we break, is it not the communion of the body of Christ?**

Jesus' *blood* was shed when He bore our sins, so that we would not have to bear them, but could be saved from them and be delivered from the power of sin in our lives.

Jesus' *body* was striped when He bore our sicknesses, so that we would not have to bear them, but could be healed of them and be delivered from the power of sickness in our lives.

By knowing God's word, we discover our deliverance from the power of sickness in our lives because of the striped body of Christ. In the same way, we learn to discern our deliverance from the power of sin in our lives because of the shed blood of Christ. We are as free from sickness as we are from sin.

Sickness then has no more power over us than sin does. We learn that sickness is no more for God's glory than sin is. We no more accept sickness in our lives than we accept sin.

We learn that both sin and sickness were done away with, being borne by our perfect substitute, Jesus, the Lamb of God, who was pierced and scourged on our behalf individually.

Partaking of the Communion

When the emblems of the Lord's Supper are brought to us in commemoration of our Lord's death, we take the cup of wine and drink it. We express gratitude to our Father for the blood of Christ which washes away our sins. We rejoice because the power of sin in our lives has been broken, that sin has no more dominion over us.

But how do we know these things? Because the Bible says: **The blood of Jesus Christ his Son cleanses us from all sin** (1 John 1:7).

We are free from sin. Once and for all, we have been saved from a life of sin; and we believe that sin shall no longer have dominion over us because we are saved. (Rom. 6:14.) The wine symbolizes **the blood of Christ, shed for the remission of our sins.**

But what about the bread? We take it and eat it as a token of the body of our lamb, Jesus, just as the Israelites partook of the body of the lamb that was slain in Egypt. Then we offer thanks for the sacrifice of Jesus. We thank God that Christ's body was offered for us, but that is as far as some have been taught.

Many have been taught that the body of Jesus was pierced for us, but have not been told about the benefits they could receive because His body was also beaten for them and why the stripes were laid on Him.

Who heals all your diseases (Ps. 103:3) has usually been overlooked in the Communion service, and because the church has not properly discerned the Lord's body, many are weak and sickly today.

The Cup and the Bread

In the Communion service, the cup of wine is a type of the blood of Christ, **shed for many for the remission of sins**. When I partake of it, I rejoice in the fact that my sinful nature has been changed, that I have been re-created and made new, that I am saved. In this way, I discern or understand the Lord's blood.

In the same Communion service, the piece of broken bread is a type of the body of Christ, beaten with stripes by which my sicknesses were healed. When I eat the bread, I rejoice in the fact that my sick, weak body has been changed; that it has become **bone of his bone, flesh of his flesh, and body of his body** (Eph. 5:30); that **the life of Christ has been made manifest in my mortal flesh** (2 Cor. 4:11); that sickness no longer has power over me; that I am healed. In this way, I **discern the Lord's body**. Multitudes have not done this today.

Why Serve the Bread?

I have often wondered why those who do not teach divine healing for the body serve the bread to the congregation. The bread represents the body of Christ, on which was laid the stripes by which we were healed. (Is. 53:5; 1 Peter 2:24.)

It would be consistent for them, to serve the **cup**, which typifies the blood shed for the remission of sins, because they discern and are benefited by the blood of Christ. But it seems useless for them to serve the bread which typifies the body of our Lord scourged for our physical healing, then proceed to teach that divine healing for the body is no longer for us. *RELIGIONS LIES)*

Many are sick or infirm because, although they partake of the Lord's body, they do not understand it.

When Jesus said of the bread, **This is my body, which is broken for you**, He expected us to understand that it was on His body that the stripes by which we were healed were laid. (1 Cor. 11:24.)

Some take the Lord's Supper **unworthily** and are, therefore, unable to discern or appropriate with faith the Lord's body for healing. If those in need of healing will first **examine** themselves and be sure that they know why Jesus Christ suffered and died, then **eat the bread and drink the cup worthily** as Paul instructed, they will then discern the Lord's body with faith for their own healing.

The benefits of healing in the lacerated body of our Lamb are just as clearly taught in the scriptures as the benefits of salvation in the blood of our Lamb.

Discern the body as having been beaten and lacerated with stripes — stripes by which your sicknesses were borne and you were healed — and health will be yours. It is as certain as when you discern His blood as having been shed for you the sacrifice by which your sins were borne — and salvation is yours.

Sickness will lose its power over your body just as sin loses its power over your spirit. You will be as free from sickness as you are from sin. Christ, your substitute, bore both for you, so you do not have to bear them. By believing this portion of the word and acting accordingly, you are as free from sickness as you are from sin.

We Are Set Free

Sin and sickness need be borne only once; and since Jesus Christ has already borne them, you need not bear them. If you bear them, then Jesus' bearing of them was in vain. Since Jesus bore them, you and I need never bear them. So, **with his stripes, we are healed** and, through His blood, **we have remission of sins**.

We now have no more faith in the right of sickness to dominate us or dwell in our body than we have in the right of sin to dominate us or dwell in our spirit.

Claim both of these provisions by faith. Accept them as yours. Accept Jesus as healer, just as you accept Him as Savior, and you will be as free from sickness as you are from sin.

No person ever appealed in vain to Christ for help in bodily suffering. As multitude after multitude pressed upon Him for physical healing, the record is always the same: **He healed them all** (Matt. 4:23; 8:16; 12:15; 14:14; Luke 4:40; 6:19).

He laid his hands on every one of them, and healed them.

Luke 4:40

Revealing God's Will

He came **to do His Father's will** (John 6:38; Heb. 10:7,9); therefore, He preached the gospel and **healed all that were sick** (Matt. 8:16).

185

Jesus of Nazareth went about healing all that were oppressed of the devil.

Acts 10:38

His reason for healing them all is His redemptive work for everyone in His death. **Himself** (vicariously) **took our infirmities, and bore our sicknesses** (Matt. 8:17). That includes everyone.

It was our sicknesses He bore. Nothing short of healing them all would fulfill God's promise.

When Jesus healed the woman with the issue of blood, it was for that one woman. But what He did as our substitute on the cross was for everybody.

Since Christ's redemptive sacrifice was God's reason for His healing them all, He must continue to heal all who accept Him, because what His sacrifice provided for those who lived in that day, it does for us in our day. He tasted death for every person. (Heb. 2:9.)

His purpose in commanding that the gospel be preached to **every creature** (Mark 16:15-18) is so that **every creature** may receive its benefits. That includes you — right now.

Chapter 34

SOME ENEMIES OF FAITH

1. Desiring To Read About the Word, Instead of Reading the Word Itself

Faith comes by hearing, and hearing by the word of God.

Romans 10:17

Reading about faith, and about people of faith, only produces a deep desire for faith. However, reading or hearing God's word will produce real faith.

2. Ignorance of What Believing Is

There is a difference between a noun and a verb. A noun is "the name of a person, place, or thing." A noun can be dead. "Corpse" is a noun. "Casket" is a noun. But a verb shows action.

"Faith" is a noun, but "believe" is a verb.

I have seen people who claimed to have great faith. Some said they had all the faith in the world. That may be true; but all the faith in the world, if not accompanied by corresponding action, is dead faith.

Faith without works is dead (James 2:20). It is possible to have faith and yet receive nothing from God.

But when you say you believe, that is a different thing, because the word "believe" is a verb and a verb is an action word.

If you believe, that means you are acting on God's promise; and when you couple action with your faith, that is believing. Your acting on God's promise always puts Him to work bringing about the fulfillment of that promise.

Believing the word is simply acting on the word. Believing is acting; faith is the cause of the action.

3. Having the Wrong Confession

You do not act one thing and confess another.

Paul says that **with the mouth confession is made to salvation** (Rom. 10:10). You would not confess Jesus Christ as your Lord and act

187

like an unbeliever. If you did, your confession would mean nothing. It would be empty words.

If you were to confess, **By his stripes, I was healed,** you would not remain in bed because of a fever. You would ignore the fever and make your action correspond with your confession. You would ignore symptoms and **hold fast the confession of your faith without wavering** (Heb. 10:23).

Jesus is the High Priest of our confession (Heb. 3:1). This means He will fulfill His priestly responsibilities of seeing that we receive the fulfillment of every one of God's promises that we steadfastly confess with our mouths and believe with our hearts.

God's word in our mouths and in our hearts is equivalent to His voice and excludes all reason for doubt. The **seed**, which is the word of God, when planted in **good ground**, always brings forth fruit. There can never be failure when we get in harmony with God's word. It is in this way that we prove Christ's words to be **spirit and life** (John 6:63) as He says they are. These words, **I am the Lord who heals you** (Ex. 15:26), in your mouth and in your heart, will do away with all sickness.

When Mary said to the angel Gabriel, **Be it done to me according to your word** (Luke 1:38), that was **the word of faith** in her heart and in her mouth (Rom. 10:8); and it turned the words of the angel into creative power and gave to the world a Savior. All our blessings have been the result of **the word of faith** in Mary's heart.

God's word in our hearts and on our lips is as effective as when God said, **Let there be light**, and when **the worlds were framed by the word of God** (Gen. 1:3; Heb. 11:3).

In the face of what was humanly impossible, Mary said with faith: **Be it done to me according to your word.** This was **calling those things which be not as though they were** (Rom. 4:17), as Abraham had done.

Every Bible promise is God speaking to us. Therefore, instead of neglecting them, let us say with Mary of each promise, **Be it done to me according to your word**. We then prove that **no word of God is void of power** (Luke 1:37 RV).

4. Hope Is Never Faith

The hope I refer to here is the natural human emotion that is without a basis for expectancy.

Many people mistake hope for faith.

People will say, "I hope I get healed." "I hope I will be better." "I hope I am saved." "I hope God answers prayer."

That empty, human emotion is never faith.

There is a real Bible *hope* which is a virtue from God as much as *faith* and *love* are. **Now abides faith, hope, charity** (love), **these three** (1 Cor. 13:13).

For example, we hope for blessings which God has prepared for our future such as heaven and a crown of righteousness. But we must exercise faith for blessings which God has provided for us now.

Healing, like forgiveness, is a provision for all and is freely offered to all now. We need not hope for the blessings which Christ died to provide. We claim those gifts by faith now.

There are promises in the Bible, and there are also statements of fact. A promise is for the future; a statement of fact is for the present.

The second coming of Christ is a hope. It is in the future. The mansions of heaven which we shall someday inhabit constitute a hope. They are for the future. Heaven is a hope. The crown of righteousness, which the Lord has laid up for us, is a hope. It is for the future.

Hope keeps us from being ashamed (Rom. 5:5). Hope pertains to things in the future. You do not hope for something that you already have. (Rom. 8:24.)

Faith recognizes things that the scriptures declare are ours now and claims them, regardless of physical evidence. For example: **With his stripes, we are healed**. This is not a promise; it is a statement of fact. You do not hope for that. Faith claims it now, believes it, and acts upon it as a statement of fact.

You get out of bed. You discard your aids. You act your deliverance, just like you would act upon the word of a lawyer who said you had a thousand dollars in the bank which had been left to you in a person's will. You would not hope his words were true or that someday you might have a thousand dollars; you would act on his words.

Never say, "I hope I will be healed someday." You were healed. Believe that, act accordingly, and health will be yours.

5. Praying for Faith

I have heard people pray: "Lord, help me to have faith. Help me to believe Your word." They forget that the Bible says, **Faith comes by hearing** the word of God (Rom. 10:17), not by praying for faith.

Praying for faith would be to say, "Father, help me to be convinced that You meant what You said when You made that promise." Those who pray for faith are also ignoring the fact that Jesus says we are believers. You cannot be a believer and a doubter at the same time.

Jesus said, **whoever believes shall have everlasting life** (John 3:16) — or be saved. If you are saved, then you are a believer. Never ask the Father to help you believe. You are a believer. Now act on His word.

6. Mentally Agreeing With the Word

Many who say they have all the faith in the world prove the opposite by their next sentence. They will say: "Oh yes, I have all the faith in the world. I have always believed God's word. But somehow I just cannot get healed. I never have been well. I try and try to believe, but it seems I never receive healing."

God says that we were healed when Christ bore our diseases. Believe that you were made well when He bore the stripes by which you were healed. Agree with God's word. Believe it with your heart and act on His promises.

Some people only talk about their faith. But the fact is that faith is expressed in actions not in words.

When those four men in Mark, chapter 2, carried that man who was sick with palsy and let him down through the roof, Jesus **saw their faith**. It did not say He heard them brag on how much faith they had; but rather **He saw their faith**, and He healed the man. He saw faith in their actions.

Never talk about or boast about your faith. **Without faith it is impossible to please him** (Heb. 11:6). But don't talk about it all the time. Act your faith. That is believing.

If God says, **I am the Lord who heals you**, and **who heals all your diseases**, then act on that and put God to work making it good. Do not lie in bed, boasting about your faith, yet complaining about your pain. Rise up and take God at His word. Act your faith, and God will make His word good to you.

7. Depending on the Faith of Others

Have your own faith. Everyone should build their own faith. Most people wait until they meet some crisis: They become sick, a loved one becomes ill, or some financial problem confronts them that may affect their future.

Then they frantically search for someone who can pray for them, but to no avail because their expectancy is based on another person's faith rather than on God's word.

Had there been faith, they would have made their request known to God and would have rejoiced, knowing that whatever they were asking of the Father in Jesus' name, He would do.

Chapter 35

TO DO OR NOT TO DO

1. *Do not try* to believe. Act on the word. That is believing.

2. *Do not make* a confession that contradicts God's word. Make your testimony and confession agree with God's word, regardless of symptoms. Keep His word on your lips.

3. *Do not trust* in other people's faith. Have your own faith. You are a believer. You have faith. God has given to each person a measure of faith. (Rom. 12:3.)

4. *Do not talk* doubt and unbelief. Quote the scriptures steadfastly, and they will be yours. **They overcame him** (the adversary) **by the blood of the Lamb, and by the word of their testimony** (Rev. 12:11).

5. *Do not talk* sickness and pains. Talk about your healing. When you talk about sickness, you magnify and glorify the devil whom you admit by your words is able to make you sick. Make your adversary listen to your praise to God and to your conversation about the living word and the promises of God, and he will leave you. (Matt. 4:11; James 4:7.)

While Jesus was being tempted, He defeated Satan by saying, **It is written**, and then by repeating His Father's words. You can defeat in the same way.

6. *Do not be* a doubting Thomas. It must have grieved the heart of Jesus for Thomas to doubt His resurrection. Unbelief in the redemptive work of Jesus Christ is not a small thing. Your attitude toward the substitutionary death of Christ must be: since He bore my diseases, I am healed.

7. *Do not talk* failure, inability, or about what you cannot do. Say, **I can do all things through Christ which strengthens me** (Phil. 4:13). **In all these things, we are more than conquerors** (Rom. 8:37). These were the words of Paul who **fought a good fight** (and) **kept the faith** (2 Tim. 4:7). Always say, "I can"; never Say, "I cannot."

You can never prove your faith if you never practice the word — if you never act on the word and let it live and have its rightful place in you.

Be doers of the word, and not hearers only, deceiving your own selves.

James 1:22

191

Faith cannot be built by sympathy. It is only built by acting on the word and letting the word live in you as it lived in Jesus. By doing what the word of God says, you prove your faith. You become a **doer of the word.**

God is no closer to anyone than He is to you. He will answer no one any quicker than He will answer you. He is your God. The word is yours when the pastor is out of town and the telephone is disconnected.

Chapter 36

THE POWER OF GOD'S WORD

In the beginning God *created* **the heaven and the earth** (Gen. 1:1). Notice how God **created** the heaven and earth:

And God *said,* **Let there be light: and there was light** (Gen. 1:3). God just spoke the words: **Let there be light.** What God said came to pass.

> **And God** *said,* **Let there be a firmament, and** *it was so.*
>
> **Genesis 1:6-7**

> **And God** *said,* **Let the waters under the heaven be gathered together to one place, and let the dry land appear:** *and it was so.*
>
> **Genesis 1:9**

> **And God** *said,* **Let the earth bring forth, and** *it was so.*
>
> **Genesis 1:11**

> **And God** *said,* **Let there be lights in the firmament, and** *it was so.*
>
> **Genesis 1:14-15**

How God Created What He Made

Now we see what brought things into existence.

> **Through faith we understand that the worlds were framed by** *the word of God,* **so that things which are seen were not made of things which do appear.**
>
> **Hebrews 11:3**

When we, as sons and daughters of the living God, begin to realize the creative power that is contained in what God says when He speaks, we then understand a truth which will make impossibilities become possible and make difficult things easy.

Until we learn the power of God's word, that word has no life for us. It has not taken on vitality; it has been only a beautiful doctrine, a creed, a dogma. It has been dead and useless — the product of a printer, the combination of paper and ink.

Jesus says,

> **The words that I speak to you, they are spirit, and they are life.**
>
> **John 6:63**

When God Speaks

When God speaks, the same creative power that was drawn upon when He spoke the world into existence goes into action again.

His word today is just as effective, just as powerful, just as creative, as **when the worlds were framed by the word of God.**

> **I am the Lord: I will speak, and the word that I shall speak shall come to pass.**
>
> **Ezekiel 12:25**

> **And he (God) has confirmed his words, which he spoke.**
>
> **Daniel 9:12**

> **Heaven and earth shall pass away, but my words shall not pass away.**
>
> **Matthew 24:35**

> **The word of the Lord endures for ever.**
>
> **1 Peter 1:25**

> **The promise (is) sure to all the seed.**
>
> **Romans 4:16**

> **What he (God) had promised, he was able also to perform.**
>
> **Romans 4:21**

> **No word from God is void of power** (ability).
>
> **Luke 1:37** RV

Act on the Word

Believe God's word. Trust His word. Know the power — the creative power — of His word; then you can, and will, act on His word.

If God says **I am the Lord that heals you,** and you dare to believe the power of these wonderful words, you will act on them.

The bedridden will arise by faith and be made whole; the lame will leap like a deer; the tongue of the dumb will begin to sing; the deaf ears will be unstopped; pains will leave; and darkness will vanish. You will begin to do the very things you could not do before you took God at His word, acted on that word, and were healed.

The creative power of God's word will create the very thing in your body that you need in order to be well and strong.

Weakness will be transformed into strength. Death will be transformed into life. Sickness will be transformed into health. Impossibilities will be turned into possibilities.

If you need healing, you can believe God's word now and receive new strength and health in your body. You can experience personally the wonderful creative power of God's word by simply believing it enough to act on it.

Faith Proved by Actions

Act on God's word because **faith without works** (or actions) **is dead** (James 2:20). This scripture means that we have only as much faith as we demonstrate with actions. Faith never boasts; faith always acts.

It would be foolish to say that we believe something, then refuse to act accordingly. It would be useless to express confidence in the strength of a bridge which spans a chasm, then refuse to drive across it.

James says of Abraham: **Faith joined with his works, and by his actions** (Abraham's) **faith was made perfect** (James 2:22).

You prove your faith by actions that correspond.

Your actions justify your faith.

Faith in Action Always Wins

For over four decades, we have conducted great mass evangelism crusades out in open stadiums or great parks or fields where up to 250,000 or more could attend. But in our early years, we sometimes used public auditoriums.

I remember one of our crusades which was held in a large auditorium in Jamaica. The crowd packed around the wall of the grounds leading to the auditorium from mid-afternoon waiting for the gates to be opened.

A poor woman carried her husband on her back all the way from the country. He had suffered a paralytic stroke and could neither walk nor stand alone.

When she reached the auditorium grounds, she found the gates were locked. Hundreds of others were climbing the walls to get closer to the building. She shoved her husband over the high wall, climbed the wall herself, picked him up, carried him into the building, and brought him to us for prayer. She was acting her faith. Needless to say, he walked out, healed by God's power. Faith put into action always wins.

A woman, dying of cancer, was carried into one of our meetings and laid in a side room, not expected to live through the service. For six months she had been unable to sit up. Her feet and legs were totally paralyzed.

After teaching the word of God to the people, we went in and laid our hands on the woman, rebuking the cancer.

I asked her, "When do you want to be well?" She said, "Now." I said, "Rise up, in the name of Jesus, and be made whole." Slowly she moved her feet off the bed, sat up, stood up, threw up her arms, and walked out alone before the audience, shouting and praising God. She acted her faith, and she was miraculously healed.

The very minute real faith goes into action, depending on what God has said in His word, creative power begins its work and sickness must leave. Never be afraid to believe God and to act on His word.

Remember the words Jesus spoke to the father of the little girl who was reported by the skeptics to be dead: **Be not afraid, only believe** (Mark 5:36).

It helps a lot of people when they discover that the word "believe" is a verb. A verb shows action.

James knew that when he wrote: **Faith, if it has not works, is dead, being alone** (James 2:17) and, **What does it profit, though a person say he or she has faith, and have not works?** (James 2:14) and, **Show me your faith without your works, and I will show you my faith by my works** (James 2:18).

If God could create the worlds with His words, then He can heal your sick body with His word.

He sent his word, and healed them (Ps. 107:20).

The Authority of God's Word

In the beginning was the Word, and the Word was with God, and the Word was God. The same was in the beginning with God. All things were made by him; and without him was not any thing made that was made.

John 1:1-3

God linked Himself with His WORD.

He made Himself a part of His WORD.

He is not only *in* His WORD, but He is *back* of His WORD.

You cannot separate God from His WORD.

He not only called into being things which were not and compelled them to come into existence with His words, but He watches over His word to see that not one word fails. **I will hasten** (stand behind or back up) **my word to perform it** (Jer. 1:12).

God says, **I am the Lord that heals you** (Ex. 15:26). That promise will endure forever. (1 Peter 1:25.) It has been said that the word is like its Author: eternal, unchanging, and living.

The word of a person is what a person is.

The word of God is what God is.

Unbelief in this word is unbelief in God Who is its Author.

196

Our attitude toward the word of God determines everything.

When Mary was told that she would conceive of the Holy Ghost and bring forth a son, she could not understand how such a thing could be. In the natural it was impossible.

Reason will take the word's place if we allow it to, because acting on the supernatural word of God does not appeal to our natural senses.

Mary gave us the secret of finding favor with God when she said, **Be it done to me according to your word** (Luke 1:38). That pleased the Father, and it was done.

Learn to put aside your reasonings and your head knowledge, knowing that **the carnal mind is enmity against God: for it is not subject to the law of God, neither indeed can be** (Rom. 8:7).

Do like Mary and say: **Be it done to me according to your word,** then act accordingly, and God will bring it to pass.

Astonished at Jesus' Words

After Jesus had been baptized by John in the Jordan River, He was led of the Spirit into the wilderness for forty days. **Then Jesus returned in the power of the Spirit** (Luke 4:14) to begin His earthly ministry.

The first thing that amazed the people was the fact that Jesus spoke with such power and authority.

They were astonished at his doctrine: (Why?) **for his word was with power** (Luke 4:32).

They exclaimed: **What a word is this! For with authority and power he commands the unclean spirits, and they come out** (Luke 4:36).

Jesus stood in a fisherman's boat that was tossing and plunging in the raging waves of the sea, and in the face of a black sky and the fury of sweeping winds, He said to the storm, **Peace, be still** (Mark 4:39), and there was a great calm.

Then the disciples exclaimed: **What manner of man is this, that even the wind and the sea obey him?**

When Jesus first appeared in the temple, He read from the book of Isaiah: **The Spirit of the Lord is upon me, because he has anointed me to preach the gospel to the poor; he has sent me to heal the brokenhearted, to preach deliverance to the captives, and recovering of sight to the blind, to set at liberty them that are bruised** (Luke 4:18).

That same chapter states how **they wondered at the gracious words which proceeded out of his mouth** (Luke 4:22).

Many times the people were amazed when Jesus spoke with authority and power. Wherever and whenever they believed His words, the impossible became possible, the difficult became easy, things unheard of began to happen, glorious miracles became commonplace.

His word was with power. It is still the same, because He is still the same.

The Key to Victory

To the father of the lunatic son, Jesus said: **If you can believe, all things are possible to the one that believes** (Mark 9:23).

You can believe Christ's word now. Believe that what He says will come to pass. Doubt nothing; but, rather, only believe.

All things are possible to the one that believes. If you will only believe, you can be delivered and healed right now, where you are.

Act on God's word right now and rise above all your doubts and fears. Let your faith set you free by putting it into action. You have the faith inside you right now, just let it act, bringing deliverance to you. Do not hold it prisoner. Do not keep it bound. It will lie dormant within you if you do not act on God's word.

You have known that God's word was true; now let your faith act, so healing will come to you.

Act your faith, and God's word will impart creative power and divine life to your body.

Do you believe this? (John 11:26). All things are possible to the one that believes. Act on God's words. **Himself took our infirmities, and bore our sicknesses** (Matt. 8:17).

If you can only believe, it will be done right now right where you are and you will be set free.

Your sicknesses and your pains will begin to vanish; your weakness will begin to be transformed into strength. Light will begin to appear to that blinded eye. Sound will begin to come to those deaf ears. Life will start flowing into that paralyzed limb. Believe it, and it is done right now.

Rise up, and walk in Jesus' name. Do it right now.

Do the thing you could not do, and you will be healed. Do it in Jesus' name, commanding weakness or sickness or lameness to leave you.

What Opened My Eyes?

I shall always remember what happened to me when, for the first time, I saw the power of God's word demonstrated like this. I looked on while a believer commanded deaf and dumb spirits to come out of many that were bound by them, and I saw them both hear and speak.

I was thoroughly convinced that this was the Bible way. The power of the name of Jesus was revealed to me. I saw, proven before my eyes, that the same things could be done now that were done by the apostles and by Jesus Himself.

I found that we can do everything that Jesus said we could do, by doing it in His name.

We went back to the church which we were then pastoring and announced a divine healing meeting, telling everyone to bring their sick, assuring them that they would be healed. Many miracles of healing were witnessed that first night, and the news spread far and wide.

Since then, we have seen many thousands of miracles and healings in crusades around the world and have proven thousands of times that **Jesus Christ** (is) **the same yesterday, and today, and forever** (Heb. 13:8). If He is the same, His word is the same. It still conveys power when spoken.

Launch Out Into the Deep

In the gospel of Luke, we read how the disciples toiled all night with their fishing nets, but caught nothing. Jesus came along and said: **Launch out into the deep, and let down your nets. And Simon said to him, Master, we have toiled all night, and have taken nothing: nevertheless at your word I will let down the net** (Luke 5:4-5).

Peter did not argue with Jesus. He did not explain how hopeless the situation was. He did not explain that he knew those waters and knew there were no fish in that area.

Often when we speak God's promises, someone wants to explain how long they have been ill, or how many doctors and specialists have said their case is hopeless, or how many times they have been prayed for and received no help. Learn a secret from Peter: Obedience will always bring victory when we obey the word of the Lord.

Peter acted on the word of Jesus. He let down the nets as Jesus said to do, because he believed that if Jesus spoke the word, it would be as He said — and he caught a great multitude of fish.

Never be afraid to obey and to act on the word of the Lord because **there is no word from God void of power** (Luke 1:37 RV). He can fill all the nets, so let all of them down.

Perhaps you have been ill for years. Others may have prayed many times for you. Doctors may have shaken their heads in despair not knowing how to help you. They may have told you that only a higher power can heal now.

You may have tried time and again to be healed, and you may have seemed to fail. But the word still declares: **By his stripes we were healed** (Is. 53:5).

Take new courage. This time, say like Peter: "**Nevertheless, at your word, I will let down the net.** Because of Your word, I am asking again. At Your word, I shall recover. At Your word, I shall be completely healed."

God's word cannot fail you. Believe it with all your heart and, at His word, act your faith. Let down your nets and expect them to be filled with healing. Step out on God's unfailing word.

Faith always brings a complete answer, **even exceeding abundantly above all that we ask or think** (Eph. 3:20), as was Peter's experience when he let down his net at Christ's word.

Chapter 37

THREE QUESTIONS ABOUT PAUL'S THORN

Lest I should be exalted above measure through the abundance of the revelations, there was given to me a thorn in the flesh, the messenger of Satan to buffet me, lest I should be exalted above measure.

For this thing I sought the Lord three times, that it might depart from me. And he said to me, My grace is sufficient for you: for my strength is made perfect in weakness. Most gladly therefore will I rather glory in my infirmities, that the power of Christ may rest upon me.

2 Corinthians 12:7-9

One of the most prevalent objections raised today against the ministry of healing is Paul's "thorn in the flesh." One traditional idea has led to another. The widespread teaching that God is the source of disease has, no doubt, led to the idea that Paul had a sickness that God refused to heal.

We do not believe that anyone who will take time to read all that God's word has to say on the subject of healing could ever form such a conclusion.

It is with a sincere desire to help every honest reader that we present the following study concerning Paul's thorn. Thousands of people have needlessly suffered for years, believing they were pleasing God.

In order to have a better understanding of this matter, let us consider what the Bible says about this "thorn in the flesh."

FIRST: What Was Paul's Thorn?

The expression **thorn in the flesh** is used in both the Old and New Testaments as an illustration. The **thorn in the flesh** never indicated sickness.

Whenever the expression is used in the Bible, it is specifically stated what the **thorn in the flesh** was.

In Numbers 33:55, the expression **thorns in your sides** illustrated the inhabitants of Canaan.

In Joshua 23:13, the expression referred to the heathen nations of Canaan (the Canaanites).

The Bible clearly states exactly what these **thorns in the flesh** were. Both times the **thorns** were personalities.

Paul states exactly what his **thorn** was. He says it was **the messenger of Satan;** or as translated by others, **the angel of the devil, Satan's angel,** and so on. The illustration **thorn in the flesh** was a personality, **the messenger of Satan.**

This word **messenger** is translated from the Greek word *angelos* which appears 188 times in the Bible. It is translated 181 times as "angel" and 7 times as "messenger." In all 188 times, without exception, it is referring to a person and not a thing. Hell was prepared for **the devil and his angels, or messengers** (Matt. 25:41), and Paul's **thorn in the flesh** was one of these **messengers** of the devil. Paul says so.

Preachers and teachers have labeled Paul's **thorn in the flesh** as everything from an oriental eye disease ophthalmia to an unconverted wife. It seems so unreasonable to me to speculate about what the **thorn** was when Paul states that it was **a messenger of Satan.**

SECOND: What Was the Purpose of Paul's Thorn?

Paul not only tells us what his **thorn** was, **a messenger of Satan,** but he also tells us what this **messenger** or **angel of Satan** came to do: **to buffet me.**

The word **buffet** means "blow after blow," as when waves buffet a ship, or as when they **buffeted** Christ. (Matt. 26:67; Mark 14:65; 1 Cor. 4:11; 1 Peter 2:20.)

This word, used in 2 Corinthians 12:7 to describe the suffering received by Paul from this **messenger of Satan,** must harmonize with its same meaning in these other passages. In no case does it refer to sickness or disease.

This **messenger** or **angel** of Satan was sent to **buffet** Paul continually — to deal blow after blow to this faithful man of God. The use of the word **buffet** in 1 Corinthians 4:11 is translated in the Spanish Bible, **beaten with many blows.**

A sickness could never beat one with many blows nor buffet a person, but the harassing work of an **angel of the devil** certainly fits this description.

The following description of Paul's suffering during his ministry will explain how this **angel of the devil** harassed Paul's life. We do not need to add sickness to the list. Neither Paul nor the scriptures mention it in this connection.

After Paul's conversion, God sent Ananias to Paul with the information, **I will show him how great things he must suffer for my name's sake** (Acts 9:16), which came to pass in the following ways:

1. Jews determined to kill Paul right after his conversion. (Acts 9:23.)
2. He was hindered in joining the Christians. (Acts 9:26-29.)
3. He was opposed by Satan. (Acts 13:6-12.)
4. He was opposed by Jews in a mob. (Acts 13:44-49.)
5. He was expelled out of Antioch in Pisidia. (Acts 13:50.)
6. He was mobbed and expelled from Iconium. (Acts 14:1-5.)
7. He fled to Lystra and Derbe where he was stoned and left for dead. (Acts 14:6-19.)
8. He was disputing continually with false brethren. (Acts 19:8.)
9. He was beaten and jailed at Philippi. (Acts 16:12-40.)
10. He was mobbed and expelled from Thessalonica. (Acts 17:1-10.)
11. He was mobbed and expelled from Berea. (Acts 17:10-14.)
12. He was mobbed at Corinth. (Acts 18:1-23.)
13. He was mobbed at Ephesus. (Acts 19:23-31.)
14. There was a plot against his life by the Jews. (Acts 20:3.)
15. He was seized by Jews, mobbed, tried in court five times, and suffered other hardships.

In addition to the persecutions mentioned in chapter 12 of 2 Corinthians, Paul lists these buffetings in the sixth chapter of this same letter: stripes; imprisonments; tumults; dishonor; evil report; deceivers; **as dying, and, behold, we live; as chastened, and not killed.**

In the eleventh chapter, he mentions **stripes above measure, in prisons more frequent, in deaths often** (v. 23), then continues:

> **Of the Jews five times received I thirty-nine stripes. Three times I was beaten with rods, once I was stoned, three times I suffered shipwreck, a night and a day in the deep, in perils of waters, in perils of robbers, in perils by my own countrymen, in perils by the heathen, in perils in the city, in perils in the wilderness, in perils in the sea, in perils among false brethren; in weariness and painfulness, in hunger and thirst, in cold and nakedness.**
>
> **Verses 24-27**

> **Being reviled, persecuted, defamed; made as the filth of the world, the offscouring of all things to this day.**
>
> **1 Corinthians 4:12-13**

Who but Satan's angel could be responsible for all these sufferings and buffetings? In enumerating them, we see that Paul mentions almost everything one could think of *except* sickness or an eye disease.

There is no need to substitute "sore eyes" or "sickness," which Paul does not mention, for all of these buffetings which Paul does mention.

Certainly Paul's **thorn** could not have been defective sight, because Paul's eyes were healed of blindness. He received his sight. (Acts 9:18.) Surely the Bible would not say this if Paul's eyes were as poor as theologians would have us believe.

In answering these first two questions, we have based our remarks on what Paul actually said himself: What was Paul's thorn? A **messenger** (angel) **of Satan**. What was this messenger sent to do? **To buffet me** (deal blow after blow).

Too often, in discussing Paul's **thorn in the flesh**, preachers and teachers give their idea, or what they think, or what seems to be, or what someone has said.

They comfort the sick with this message: Paul was sick and prayed three times to be healed, but God did not see fit to heal him. God told Paul that His grace would be sufficient for him. Therefore, the sufferer must be like Paul — bear his "thorn of sickness" faithfully and patiently for God's glory.

The Bible says nothing about Paul being sick, about him praying to be healed, or about God requiring Paul to remain sick.

Instead of these things which the Bible does not say, this is what the Bible does say:

> **And lest I should be exalted above measure through the abundance of the revelations, there was given to me a thorn in the flesh [not a disease, but] the messenger of Satan to buffet me, lest I should be exalted above measure.**

> **For this thing I sought the Lord three times, that it might depart from me [Paul does not say: "I prayed three times to be healed"]. And he [God] said to me, My grace is sufficient for you: for my strength is made perfect in weakness.**
> **2 Corinthians 12:7-9**

God does not say, "No, Paul, I want you to remain sick."

THIRD: Why Was Paul Given a Thorn?

Now consider this third question. The answer to it is just as clear as the first two.

Why was Satan's messenger sent to buffet Paul?

Answer: **Lest I should be exalted above measure through the abundance of the revelations.**

Is it because of the abundance of their revelations that the sick today should be taught to regard their sickness as a **thorn** which must remain lest they be exalted? Paul's own reason for his **thorn** excludes practically everyone else. You should not claim that your sickness was a **thorn** like Paul's unless you, too, have received such an abundance of revelations that you need to be kept from being exalted.

If you claim the **thorn**, then you must abide by the rest of the scriptures concerning Paul's **thorn**. Paul glorified God in all of the buffetings which he suffered at the hand of Satan's messenger.

If Paul's buffetings were sickness, and if you are suffering sickness like we are told that Paul did, you should also glory in your sickness, instead of trying to get rid of it. If you glory in your **thorn** then you should not go to the best surgeon to have the **thorn** removed.

Now let's consider the scriptures which are supposed to prove that Paul's **thorn** was some sort of sickness.

Infirmities

Most gladly therefore will I glory in my infirmities.

2 Corinthians 12:9

Therefore I take pleasure in infirmities.

2 Corinthians 12:10

You know how through infirmity of the flesh I preached the gospel to you.

Galatians 4:13

I was with you in weakness.

1 Corinthians 2:3

His bodily presence is weak.

2 Corinthians 10:10

My grace is sufficient for you: for my strength is made perfect in weakness.

2 Corinthians 12:9

This word **infirmity** is translated from the same Greek word that Paul used when he wrote: **Likewise the Spirit also helps our infirmities: for we know not what we should pray for as we ought: but the Spirit itself makes intercession for us** (Rom. 8:26-31).

It is also the same word used in Hebrews which says that the prophets **out of weakness were made strong** (Heb. 11:34). It is used to express the manner in which Christ was crucified: **For though he was crucified through weakness, yet he lives by the power of God** (2 Cor. 13:4).

The word weak (or weakness) in these scriptures is the same word used when Paul said: **When I am weak. then am I strong** (2 Cor. 12:10). If the word **weak** meant he was sick, then the word **strong** would logically mean that he was well.

These words translated **infirmities** and **weakness**, with reference to Paul's life, were never intended to mean sickness or some eye disease.

Notice the use of these words **infirmity** and **weak** (translated from the same Greek root words as those above) in the following scriptures. Substitute the words **sickness** or **disease** in their places, and you will see that this idea is wrong. (Rom. 4:19; 8:3; 14:2,21; 1 Cor. 8:9; 9:22; 15:43; 2 Cor. 13:4; Heb. 5:2; 7:28.)

In several of these scriptures, the word **weakness** is contrasted with *power* or *strong* without conveying the idea of weakness through disease at all.

When Paul speaks of his **weakness** before the church, he is expressing his nothingness in his own strength and his dependence upon the Spirit and power of God: **That your faith should not stand in the wisdom of people, but in the power of God** (1 Cor. 2:5).

Temptation

And my temptation which was in my flesh you despised not.

Galatians 4:14

This word **temptation** (which is interpreted to mean some kind of sickness) is translated from the same Greek word used to express Satan's challenge to Christ in the wilderness: **When the devil had ended all the temptation** (Luke 4:13). It was used by Jesus when He said: **Pray that you enter not into temptation** (Luke 22:40). Neither of these had any reference to sickness or disease of any kind.

Paul's Large Letter

You see how large a letter I have written to you with my own hand.

Galatians 6:11

We are taught that Paul was so near blind he had to write using large letters; but let us consider the following facts:

The word **letter** which Paul wrote is translated from the same Greek word he used when he said: **the letter kills, but the spirit gives life** (2 Cor. 3:6). Surely he was not meaning a letter of the alphabet.

The word **large**, used in the English version to define Paul's letter, is translated from a Greek word meaning *a quantitative form, as how much*, not how big.

Moreover, this word **large** as translated from the Greek is not the kind of large that is used to express size, such as when speaking of a **large** upper room. (Luke 22:12.) The **large** in this scripture from Luke's gospel is translated from the Greek word *megas*, which simply means big.

Paul's letter was quantitatively large. A letter of the alphabet can be large in size, but not in quantity.

Paul undoubtedly speaks of his epistle (letter) as being large (in quantity) simply because it was not his custom to do his own writing.

They Would Have Plucked Out Their Eyes

I bear you record, that, if it had been possible, you would have plucked out your eyes, and have given them to me.

Galatians 4:15

This scripture is supposed to prove further how Paul's eyes were so diseased, according to theological speculation, with the oriental eye disease, opthalmia, that the people were willing to give him their own eyes to replace his diseased ones. But this expression by the Galatians simply indicated affection and love for Paul because of his faithful ministry to them.

At the close of one of our crusades abroad during which over a hundred deaf-mutes and over ninety totally blind people had been healed, one of the pastors said in his farewell speech to us:

"Mr. Osborn, our people love you. They are thankful to God for your coming to us. They want you to know that they would cut off their right arm and give it to you, if that were possible."

This expression of devotion did not prove that my right arm was sick or useless.

You see, traditional speculation about Paul's thorn in the flesh is based upon scriptures which do not support these suppositions at all when one reads them without theological prejudice.

If Paul indeed was nearly blind with an eye disease; if he was weak and sickly in his body; if he prayed three times to receive healing, but was refused because he had received such spiritual revelations that he needed to be kept humble by these infirmities in his eyes and in his body; then these allegations would contradict so much other Bible truth which we shall examine next.

Chapter 38
FOOD FOR THOUGHT
ON PAUL'S THORN

1. Since healing is an essential element of the gospel, how could Paul enjoy **the fullness of the blessing of the gospel** (Rom. 15:29) as he did, and remain sick? Is not healing a part of the blessing of the gospel?

2. If Paul was sick, how could the people to whom he preached at Ephesus receive faith for such **special miracles** of healing? (Acts 19:11-12.)

3. If Paul was sick, how is it that the very first sermon he preached in Lystra created such faith in the heart of a man, who was **crippled in his feet from birth** (Acts 14:8), that he was instantly and miraculously healed?

If Paul was sick, would that man have believed the first sermon Paul preached and received enough faith to be miraculously healed? Critics often ask, "What if you were sick, then what about your message?" Do we think that Paul, sick, weak, feeble, and nearly blind, could create enough faith in an unbeliever in one sermon to produce such a miracle of healing?

4. If Paul was sick or diseased, how could he **make the Gentiles obedient, by word and deed, through mighty signs and wonders, by the power of the Spirit of God?** (Rom. 15:18-19). I notice that those who are sick, claiming to have a "thorn in the flesh" like Paul, are usually incapacitated in their ministry and seldom, if ever, produce signs, wonders, and miracles.

5. If Paul was sick or diseased, how is it that when he was preaching on the Isle of Melita, the father of Publius and **all the other sick people in the island came and were cured?** (Acts 28:8-9). That is a rather remarkable result for a man who is sickly and nearly blind.

6. Since Paul's thorn did not hinder the faith of people to be healed of physical diseases in Ephesus, Melita, Lystra and almost every other place where Paul preached, why should it be used as a means of hindering faith to be physically healed today?

7. In Bible days faith came by hearing the word of God, while today faith leaves by hearing the word of someone who tells us: "Paul was sick, and God would not heal him though he prayed three times. So maybe it is not God's will to heal you."

This argument causes people to abandon the very promises of God which are meant to give us faith.

This argument forces us to seek a special revelation from the Spirit of God to determine whether or not God wills to heal every individual.

This would mean that faith does not come by the word of God alone, as Paul says, but that faith comes by praying until a special revelation comes to us that it is God's will to heal a particular individual.

Is it not strange that those who declare that Paul was sick, instead of praying and asking God to heal them, as they claim Paul did, substitute their praying by choosing the doctor whom they believe is best qualified to rid them of their thorn of sickness, whether God wants it removed or not?

Is it not strange that those who teach that Paul's thorn was some kind of sickness, recommend that their people submit to operations and medical treatment for recovery, rather than to pray until God reveals to them that it is not His will to heal them, as they claim that God revealed to Paul?

To be consistent, they should recommend that their people *glory* in their sickness as they claim Paul did, instead of trying to get rid of the thorn.

8. Paul's **thorn in the flesh** never incapacitated him in his ministry because he could testify: **I labored more abundantly than they all** (1 Cor. 15:10). It is hardly reasonable that a sick man could labor more abundantly than all the others who were well.

The person who says sickness is Paul's thorn is generally incapacitated. The assistant does much of the work, and a large percent of time is spent "resting for health's sake."

Paul, who certainly practiced what he preached, says we should be **prepared for every good work** (2 Tim. 2:21), **thoroughly furnished to all good works** (2 Tim. 3:17), **zealous of good works** (Tit. 2:14), **careful to maintain good works** (Tit. 3:8), **perfect in every good work to do his will** (Heb. 13:21), **and abound to every good work** (2 Cor. 9:8). A sick person cannot do these things.

9. If the statement, **My grace is sufficient for you**, meant that God was telling Paul to keep his sickness, it would be the only case in the Bible where God told a person He wanted them to remain sick, that He would give them **grace** for a physically sick body.

Nowhere do the scriptures state that God gives **grace** to the physical body. The word **grace** indicates that it was the inner person that needed help. The grace of God is imparted only to the inner person, which Paul says in his case was **renewed day by day**.

God's grace is for the spiritual person, but the **life of Jesus is manifested in our mortal flesh** (2 Cor. 4:11).

Chapter 39

SEVEN REDEMPTIVE NAMES

Dr. Scofield says, on pages 6 and 7 of his Bible (see footnotes on the redemptive names), that Jehovah is the redemptive name of Deity and means "the Self-existent One who reveals Himself."

These seven redemptive names, he says, "point to God's continuous and increasing self-revelation" He then says, "In His redemptive relationship to people, Jehovah has seven compound names which reveal Him as meeting every need of humankind."

Since it is God's redemptive relationship to us that these names reveal, they must each point to Calvary where we were redeemed. The blessing that each name reveals must be provided in redemption. The scriptures clearly teach this.

These seven redemptive names are:

Jehovah-shamma: **The Lord is there**, or present (Ezek. 48:35), revealing to us the redemptive privilege of enjoying the presence of Him who says, **Lo, I am with you alway** (Matt. 28:20).

That this blessing is provided in redemption is proven by the fact that we were **made nigh by the blood of Christ** (Eph. 2:13).

Jehovah-shalom: **The Lord our peace** (Judg. 6:23-24), reveals to us the redemptive privilege of having His peace. Accordingly, Jesus says, **My peace I give to you** (John 14:27).

This blessing is in redemption because **the chastisement of our peace was upon him** (Is. 53:5) when He **made peace through the blood of his cross** (Col. 1:20).

Jehovah-raah: **The Lord is my shepherd** (Ps. 23:1). Jesus became our shepherd by **giving His life for the sheep** (John 10:11,15); therefore, this is a privilege provided in redemption.

Jehovah-jireh: **The Lord will provide** an offering (Gen. 22:8,14), and Christ was the offering provided for our complete redemption.

Jehovah-nissi: **The Lord is our banner,** or victor, or captain (Ex. 17:15). It was when, by the cross, Christ triumphed over principalities and powers (Col. 2:15), that He provided for us, as our substitute, the redemptive privilege of saying: **Thanks be to God, which gives us the victory through our Lord Jesus Christ** (1 Cor. 15:57).

Jehovah-Tsidkenu: **The Lord our righteousness** (Jer. 23:6). Jesus became our righteousness by bearing our sins on the cross; therefore, our privilege of receiving **the gift of righteousness** (Rom. 5:17) is a redemptive blessing.

Jehovah-rapha: **I am the Lord your physician, or I am the Lord who heals you** (Ex. 15:26). This name is given to reveal to us our redemptive privilege of receiving the healing which was provided by Christ, our substitute. Isaiah, in the redemptive chapter, declares, **Surely he has borne our griefs** (sicknesses), **and carried our sorrows** (pains) (Is. 53:4; Matt. 8:17).

I have reserved this name, Jehovah-rapha, for the last.

The very first covenant God gave after the passage of the Red Sea, which was a type of our redemption, was the covenant of healing. It was at this time that He revealed Himself as our physician, by His redemptive and covenant name, Jehovah-rapha: **I am the Lord who heals you**. This is not only a promise; it is a statute and an ordinance. (Ex. 15:25-26.)

Corresponding to this healing covenant, we have, in the command of James (James 5:14), a positive ordinance of healing in Christ's name which is as sacred and valid for the church today as are the ordinances of the Lord's Supper and of Christian baptism.

Since Jehovah-rapha is one of God's redemptive names sealing His covenant of healing, then Christ during His exaltation could no more abandon His office as healer than His other offices as revealed by His other redemptive names.

Have any of the blessings, which His redemptive names reveal, been withdrawn from this better covenant established upon **better promises**?

Isaiah begins the redemption chapter with the question: **Who has believed our report? and to whom is the arm of the Lord revealed?** (Is. 53:1). The report follows that Christ bore our sins and our sicknesses.

The answer to the question is: Only those who have heard the report could believe it, because **faith comes by hearing**. Since Jesus died in the place of every human being, it is surely worth reporting.

In verses 4 and 5 of this redemption chapter, Isaiah reveals Jesus suffering as our substitute for:

our sicknesses

our pains

our transgressions

our iniquities

our peace

our healing

We would have to misquote the Bible to exclude ourselves from any of these blessings.

When we read Matthew's interpretation of Isaiah, chapter 53, he says **Jesus healed all that were sick** in order to fulfill Isaiah's prophecy: **Himself took our infirmities** (weaknesses), **and bore our sicknesses** (diseases) (Matt. 8:16-17). We would have to misquote these scriptures to exclude ourselves from healing for our bodies.

If, as some think, Christ is unwilling to heal as universally during His exaltation as He did during His humiliation, then He would have to break His promise (John 14:12-13); and He would not be **Jesus Christ the same yesterday, and today, and forever** (Heb. 13:8).

Since the promise of healing, which is made to the any who are sick (James 5:14), is equally as universal in its application as the promise of salvation, which is made to **whoever** is sinful (John 3:16); and since Jesus Christ, in His sacrificial death, **bore** our sicknesses (Matt. 8:17) the same as He **bore** our sins (1 Peter 2:24); then the fact is settled by the scriptures that the sick have the same right to be healed in their bodies as the sinful have to be healed in their spirits.

If the body was not included in redemption, how can there be a resurrection? How can **corruption put on incorruption or mortality put on immortality?** (1 Cor. 15:54).

If we have not been redeemed from sickness, would we not be subject to disease in heaven, if it were possible to be resurrected regardless of redemption?

Our destiny is both spiritual and physical. It is reasonable that our redemption is both spiritual and physical.

As Dr. R. A. Torrey writes in his book, *Divine Healing*:

"Just as one gets the firstfruits of spiritual salvation in the life that now is, so we get the firstfruits of our physical salvation in the life that now is."

Chapter 40

SALVATION AND
HEALING PARALLEL

by Gordon Lindsay

The most prevalent error made by people seeking healing, including those who are fully convinced of this truth, is the confusing of natural, human *hope* with *faith* based on God's word.

Sick people, when prayed for, naturally hope that they will be better; but the natural human emotion of hope is only passive, quite different from Bible faith which is active, creative.

To just hope for something indicates uncertainty. It has no basis for expectancy. But faith looks back to what Christ accomplished for us in His death as our substitute.

Faith rests with confident assurance in God's word, even while it receives no encouragement at all by what the eye can see.

The natural person is a creature of the senses. Feeling or seeing the symptoms of an affliction, he or she tends to believe what the senses register than what God's word says.

Faith, by contrast, is not influenced by what the eye sees and, indeed, is indifferent to it. It does not honor the natural senses, but draws its strength from the immutability of God's word.

If this were not the nature of faith, no such thing as faith would be necessary. Why should faith be needed for that which the eye can already see or the hand can already feel?

The Parallel Between Salvation and Healing

It is this misconception of what faith is that makes it difficult for some to understand and to appropriate physical healing. Yet there should be no reason for this lack of knowledge.

The Bible teaching concerning healing is as simple as that of salvation. The truth is that the healing of the body and the salvation of the soul involves a similar work of the Spirit and are governed by very nearly, if not exactly, identical laws.

The key to the understanding of the whole subject of divine healing lies in a recognition of the almost exact parallel between the appropriation of healing and of salvation, by faith in God's word.

If we have a knowledge of the faith by which we receive salvation, then by a simple comparison we may understand the exact same principles of faith by which we receive healing.

Let us note the similarity between the regeneration of the spirit from its sinfulness and the deliverance of the body from its sickness.

Most people entertain at least a secret hope of eventually being saved. But though someone recognizes the value of heaven and may agree that the prospect of being eternally lost is infinitely more tragic than merely being sick, this powerful incentive to repentance is not sufficient in many cases to result in accepting Christ and being converted.

After you have some appreciation of the awfulness of the disease of sin and express a willingness to forsake it, you still will not be saved without believing that Christ died in your place.

The Finished Work of Salvation

Only when you accept the finished work of redemption can you be saved. If you will not believe until you *feel* saved, you will never be saved. Have not most of us witnessed people who have made this very same mistake?

It is only in the act of believing the finished work of redemption that conversion takes place.

New Reformation of Faith

This belief in the finished work of Christ did not become the inheritance of the Christian faith without a struggle, which, indeed shook the church to its foundation. This truth came as a fruit of the Reformation.

Luther and others discovered that prayers, penances, fastings, tears, and great strugglings of the spirit did not bring them to an enjoyment of peace with God. It was only when they boldly accepted the promise of the finished work of Christ that heaven's peace came. Nor was it easy in those days to take such a stand.

All of the traditions and dogmas of the medieval church and the instincts of the natural, unconverted nature clashed and revolted against such truth. Nevertheless, those who had daring boldness fought the battle through to victory.

The truth that the just shall live by faith, once scarcely believed by anyone, eventually came to be the foundation stone for the positive faith of millions.

This truth, born of the Reformation, is understood by every success-ful soulwinner; and to lead a person to Christ, one should instruct that individual in what to do to be saved.

It is a mistake to attempt to bring an unsaved person to a decision about receiving Christ before there is a clear knowledge of God's promise concerning salvation.

The Christian realizes that if a person's mind is confused, or if one has not fully taken hold of the promises of God, there is no way to sur-vive the first temptation that comes along. For this reason, a wise soul-winner does not press for a decision too quickly. There is a preliminary work of the Spirit that needs to take place in the heart. There are instructions which must be received.

A Preliminary Work of the Spirit Necessary to Healing

The tragedy is that many Christian workers, who clearly realize these things, throw this wisdom to the winds when it comes to the matter of divine healing.

Often they are anxious to have the sick person, in whom they are interested, ministered to immediately; and, if results are not forthcom-ing in the way which they anticipate, they may even become indig-nant.

People travel thousands of miles to clinics. They spend a fortune to obtain the best of medical skill and will philosophically accept any fail-ure of physicians.

But when they come for divine healing, they want to lay down the rules. To them such scriptures as, **Faith comes by hearing** the word of God, have little significance.

Some, in ignorance of God's word, suppose that one with the gifts of healing should go from hospital to hospital, healing all that are sick.

They seem unaware of the Bible account of Jesus at the Pool of Bethesda: He healed only one and left the other lame and the sick lying there. Or that Jesus, while at Nazareth, **could not** (would not) do mighty works there because of their **unbelief**.

They overlook the fact that Christ's teaching on healing anticipated a willingness on the part of the individual to submit completely to

God, or that when the Lord replied to the Gentile woman's request to heal her daughter, He declared that healing was the **children's bread**.

If we are to understand divine healing, we must realize that it is the same power which heals both the spirit and the body. (James 5:14-16.)

The Finished Work of Healing

It only takes a moment for a person to be saved, once the heart is prepared to receive Christ, although sometimes it may take years for one to reach a place of willingness to yield to God. But when that moment arrives, salvation comes at once. This is possible because of the finished work of Christ, which accomplished full salvation once and for all on behalf of **whoever believes** on Him.

As long as the unsaved does not believe, or postpones salvation to the future, he or she will not be saved.

Once anyone believes that God does it now, the work is done.

Christians always encourage the unconverted to believe at once. There is no way for the unsaved to be regenerated until they believe that the work of forgiveness is already done.

No one accuses a Christian of using deceit if the repentant soul is urged to take God at His word and to believe that salvation is present-ly an accomplished fact.

Yet, in the matter of divine healing, just such a charge is made by Christians who are indeed sincere, but untaught in this truth.

Two Fateful Errors

We are now in a position to point out two fateful errors which the church makes in the matter of divine healing.

First: Although it is generally accepted that teaching of the word is required before ordinarily a true work of conversion may take place, often the same persons will inconsistently reproach those who deal the same way in the matter of healing.

Too often they will encourage the sick to be prayed for without teaching and may resent it if the minister advises the sick person to receive teaching from the word of God before being prayed for.

Second: Although they will encourage an unsaved person to believe in the finished work of salvation, some will inconsistently reproach those who deal the same way in securing the healing of the sick.

Some mischievously point to a person who was supposed to have been healed and who is apparently still sick. This is criminal unbelief.

It is the same as to discourage someone from getting saved by pointing to a person who was thought to be saved, but is now living in sin.

Let God be true and everyone else a liar.

According to God's word, you are *saved* if you truly believe. In the same way, you are *healed* if you truly believe. Both salvation and healing are finished works, completed in redemption. They are both appropriated by faith that the work is accomplished by Christ.

Appropriation of Faith

Healing is a finished work as far as God is concerned; but we have to appropriate it by faith, knowing that the work is done now, regardless of the symptoms which we may feel or see.

Faith is believing, confessing, and acting on the finished work of Christ according to what is written in the word of God. Peter declares: **By whose stripes you were healed** (1 Peter 2:24).

We do not pray healing down from heaven or persuade God to do what was accomplished at Calvary. What we do is appropriate healing in identically the same way that we appropriate salvation.

Those Who Receive With Joy and Fall Away

Jesus told of some who hear the gospel and **receive the word with joy, and for a while believe, and in time of temptation fall away**. Others, He said, **are choked with cares and riches and pleasures of this life, and bring no fruit to perfection** (Luke 8:13-14).

There was nothing wrong with the word that was sown in their hearts. There was nothing amiss with the encouragement it gave these people to believe, nor with the joy that came to them as a result of believing. The trouble was that they allowed something to disturb their believing, which **choked** or interrupted the work of the Spirit.

This circumstance is also true of those who believe for healing. The moment a person believes for physical deliverance, he or she receives it as far as God is concerned.

> **Whatever you desire, when you pray, believe that you receive it, and you shall have it.**
>
> **Mark 11:24**

Dr. Goodspeed translates it: "Whenever you pray or ask for anything, have faith that it has been granted you, and you shall have it."

If temptation comes and you yield to the symptoms, you do the very thing the devil wants you to do. You do exactly as a new convert, who, under temptation, gives way to the enemy's accusation that he or she never was saved. So is the person who believes for healing, then doubts and afterward declares that healing never was received.

The truth is that the majority of people who come for healing are healed as far as God is concerned. The real problem is to keep these people from the influence of unbelief, from skepticism, and those who are slaves to their sense knowledge. At this time, it is important to keep these people under the word of God and from association with unbelievers.

The problem is identically the same as a pastor experiences when a large group of people accept Christ. That pastor labors with the converts, giving them loving attention, feeding them with the sincere milk of the word. If that was not done, in many cases they would fall by the wayside.

Satan tempted Christ and said, **If you be the Son of God** (Luke 4:3).

He tempts the convert who has been saved.

He will tempt every person who has been healed.

But while the young convert is encouraged to resist temptation and the devil, and to look to Christ, the person who is healed will too often be given suggestions by friend or foe, by the weak and the well, by the preacher and church members, not to be too sure of healing, and to be on the alert for the return of the old affliction.

Those who have accepted Christ's healing by faith, like those who have accepted Christ's salvation by faith, must be nourished, encouraged, taught, and fed with the promises which their faith is claiming.

Only those who **continue in His word** and who maintain a proper attitude of faith toward God's accomplished blessings can retain the full benefits.

Sin of Unbelief

We might as well face the truth: Unbelief is sin.

Unbelief is war against the very law of being. It is a slavish loyalty to sense knowledge and a disloyalty to the word of God.

A true pastor encourages new converts to stand steady in the faith, even though they go through the fires of temptation. He or she warns them to hold fast and not give way to the wiles of the enemy.

People who have been healed should be taught that it is God's plan that **sickness should be taken from their midst** (Ex. 23:25) and that God's will is that they should **prosper and be in health, even as** (their) **soul prospers** (3 John 2).

This is the promise, and it will be fulfilled in the lives of all who are bold to believe.

Chapter 41

100 DIVINE HEALING FACTS

Many believe that God sometimes heals the sick, but they have no personal knowledge of Jesus as our in-dwelling healer. They know nothing of the many facts which prove that physical health is part of salvation.

They see others healed, but they question whether healing is God's will for them. They are waiting for a special revelation of the will of God for them. In the meantime, they are doing all within the power of human skill to get well with the use of natural means, whether it is God's will for them to be healed or not.

If it is not God's will for you to be well, it would be wrong for you to seek recovery even through natural means.

If it is God's will for you to be well, then it is only logical that the best way of recovery is by divine means.

The Bible reveals the will of God in regard to the healing of the body as clearly as it reveals the will of God in regard to regeneration of the spirit. God need not give any special revelation of His will when He has plainly given His revealed will in His word. He has definitely promised to heal you.

God's promises to heal are as much a revelation of His will to heal as His promises to save reveal His will to save.

A careful study of the scriptures by an unprejudiced person will clearly show that God is both the Savior and the healer of His people — that it is always His will to save and to heal all those who believe on Him. In evidence of this, we call your attention to the following 100 facts:

1. Sickness is no more natural than sin. God made all things **very good** (Gen. 1:31). Therefore, we should not look for the remedy of sin or sickness in the natural, but from God who created us happy, strong, healthy, and to fellowship with Him.

2. Both sin and sickness came into the world through the fall of the human race. Therefore, we must look for the healing of both in the Savior of the human race.

223

3. When God called His children out of Egypt, He made a covenant of healing with them. (Ex. 15:26; 23:25.) Throughout their history, we find them in sickness and in pestilence, turning to God in repentance and confession; and, always, when their sins were forgiven, their sicknesses were healed.

4. God healed those who were bitten by fiery serpents as they looked at a brazen serpent on a pole, which is a type of Calvary. (Num. 21:8.) If everyone who looked at the brazen serpent was healed then, it is logical that everyone who looks at Jesus now can be healed.

5. Jesus said: **As Moses lifted up the serpent in the wilderness, even so** (for the same purpose) **must the Son of man be lifted up** (John 3:14-15; Num. 21:4-9).

6. The people had sinned against God then. Humankind has sinned against God today.

7. The poisonous serpent's bite resulted in death then. Sin results in death today. (Rom. 6:23.)

8. The people cried to God then, and He heard their cry and provided a remedy — *the serpent lifted up.* Those who cry to God today discover that God has heard their cry and has provided them a remedy — *Christ lifted up.*

9. The remedy was **for everyone that is bitten** then. The remedy is for **whoever believes** today. (John 3:16.)

10. In their remedy they received both forgiveness for their sins and healing for their bodies. In Christ, we receive both forgiveness for our sins and healing for our sick bodies.

11. There were no exceptions then — their remedy was for **everyone that is bitten.** There are no exceptions today — our remedy is for **whoever believes.**

12. Everyone was commanded to individually look at the remedy then. Everyone is commanded to individually believe on Christ today.

13. They did not need to beg nor make an offering to God then. There was only one condition: **When they look.** We do not need to beg nor make an offering to Christ today. There is only one condition: **Whoever believes.**

14. They were not told to look to Moses, but rather to the remedy then. We are not told to look to the preacher, but to Christ today.

15. They were not to look to the symptoms of their snake bites then, but rather to their remedy. We are not to look to the symptoms of our sins and diseases today, but to our remedy, Christ.

16. **Everyone that is bitten, when he or she looks upon it, shall live** was the promise to all then, without exception. **Whoever believes in him should not perish, but have everlasting life** is the promise to all today, without exception.

17. Since their curse was removed by the lifting up of the "type" of Christ, our curse was certainly removed by Christ Himself. (Gal. 3:13.)

18. The "type" of Christ could not mean more then to those Israelites, than Christ means to us today. Surely they, through only a "type" of Christ, could not receive more blessings which we cannot receive today through Christ Himself.

19. God promises protection for our bodies as well as for our spirits if we live in Him. (Ps. 91.) In the New Testament, John wishes **above all things that you may prosper and be in health, even as your soul prospers** (3 John 2). Both scriptures show that God's will is that we be as healthy in our bodies as we are in our spirits. It is never God's will for our spirits to be sick. It is never God's will for our bodies to be sick.

20. Asa died in his sickness because he sought not the Lord, but to the physicians (2 Chron. 16); while Hezekiah lived because he sought not to the physicians, but to the Lord. (Is. 38.)

21. The removal of our diseases is included in Christ's redemptive work, along with the removal of our sins. (Is. 53.) The word *bore* implies substitution (suffering for), not sympathy (suffering with). If Christ has *borne* our sicknesses, why should we bear them?

22. Christ fulfilled Isaiah's words: **He healed all that were sick** (Matt. 8:16-17).

23. Sickness is revealed as coming directly from Satan. So Satan went forth and smote Job with sore boils from the sole of his foot to his crown. Job maintained steadfast faith as he cried out to God for deliverance, and he was healed. (Job 42:10,12.)

24. Christ declared that the infirm woman was bound by Satan and ought to be loosed. He cast out the **spirit of infirmity**, and she was healed. (Luke 13:16.)

25. A devil which possessed a man was the cause of his being both blind and dumb. When the devil was cast out, he could both see and talk. (Matt. 12:22.)

26. A demon was the cause of a boy being deaf and dumb and also the cause of his convulsions. When the demon was cast out, the boy was healed. (Mark 9:17-27.)

27. It is written: **Jesus of Nazareth went about doing good, and healing all that were oppressed of the devil** (Acts 10:38). This scripture shows that sickness is Satan's oppression.

28. We are told: **The Son of God was manifested, that he might destroy the works of the devil** (1 John 3:8). Sickness is part of Satan's works. Christ, in His earthly ministry, always treated sin, diseases, and devils the same. They were all hateful in His sight. He rebuked them all. He was manifested to destroy them all.

29. He does not want the **works of the devil** to continue in our physical bodies. He was manifested to destroy them. He does not want a cancer, a plague, a curse, **the works of the devil**, to exist in His own members. **Know you not that your bodies are the members of Christ?** (1 Cor. 6:15).

30. Jesus said, **The Son of man is not come to destroy human lives, but to save them** (Luke 9:56). Sickness destroys; therefore, it is not from God. Christ came to *save* us (Greek: *sozo*, meaning to deliver us, to save and preserve us, to heal us, to give us life, to make us whole), but never to *destroy* us.

31. Jesus said: **The thief** (speaking of Satan) **comes not, but to steal, and to kill, and to destroy: I am come that they might have life, and that they might have it more abundantly** (John 10:10).

32. Satan is a killer; his diseases are the destroyers of life. His sicknesses are the thieves of happiness, health, money, time, and effort. Christ came to give us abundant life in our spirits and in our bodies.

33. We are promised the life of Jesus in **our mortal flesh** (2 Cor. 4:10-11).

34. We are taught that the Spirit's work is to quicken our **mortal** bodies in this life. (Rom. 8:11.)

35. Satan's work is to *kill*. Christ's work is to give *life*.

36. Satan is bad. God is good. Bad things come from Satan. Good things come from God.

37. Sickness is, therefore, from Satan. Health is, therefore, from God.

38. All authority and power over all devils and diseases was given to every disciple of Christ. (Matt. 10:1; Mark 16:17.) Since Jesus said, **If you continue in my word, then are you my disciples indeed** (John 8:31), these scriptures apply to you today, that is, **if you continue in** (act on) His word.

39. The right to pray and receive the answer is given to every believer. (John 14:13-14.) **If you shall ask anything in my name, I will do it.** This logically includes asking for healing, if we are sick.

40. **Everyone that asks receives** (Matt. 7:7-11). That promise is for you. It includes everyone who is sick.

41. The ministry of healing was given to **the seventy**, who represent the future workers of the church. (Luke 10:1,9,19.)

42. It was given to all **them that believe** the gospel, them that act on the gospel, or the practicers or doers of the word. (Mark 16:17.)

43. It is committed to **the elders** of the church. (James 5:14.)

44. It is bestowed upon the whole church as one of its ministries and gifts, until Jesus comes. (1 Cor. 12:9-10.)

45. Jesus never commissioned anyone to preach the gospel without including healing for the sick. He said, **Whatever city you enter, heal the sick that are there** (Luke 10:8-9). That command still applies to the ministry today.

46. Jesus said that He would continue His same works through believers while He is with the Father. **Verily, verily, I say to you, the person that believes on me, the works that I do shall he or she do also; and greater works than these shall they do; because I go to my Father** (John 14:12). This certainly includes healing the sick.

47. In connection with the Lord's Supper, the cup is taken **in remembrance** of His blood which was shed for the **remission of our sins** (1 Cor. 11:25). The bread is eaten **in remembrance** of His body on which were laid our diseases and the stripes by which **we are healed** (1 Cor. 11:23-24; Is. 53:5).

48. Jesus said that certain teachers were **making the word of God of no effect through** (their) **tradition** (Mark 7:13). Human ideas and theories have for centuries hindered the healing part of the gospel from being proclaimed and acted upon as it was by the early church.

49. One tradition is that God wills some of His children to suffer sickness and that, therefore, many who are prayed for are not healed because it is not His will to heal them. When Jesus healed the demon-possessed boy whom the disciples **could not** heal (Mark 9:18), He proved that it is God's will to heal even those who fail to receive healing; furthermore, He assigned the failure to the disciples to cure the boy, not to God's will, but to the disciples' **unbelief** (Matt. 17:19-20).

50. The failure of many to be healed today when prayed for is never because it is not God's will to heal them.

51. If sickness is the will of God, then every physician would be a law-breaker, every trained nurse a defier of the Almighty, and every hospital a house of rebellion instead of a house of mercy.

52. Since Christ came to do the Father's will, the fact that He **healed them all** is proof that it is God's will that all be healed.

53. If it is not God's will for all to be healed, how did *everyone* in the multitudes obtain from Christ what was not God's will for some of them to receive? The gospel says, **He healed them all**.

54. If it is not God's will for all to be healed, why do the scriptures state: **With his stripes we are healed** and **by whose stripes you were healed**? (Is. 53:5; 1 Peter 2:24). How could **we** and **you** be declared healed, if it is God's will for some of us to be sick?

55. Christ never refused those who sought His healing. Repeatedly, the gospels tell us that He healed them all. Christ the healer has never changed.

56. Only one person in the entire Bible ever asked for healing by saying, **If it be your will**. That was the poor leper to whom Jesus immediately responded, **I will; be clean** (Mark 1:40-41).

57. Another tradition is that we can glorify God more by being patient in our sickness than by being healed. If sickness glorifies God more than healing, then any attempt to get well by natural or divine means would be a effort to rob God of the glory that we should want Him to receive.

58. If sickness glorifies God, then we should rather be sick than well.

59. If sickness glorifies God, Jesus robbed His Father of all the glory that He possibly could by healing **everyone** (Luke 4:40), and the Holy Spirit continued doing the same throughout the Acts of the Apostles.

60. Paul says, **You are bought with a price: therefore glorify God in your body, and in your spirit, which are God's** (1 Cor. 6:20).

61. Our bodies and our spirits are bought with a price. We are to glorify God in both.

62. We do not glorify God in our *spirit* by remaining in sin. We do not glorify God in our *body* by remaining sick.

63. John's gospel is used to prove that sickness glorifies God (John 11:4); but God was not glorified in this case until Lazarus was raised up from the dead, the result of which was, **Many of the Jews believed on him** (John 11:45).

64. Another tradition is that while God heals some, it is not His will to heal all. But Jesus, who came to do the Father's will, **did heal them all**.

65. If healing is not for all, why did Jesus bear *our* sicknesses, *our* pains, and *our* diseases? If God wanted some of His children to suffer, then Jesus relieved us from bearing something which God wanted us to bear. But since Jesus came to do the **will of the Father**, and since He **has borne our diseases**, it must be God's will for all to be well.

66. If it is not God's will for all to be healed, then God's promises to heal are not for all. That would mean that faith does not come by hearing the word of God alone, but by getting a special revelation that God has favored you and wills to heal you.

67. If God's promises to heal are not for all, then we could not know what God's will is by reading His word alone. That means we would have to pray until He speaks directly to us about each case in particular. We could not consider God's word as directed to us personally, but would have to close our Bibles and pray for a direct revelation from God to know if it is His will to heal each case.

68. God's word is His will. God's promises reveal His will. When we read of what He promises to do, we then know what it is His will to do.

69. Since it is written, **Faith comes by hearing** the word of God, then the best way to build faith in your heart that God is willing to heal you is for you to hear that part of God's word which promises you healing.

70. Faith for spiritual healing **comes by hearing** the gospel: **He bore our sins**. Faith for physical healing comes by hearing the gospel: **He bore our sicknesses**.

71. We are to **preach the gospel** (that He bore our sins) **to every creature**. We are to **preach the gospel** (that He bore our sicknesses) **to every creature**.

72. Christ emphasized His promise, **If you shall ask anything in my name, I will do it**, by repeating it twice (John 14:12-14). He did not exclude healing from this promise. **Anything** includes healing. This promise is for all.

73. If healing is not for all, Christ should have qualified His promise when He said, **Whatever you desire** (except healing) **when you pray, believe that you receive it, and you shall have it** (Mark 11:24). But He did not. Healing, therefore, is included in the **whatever**. This promise is made to you.

74. If it is not God's will to heal all, His promise would not be dependable where Christ said, **If you live in me, and my words live in you, you shall ask what you will, and it shall be done to you** (John 15:7).

75. James says: **Is any sick among you? Call for the elders of the church; and let them pray over them, anointing them with oil in the name of the Lord: and the prayer of faith shall save the sick, and the Lord shall raise them up** (James 5:14-15). This promise is for all, including you, if you are sick.

76. If God today has abandoned healing in answer to prayer in favor of healing only by medical science, as modern theology speculates, that would mean that He requires us to use a less successful method during a better dispensation. He healed them all then, but today many diseases are incurable by medical science.

77. Paul tells us that God would have us **prepared to every good work** (2 Tim. 2:21), **thoroughly furnished to all good works** (2 Tim. 3:17), **that we may abound to every good work** (2 Cor. 9:8). A sick person cannot measure up to these scriptures. These conditions would be impossible if healing is not for all. Either healing is for all, or these scriptures do not apply to all.

78. Bodily healing in the New Testament was called a mercy, and it was God's mercy which always moved Him to heal all the sick. His promise is that He is **plenteous in mercy to all that call on Him** (Ps. 86:5). That includes you, today.

79. The correct translation of Isaiah 53:4 is: **Surely** (or certainly) **He has borne our sicknesses, and carried our pains**. To prove that our sicknesses were carried away by Christ, just like our sins were carried away, the same Hebrew verb for **borne** and **carried** is used to describe both. (Is. 53:4, 11-12.)

80. Christ was **made to be sin for us** (2 Cor. 5:21) when He **bore our sins** (1 Peter 2:24). **He was made a curse for us** (Gal. 3:13) when He **bore our sicknesses** (Matt. 8:17).

81. Since Christ **bore our sins**, how many is it God's will to forgive? Answer: **Whoever believes**. Since Christ **bore our sicknesses**, how many is it God's will to heal? Answer: **He healed them all**.

82. Another tradition is that if we are righteous, we should expect sicknesses as a part of our life. They quote the scripture: **Many are the afflictions of the righteous** (Ps. 34:19), but this does not mean sicknesses as some would have us believe. It means trials, hardships, persecutions and temptations, but never sicknesses or physical disabilities.

83. It would be a contradiction to say, "Christ has borne our sicknesses, and with His stripes we are healed," but then add, "Many are the sicknesses of the righteous, which He requires us to bear."

84. To prove this tradition, theologians quote, **But the God of all grace, who has called us to his eternal glory by Christ Jesus, after that you have suffered a while, make you perfect, establish, strengthen, and settle you** (1 Peter 5:10). This suffering does not refer to suffering sickness, but to the many ways in which God's people have so often had to suffer for their testimony. (Acts 5:41; 2 Cor. 12.)

85. Another tradition is that we are not to expect healing for certain afflictions. People quote the scripture, **Is any among you afflicted? let him or her pray** (James 5:13). This again does not refer to sickness, but to the same things pointed out in number 82 above.

86. Another tradition is that God chastises His children with sickness. The scripture is quoted, a part of which says, **Whom the Lord loves he chastens** (Heb. 12:6-8). God does chasten those whom He loves, but it does not say that He makes them sick. The word **chasten** here means "to instruct, train, discipline, teach, or educate," like a teacher "instructs" a pupil, or like a parent "trains and teaches" a child.

87. When a teacher "instructs" a student, various means of discipline may be employed, but never sickness. When a parent "trains" a child, there are many ways to chasten, but never by imposing a physical disease upon it. For our heavenly Father to **chasten** us does not require that He lay a disease upon us. Our diseases were laid upon Christ. God could not require that we bear, as punishment, what Jesus has substantially borne for us. Christ's sacrifice freed us forever from the curse of sin and disease which He bore on our behalf.

88. The most common tradition is the worn-out statement: The age of miracles is past. For this to be true, there would have to be a total absence of miracles. Even one miracle would prove that the age of miracles is not past.

89. If the age of miracles is past, no one could be born again because the new birth is the greatest miracle a person can experience.

90. If the age of miracles is past, as some claim, that would mean that all the technical evidence produced in hundreds of laboratories of the world, concerning innumerable cases of miraculous healings, is false and that God's promises to do such things are not for today.

91. Anyone who claims that the age of miracles is past denies the need, the privileges, and the benefits of prayer. For God to hear and answer prayer; whether the petition is for a postage stamp or for the healing of

a paralytic, is a miracle. If prayer brings an answer, that answer is a miracle. If there are no miracles, there is no reason for faith. If there are no miracles, prayer is mockery and only ignorance would cause anyone to either pray or expect an answer. God cannot answer prayer without a miracle. If we pray at all, we should expect that prayer to be answered. If that prayer is answered, God has done it; and if God has answered prayer, He has performed something supernatural. That is a miracle. To deny miracles today is to make a mockery of prayer today.

92. The age of miracles is not past because Jesus, the miracle-worker, has never changed: **Jesus Christ the same yesterday and today and forever** (Heb. 13:8).

93. When Jesus sent His disciples to preach the gospel, He told them: **These** (supernatural) **signs shall follow them that believe.** This was for **every creature,** for **all nations,** until **the end of the world.** The end of the world has not yet come, so the age of miracles has not passed. Christ's commission has never been withdrawn or canceled.

94. Christ's promise for the spirit — that it shall be saved — is in His commission and is for all. His promise for the body — that it shall recover — is in His commission and is for all. To deny that one part of His commission is for today is to deny that the other part is for today. As long as Jesus' commission is in effect, the unsaved can be healed spiritually and sick people can be healed physically by believing the gospel. Multiplied thousands of sincere people all over the world are receiving the benefits of both physical and spiritual healing through their simple faith in God's promises.

95. Christ bore your sins so that you may be forgiven. *Eternal life is yours.* Claim this blessing and confess it by faith; God will make it good in your life.

96. Christ bore your diseases so that you may be healed. *Divine health is yours.* Claim this blessing and confess it by faith; God will manifest it in your body.

97. Like all of Christ's redemptive gifts, healing must be received by simple faith alone without natural means and, upon being received, must be consecrated for Christ's service and glory alone.

98. God is as willing to heal believers as He is to forgive unbelievers. (Rom. 8:32.) That is to say, if when you were unsaved, God was willing to forgive you, now that you are His child, He is willing to heal you. If He was merciful enough to forgive you when you were unconverted, He is merciful enough to heal you now that you are in His family.

99. You must accept God's promise as true and believe that you are forgiven before you can experience the joy of spiritual healing. You must accept God's promise as true and believe that you are healed

before you can experience the joy of physical healing.

100. **As many** (sinners) **as received him were born of God** (John 1:12-13). **As many** (sick) **as touched him were made whole** (Mark 6:56).

When we preach that it is always God's will to heal, the question is immediately raised: "How then could we ever die?"

God's word says: **You take away their breath, they die, and return to their dust** (Ps. 104:29). The Bible says: **You shall come to your grave in a full age, like as a shock of corn comes in its season** (Job 5:26).

For us to come to our full age and for God to take away our breath does not require the aid of a disease. God's will for your death as His child is that, after living a fruitful life, fulfilling the number of your days, you simply stop breathing and fall asleep in Christ to awaken on the other side and live with Him forever. **So shall** (you) **ever be with the Lord** (1 Thess. 4:17). Indeed, this is the blessed hope of the righteous.

> **Because you have set your love upon me, God says, therefore will I deliver you: I will set you on high because you have known my name. You shall call upon me, and I will answer you: I will be with you in trouble; I will deliver you, and honor you. With long life will I satisfy you, and show you my salvation.**
>
> **Psalm 91:14-16**

ACKNOWLEDGMENT: In presenting these 100 Divine Healing Facts, we are indebted to the resourceful writings of F. F. Bosworth, from which many of the thoughts expressed have been gleaned.

Chapter 42

PRAYER FOR HEALING

Once you have accepted Christ as Savior, you are a child of God and have the right to the fulfillment of any and all of God's promises.

If you need healing, you may pray right now and be healed in the same way in which you have been saved.

Now that you realize where sickness came from and that it is not the will of your loving, heavenly Father that you suffer, it is time to approach Him in humility and in faith.

Jesus said, **These signs shall follow them that believe, in my name they shall cast out devils; . . . they shall lay hands on the sick, and they shall recover** (Mark 16:17-18).

Remember that He invites you:

Call unto me, and I will answer you.

Jeremiah 33:3

Ask, and you shall receive, that your joy may be full.

John 16:24

For every one that asks receives.

Matthew 7:8

The reason you can call on the Lord right now and be healed of your physical infirmities and diseases is that Jesus Christ Himself suffered all of them for you. He did it willingly, as your substitute, so that you could be healed of them.

He took upon Himself all the physical consequences of your sinful nature so that He could come into your life as your PHYSICAL HEALER and as your spiritual Savior.

So, right now, pray this prayer:

HEAVENLY FATHER, I thank You that You have made known to me Your salvation and healing plan. I thank You that Christ has redeemed me from sickness, being made sick for me, and that by His stripes I was healed.

I am so thankful that I no more need to bear my own sickness than I need to bear my sins, because You have revealed Christ to me.

Before I understood that sickness and disease, suffering and pain resulted from that first sin and rebellion of Adam and Eve, I presumed that there was no escape from the ever-present threat of physical disease in my life.

I knew that in spite of the wonders of modern medical science, our world is still full of sickness, suffering and crippling diseases.

I AM SO GLAD to know the truth; that Satan is to blame for my sickness, and that I have covenant rights and authority over all devils and diseases.

I marvel that You did not leave humanity in bondage to Satan. After I had rebelled against You and violated Your laws of life, I deserved to die. Oh, what love You manifested toward me in sending Your Son as the sacrifice for my sins. (Rom. 3:24-25.)

Why did You love me so much? There was nothing in my nature that merited Your favor. Thank You for Your infinite love for me, when I was not worthy of Your love.

Sin had taken its awful toll in my life so that my physical body was totally vulnerable to every kind of disease and sickness conceived by the devil to torture me and to destroy my usefulness.

NOW I UNDERSTAND that Jesus not only suffered the full punishment for all my sins, but He also bore all the consequences of my sinful nature.

Now I know that He, of a certainty, took upon Himself all of my diseases and suffered all my pains — my PHYSICAL diseases and pains — so that I could be completely healed.

His physical body was tortured. He was beaten beyond recognition. **His visage was so marred more than any other man** *(Is. 52:14). His back was striped. When they beat Him,* **they plowed his back: they made long their furrows** *(Ps. 129:3). He was bruised and torn. (Is. 53:5.) Now I know that all my sicknesses were laid on Him. He suffered them for me so that I could be free.*

I understand that all sickness as well as sin has the same evil source — Satan, the deceiver. I turn away from him with total resolution, and I welcome the presence and peace, life and health of my Lord into my life.

NOW, FATHER, I come according to Your word, knowing that You always make Your word good and fulfill Your promises. You said: **I am the Lord that heals you.**

Thank You for the fact that when I believe the good news of what Jesus did on my behalf, and when I receive Him into my heart, Satan has no more place in my life. That is why You said: **Behold, I give you power over all the power of the enemy; and nothing shall by any means hurt you** *(Luke 10:19). You gave me power and authority over all devils, and to cure diseases. (Luke 9:1.) You promised that as a believer of the gospel, I can, in*

Your name, cast out devils; I can lay my hands on the sick and they shall recover. (Mark 16:18.)

I do now take You at Your word. I rebuke the enemy which has caused my suffering. I resist this oppression of the devil. (Acts 10:38.)

In the name of Jesus Christ, I command the sickness, which is a spirit of infirmity, to leave, and every symptom to be destroyed in the name of Jesus who is present now.

FATHER, I thank You that You have heard my prayer and have granted the answer.

*You bore my sins and my diseases. Now I am free of them. When You suffered my sicknesses, **by your stripes I was healed** (Is. 53:5; 1 Peter 2:24).*

The grace and life of Jesus Christ which now live in me, heal me of all sin and disease. I am saved. I am healed. I am free.

I now understand that Satan has lost all dominion over me. Therefore, no sin can condemn me, and no sickness has the right to live in my body which has now become the temple of the Holy Spirit.

I claim the promise of healing for my body now, by faith in Your word; and I thank You that the very source of my sickness is destroyed and that, according to Jesus' promise, I shall recover.

In Jesus Christ's name, I have prayed.

OH, JESUS, YOU ARE LORD. Your life is mine. Your health is mine. I am saved and I am healed. Every symptom of my old life, my old sins and mistakes, my old pains and sicknesses must now disappear, because the life and power of Christ are healing and making me whole NOW.

From today, I shall walk in Your new life and health, because You are my life, my all. You are with me and in me NOW.

Thank You, Lord. AMEN.

* * *

Now you have prayed and rebuked the source of your trouble. You accept, by faith in God's word, that He has answered your prayer. Now, **hold fast the profession of** (your) **faith without wavering; for he is faithful that promised** (Heb. 10:23).

Allow the devil to hear nothing spoken from your lips other than the confession of God's word. Allow yourself to think nothing contrary to what God has promised in His word.

Remember that your faith can never rise higher than your words. The promises of God become real and living only as we confess them. To enjoy the Christian life, you must learn the value of God's word on your lips.

You cannot talk contrary to God's word and win His blessings.

Your words are your standard of faith. They express what you really believe.

Anything other than *You shall recover* (Mark 16:18) is a lie from the devil. Treat it as such and stand on God's word, for God will make it good in you.

Do as Abraham did: Be strong in faith by looking to the promise.

Keep the word before your eyes. Look at the promises continually.

Never consider symptoms that contradict the word as grounds for doubting the word of God because it is written: **I will watch over my word to perform it** (Jer. 1:12; Ezek. 12:25,28; Is. 38:7; Rom. 4:21).

Chapter 43

LIFE'S GREATEST QUESTION

Jesus said, **You shall know the truth, and the truth shall make you free** (John 8:32). Knowledge of these great truths of redemption makes it possible for God to fulfill all of His promises for you, if you will accept Jesus Christ as Savior.

A man asked me: "Will you pray for me to be healed?"

"Certainly," I replied, and then asked, "Are you a Christian, a born-again believer?"

"No," was his reply.

"Then," I asked, "why do you ask God to heal you when you do not love Him enough to serve Him?"

"Well, I just thought I could be healed," he answered.

"You may be healed, and you will be healed; but first, accept Christ as Savior, then He will be delighted to heal you," I reasoned, and then continued, "Why should you ask God for more strength to serve the devil? If you will serve God, He is Jehovah-rapha — the Lord that heals you; He will not only heal you, but will fulfill every one of His promises to you and keep you happy the rest of your life."

The man thought it over intelligently, accepted Christ, was joyfully converted and healed completely.

You may be one who desires healing for your body, yet you may not have the joy of knowing that all is well with your soul. If you are, remember that no time is as good as the present to be saved.

Now is the accepted time; behold, now is the day of salvation.
2 Corinthians 6:2

God is waiting to bless your life. He longs to reveal Himself to you in His fullness.

Every person who has never accepted Christ as Savior must remember that **all have sinned, and come short of the glory of God** (Rom. 3:23).

Except you repent, you shall all likewise perish.
Luke 13:5

Jesus said, **You must be born again** (John 3:7).

Paul said, **If anyone be in Christ, he or she is a new creature: old things are passed away; behold, all things are become new** (2 Cor. 5:17).

You are able to *know* that you are saved, and every person should know this. The Bible says, **We *know* that we have passed from death to life** (1 John 3:14). There are many things which we shall never know; but, thank God, we can know we have passed from death to life.

The moment you become definite in your actions and follow the scriptural pattern, you will know this.

Some may ask, How may I know that I am saved? How may I be sure that my sins are forgiven?"

This Is Life's Greatest Question

The Philippian jailer asked, **What must I do to be saved? And they** [Paul and Silas] **said, Believe on the Lord Jesus Christ, and you shall be saved** (Acts 16:30-31).

Jesus said, **The one who believes and is baptized shall be saved** (Mark 16:16).

Paul said, **If you shall confess with your mouth the Lord Jesus, and shall believe in your heart that God has raised him from the dead, you shall be saved** (Rom. 10:9).

Peter said, **Whoever shall call on the name of the Lord shall be saved** (Acts 2:21).

Each scripture which we have just quoted contains a definite promise: **You shall be saved**. If you will be definite in meeting the conditions, **you shall be saved.**

Chapter 44

JESUS CHRIST — THE WAY

The master key to the God-life within you is to understand and personally relate to what Christ did for you when He died on the cross in your place.

Believe what the Bible says: **You have been crucified with Christ** (Gal. 2:20).

When Christ died, it was not for sins He had committed. The punishment He endured was your sins being judged — once and for all.

> **Knowing this, that your old person was crucified with him, that the body of sin might be done away, that we should no longer be in bondage to sin.**
>
> **Romans 6:6**

Remember, God promised that if you believe what His word says about Christ dying for you, His power would come and transform you into His child again by His life being reborn in you. (John 1:12 Ph.)

The Bible says,

> **You were dead and buried with him, so that just as he was raised from the dead by the Father's power, so you too might rise to life on a new plane altogether .**
>
> **If you have shared his death, you shall also share His resurrection life.**
>
> **Never forget that your old self died with him on the cross so that the tyranny of sin over you might be broken — for a dead person is free from the power of sin.**
>
> **Look upon yourself as dead to the appeal and power of sin but alive to God through Christ Jesus.**
>
> **Romans 6:4-6,8,11 Ph**

Understand and relate yourself to God's plan of salvation for you. It is personal. It was carried out on *your* behalf. He opened the way for you and Him to live together again.

You Have the Right To Choose

He loves you and paid for you.

Jesus Christ is your link with God. He removed your judgment by suffering in your place.

Now, all you have to do is to believe. You have the right and freedom to choose to believe.

The moment you decide to BELIEVE that Christ's death was on *your* behalf, then He will come in and live with you forever; you will be saved. The key to your new lifestyle is to relate yourself to God through Christ, and to do it RIGHT NOW.

Behold, *now* is the accepted time; behold, *now* is the day of salvation — for YOU (2 Cor. 6:2).

God's SALVATION PLAN is written in the Bible for YOU.

> **I have spoken to you, that in me you may have peace.**
>
> John 16:33

God wants you to be at peace with Him. He created you. He loves you. He values you.

The Bible says, **There is no peace for the** (unbeliever) (Is. 57:21). Why? Because when Adam and Eve questioned the integrity of God's word, they abandoned the lifestyle and friendship of God. There could be no peace. Fear replaced confidence. Disease destroyed health. Grief and sorrow superseded happiness and tranquillity. Loneliness reigned instead of friendship. Guilt and condemnation ruled instead of peace and assurance.

Sin separates you from God. (Is. 59:2.)

Confusion and insecurity take the place of faith and love.

But when you know that God loved and valued you enough to give His Son to be judged in your place so that you could be restored to Him as though no sin had ever been committed, then you realize that there is nothing left to stand between you and God. **There is therefore now no condemnation to those who are in Christ Jesus** (Rom. 8:1).

Restored to self-dignity, you open your arms and welcome Jesus Christ as He brings God's life back home to your heart where you and He become friends again.

Quality Quotations

Now I want to share with you some Bible quotations which will confirm to you God's salvation plan.

The first quotation shows you how God wants to have you near Him and how He wants to be near you.

God is faithful, by whom you were called to the fellowship of his Son.

1 Corinthians 1:9

The next quotation reminds you that God's salvation plan is, and has always been, based on your confidence in the integrity of His word.

Without faith [if you distrust God], it is impossible to please God: for anyone who comes to him *must believe* that he exists, and that he always rewards those who diligently seek him.

Hebrews 11:6

The next group of quotations enumerate the ways Jesus Christ became *your* personal substitute, assumed *your* guilt and suffered the penalty of *your* sins in His death for you on the cross.

Surely Jesus Christ has borne *our* sicknesses and carried *our* sorrows.

Isaiah 53:4 ML

Jesus Christ was wounded and bruised for *our* sins. He was chastised that *we might have peace.*

Isaiah 53:5 LB

God has laid on Jesus Christ the guilt and sins of every one of us.

Isaiah 53:6 LB

For the transgression of *people* was Jesus Christ stricken.

Isaiah 53:8 RS

He made his soul an offering *for [our] sin.*

Isaiah 53:10

Himself [Jesus Christ] took *our* infirmities and bore our sicknesses.

Colossians 1:20 LB

Brought Back as God's Friend

The Bible quotations which follow explain the results you can experience when you understand and believe that Jesus Christ actually died in your place and endured all of the punishment and condemnation you deserved to bear.

It was through what God's Son did that he cleared a path for everything to come to him for Christ's death on the cross has made peace with God for all by his blood.

This includes YOU who were once so far away from God. Now he has brought you back as his friend.

He has done this through the death on the cross of his own human body [substituting for you], and now as a result, Christ has

243

brought you into the very presence of God, and you are standing there before him with nothing left against you.

The only condition is that you *fully believe* the Truth, and be convinced of the Good News that Jesus died for you.

Colossians 1:20-23 LB

Identified With Christ

The following Bible quotations explain how you are personally identified with Jesus Christ in His death, burial and resurrection.

Jesus Christ, was wounded for OUR transgressions. He was bruised for OUR iniquities.

Isaiah 53:5

Our old person is crucified with Jesus Christ so that the body of sin might be destroyed, that henceforth we should not serve sin.

Romans 6:6

We have been planted together in the likeness of his death.

Romans 6:5

Jesus Christ was raised again for *our* justification.

Romans 4:25

God has raised *us* up *together with Christ.*

Ephesians 2:6

Now if we be dead with Christ, we believe that we shall also LIVE WITH HIM. [That is not just in heaven, but here and now.]

Romans 6:8

Jesus said: Lo, I am with you alway, even to the end of the world (Matt. 28:20).

God says: I will dwell in them, and walk in them; and I will be their God, and they shall be my people (2 Cor. 6:16).

And you did God *make alive together with Jesus Christ.*

Colossians 2:13 AR

God made us *alive together with Christ* and *raised us up with him.*

Ephesians 2:5-6 AR

Here is a verse that summarizes these IDENTITY facts:

I am crucified with Christ: nevertheless I *live*; yet not I, but *Christ lives in me*: and *the life which I now live* in the flesh I live by the faith of the Son of God, who loved me, and gave himself for me.

Galatians 2:20

Sharing God's New Life

The *next quotations* from the Bible will encourage you to always trust in God's plan of salvation.

So look upon your old sin nature as dead, and instead *be alive to God* through Jesus Christ.

Romans 6:11 LB

When God the Father, with glorious power, brought Jesus Christ back to life again, *you were given his wonderful new life to enjoy.* Now *you share his new life.*

Romans 6:4-5 LB

Whoever *believes* in Jesus Christ shall not perish, but have eternal *life.*

John 3:16

Anyone who believes on the Son has everlasting *life.*

John 3:36

Jesus said, I am come that *you* might have *life more abundantly.*

John 10:10

Salvation is not a reward for the good we have done.

It is God himself who has made us what we are and *given us new lives from Jesus Christ.*

Ephesians 2:9,10 LB

God gave you a share in *the very life of Christ,* for he forgave all of your sins, and blotted out the charges proved against you. In this way God took away Satan's power to accuse you of sin, and He openly displayed to the whole world Christ's triumph at the cross where *your sins* were taken away.

Colossians 2:13-15 LB

So you have everything *when you have Christ,* and *you are filled with God* through your union with Christ.

Colossians 2:10 LB

For all things are yours, and you are Christ's, and Christ is God's.

1 Corinthians 3:21,23

Jesus Christ's divine power *has given unto us all things that pertain unto* LIFE.

There is given to us exceeding great and precious promises: that by these we might be *partakers of the divine nature.*

2 Peter 1:3, 4

Chapter 45

INTRODUCTION
TO NEW LIFE FACTS
(To the Next Seven Chapters)

God's salvation plan is His *new life plan* for you. He created you for life — His kind of life. Jesus Christ came **that you might have** *life* **more abundantly** (John 10:10).

God's life, being restored to you, depends on your knowledge of certain facts.

In the next seven vital chapters of this book, I share with you the seven essential facts which open the way to God's lifestyle.

Know these facts and live.

Chapter 46

NEW LIFE FACT I

BELIEVE YOU ARE VALUABLE
AS GOD'S CREATION

You are created in God's image to share His life, love, purpose and creative plan. You are therefore infinitely valuable to Him.

He is saying to you, right now:

"I love you. I created My best when I created you. I paid a price for you, and you are worth all I ever paid for you. I have destined My best for you."

God created humankind in his own image, in the image of God created he him; male and female created he them.

Genesis 1:27

In the likeness of God he created male and female.

Genesis 5:1-2

God made nothing inferior. He is first class all the way. He created you unique. You are exceptional — one-of-a-kind.

Before you were born, you existed in God's mind. He knew this world would need you at this time. He planned you with a special purpose that no one but you could fulfill because no one on earth could do what you are here to do.

Your God-given value does not depend on special genes from superior parents. Your worth before God is not measured by your assets, the color of your skin, super intelligence or formal education.

All sorts of miracles start happening when you discover and accept your value and your potential.

The Bible says, **You are God's workmanship** (Eph. 2:10).

The man who wrote most of the Psalms was wonderstruck by how God made human persons.

The Lord made people a little lower than *God*, and crowned them with glory and honor (Ps. 8:5). (KJV **a little lower than the**

249

angels. The original Hebrew word used is "Elohim" — God, as used in Gen. 1:1.)

The Lord gave them dominion over the works of his hands; he put all things under their feet.

The bottom line of positive and stable self-esteem is when you can say:

"I accept the value that God has put on me."

When you do that, you will then cooperate with God to develop the best possible you in this world.

Self-value will rid you of all jealousy because you will never again want to be anyone else. (John 15:15; Is. 62:3.)

Self-value will wipe out inferiority because you are in God's class of being and He, in you, is greater than any person or any power outside of you. (1 John 4:4.)

Self-value will eliminate fear of failure or defeat because nothing can stop you and God working together. (Is. 41:10; Deut. 31:6.)

Self-value will give you courage because you discover that with God at work in you, you become indomitable. (Jos. 1:9; 1 John 4:4.)

Self-value will cause you to stand up tall, to square your shoulders, to look out into the future with new confidence, to walk with a steady stride, and to rise to the level of importance for which God created you. (Ps. 91:1-2; 46:1-3.)

God created human persons as much like Himself as any child can be like its natural parents.

God planned that whatever could be said about *Him*, could be said about *you*. (1 John 4:17.)

God never planned you or me for poverty, inferiority, sickness, depression, want or insecurity. (1 Peter 2:9.)

God never created anything inferior — not you — not any human person. (Ps. 8:4-6.)

As this powerful principle takes root, you begin to see and respect yourself as a member of divine royalty. (Gal. 4:6-7.)

God's family is supposed to represent Him and to reflect His lifestyle on earth.

Recognize your value. When you do, you cause the seeds of greatness to germinate in you. (Gal. 3:29; 1 Peter 1:23; 1 John 3:9.)

Keep those seeds watered by thinking on them and reaffirming your value until your attitude and conduct are transformed.

Now say this to God, out loud.

PRAYER:

I RECOGNIZE my value, that You created me in Your own image and likeness. Whatever can be said about You can be said about me as Your off-spring.

My life is Your very breath — Your life in human form. Your best material is in me. I am the product of love. I am created for greatness, crowned with glory and honor, to have dominion over all of Your works.

THANK YOU, LORD. I have had a rebirth of self-worth. Knowing that I am created in Your image and likeness reminds me of my divine origin, of my high purpose, of my infinite value.

I shall never again depreciate the me that You value so much. I shall never again put down what You have lifted up. I am not a nobody. I am a real somebody.

AMEN!

My Value . . .
by Dr. T. L. Osborn

I am VALUABLE to God and to people because I am created in His class of being.

I am VITAL because **God's plan involves me.**

My HERITAGE is **to have God's best**, to **enjoy His companionship** and to **use His wealth and power** for the good of myself and others.

I am CREATED for **life, love, power, prosperity, success** and **dignity.**

The Seeds of Greatness **are in me.** God never created me to be a **nobody**, but a real **somebody.**

I therefore **recognize my self-value**, that God designed me **for His lifestyle** and now know that **He planned Life's BEST for me as His child.**

I shall no longer **discredit** or **demean** or **destroy** what God created in His own image and **values so much.**

I welcome **God's friendly voice.** He reminds me of my **divine origin**, of my **high purpose**, and of **His Love-Plan** to help me **achieve, enjoy** and **share** His best in life.

Chapter 47

NEW LIFE FACT II

KNOW THAT DISTRUSTING GOD'S WORD IS THE ORIGINAL AND BASIC PROBLEM

God's dream for humanity is recorded in the Bible book of Genesis. His plan was to reproduce Himself in Adam and Eve and to have companionship with them.

But their friendship had to be two-way. God would need to be sure that Adam and Eve wanted Him, like He wanted them. They were not required or forced to respect Him any more than you are.

God placed them in the garden of Eden and gave them **every tree that is pleasant to the eye, and good for food, and the tree of life also in the midst of the garden** (Gen. 2:9).

The only condition: Since they were created in God's image, to share His lifestyle, they were to trust what He said.

God made one single restriction to measure their faith and confidence in His dream for them. He said:

Of every tree of the garden you may freely eat; but of the tree of the knowledge of good and evil, you will not eat of it; for in the day that you eat of it *you will surely die.*

Genesis 2:16-17

They were expected to have confidence in what God said and that is all that He expects of you and me.

Satan, God's enemy, heard of God's dream and conceived a scheme to induce Adam and Eve to betray God's trust.

Satan came into the garden. (Gen. 3:1.) He contradicted God, asserting himself as an authority, and said: **If you eat of that tree, you will** *not* **surely die** (Gen. 3:4).

Eve took of the fruit and *ate it,* **and gave some to her husband with her; and** *he ate it.*

Genesis 3:6

That was the original sin — distrusting God's word.

Say this to God.

PRAYER:

LORD, now I understand why faith is so important. That is all You ask of me — just to believe Your word.

I now realize that lack of confidence in Your word was the original sin. Your friendship and companionship with me depend on our mutual trust. You want to know that I desire Your company and Your lifestyle, just like You have proven that You desire mine. And the only way I can prove my affection for You is to trust what You say.

I have not done that In the past. I now realize why I have had to walk alone. I have played into the enemy's hands by abusing the trust of life You placed in me.

WITH THE KNOWLEDGE of this basic problem, I come to You, O Lord, convinced that Your word and Your way are the only basis for the abundant and blessed life You created me for.

From today, my choice shall always be to totally trust in Your living word.

AMEN!

Chapter 48

NEW LIFE FACT III

UNDERSTAND THAT DISAVOWING GOD'S INTEGRITY RESULTS IN DEATH

God's original dream for Adam and Eve was that if they trusted in His integrity, they would live and prosper with Him forever. If they abused His trust and disbelieved His word, the process of deterioration would begin and they would die.

After Adam and Eve rejected God's trust, He came into the garden and spelled out what the results would be.

There would be no grounds for a relationship with God. Adam and Eve had exercised their free wills and had, by their action, disregarded and disbelieved what God had said. The good life ended. Dignity was desecrated.

God said, in the day that you disavow my instructions and eat the fruit I forbade, you will surely die.

Genesis 2:17

Without trust in God's integrity, human persons sink into despair and disgrace, degeneration and disease, destruction and oblivion, deterioration and death.

Their lack of trust in the integrity of what God said was later called *sin*.

The simple rule that God made was: **The person who sins will die** (Ezek. 18:4,20).

Later it was repeated in another way:

The wages of sin [disavowing the integrity of God's word] **is death.**

Romans 6:23

Adam and Eve were no longer qualified to dwell in the garden with God. Separated from His plenty and beyond His protection, they were now subject to their new master who came **to steal, to kill and to destroy** (John 10:10).

That was the beginning of suffering, disease, pain, hate, lust, envy, murder, jealousy, loneliness, guilt, poverty, hunger, destruction and death.

Sin had entered the human race. It would be passed on to all generations.

Whereas, by one person sin entered into the world, and death by sin, so death passed upon all persons, for that all have sinned.

Romans 5:12

The fundamental sin that severed God's relationship with mankind was not murder or adultery or lying or stealing or hatred or abuse.

It was the assumption or philosophy or attitude that *God did not mean what He said.*

When that position is taken, deterioration sets in like a cancer and is terminal.

When you do not trust God, you do not trust yourself, or anyone else.

When you decide that God has no integrity, your own integrity is abandoned. Conscience is calloused. Dignity is desecrated. The human person deteriorates and dies. Honor is gone. The lights go out. There is only darkness.

Say this to God.

PRAYER:

DEAR LORD, I thank You for helping me to understand the final consequences of unbelief in Your word.

Now I realize why the wages of sin is death.

I now understand that the original and the ultimate sin is to disavow Your integrity, to disbelieve Your word. When I do that, my own dignity as a human created like You is repudiated. If I do not believe in You, I do not believe in me. Excellence is bartered for mediocrity. Deterioration sets in like a terminal disease, and I die.

O GOD, I thank You for helping me to realize that, since I am created by You, the God of faith, I can experience Your lifestyle and know true living by believing in Your integrity.

Your word is Your bond. You intended for words to weld society together in mutual trust and inter-relationships. But when faith in Your integrity was abandoned, human life crumbled and fell apart. The lack of integrity turned inward, and the divine dignity of God's creation died.

I THANK YOU, Lord, that Your dream for me is so beautiful. You created me to live on Your level. Confidence in Your word and Your way is the bond that unites me with You.

I now realize that the integrity of Your word is the foundation of real life as You planned it for me.

I do, here and now, honor Your word and pledge myself to trust what You say. And I believe that this faith will lead me to the discovery of the abundant life You originally created me to enjoy.

AMEN!

HER LEG was 4'' shorter than the other, and paralyzed — the result of a birth defect. She was instantly healed in the Osborn Crusade at Bogota, Colombia.

ABOVE: Miracle scenes in the Osborn Crusade.

BELOW: A young man shows how God healed him. A bullet through his spine left him paralyzed. Doctors put him in a brace from his shoulders to his hips and said he would never walk. He attended the Osborn Crusade in his wheelchair, believed on Jesus Christ, and was instantly healed. His friends carried his wheelchair aloft as he walked to the platform to testify.

OSBORN CRUSADE — Madurai, S. India

THIS INDIAN GIRL had been crippled by polio, using braces, a built-up shoe and a cane to walk.

She was instantly healed during the Osborn Crusade at Madurai and could walk as well as any normal child.

T. L. OSBORN shows the audience at Embu the crutches, canes and braces discarded by those who have been healed during the teaching of the gospel and during the mass prayer.

* * *

JUAN SANTOS, shot through his spine, was left dead below his waist. One arm was partially paralyzed, his head shook, and both legs became rigid.

For 16 years, to move about, he swung his body between his hands. All of the city knew him.

He was instantly and totally healed in the Ponce Crusade.

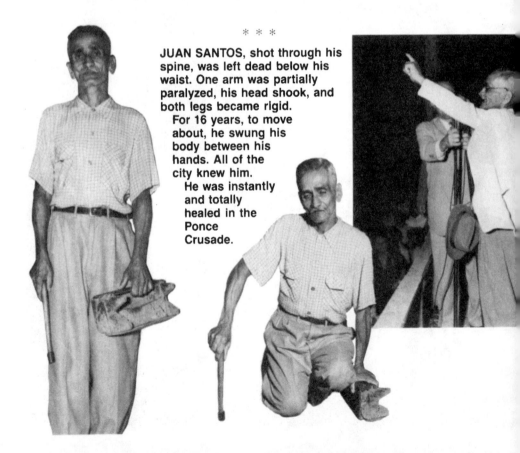

This man's legs have been healed during the Osborn Crusade, and he is proud to show the proof of his miracle.

More miracles are witnessed as T. L. and Daisy teach faith and minister to the people.

WHILE everyone waited for the person who had discarded the crutches and braces to arrive at the platform, suddenly Dr. Osborn spotted another pair of crutches being held aloft, and pointed toward them to signify another miracle God had performed among the people.

AT LAST, the woman whose braces and crutches Dr. Osborn had been holding arrived to show what God had done for her. Crippled by polio when she was a child, she had been left paralyzed. Now she is healed and her legs are strong. Thousands glorified God, saying like the people at Capernaum, *We never saw it on this fashion.* (Mk.2:12)

CRUSADE — Lubumbashi

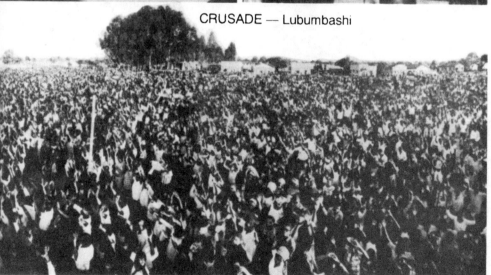

*THE HAROLD KHAN MIRACLE

DUE TO AN INJURY when he was 12 years old, Harold Khan's left leg stopped growing. By the time he reached age 14, his left leg was 5-1/2 inches shorter than the other one. At great risk, his mother brought Harold to the Osborn Crusade — where he was miraculously healed. Harold's Moslem father believed on Jesus when he saw the miracle He did for his son.

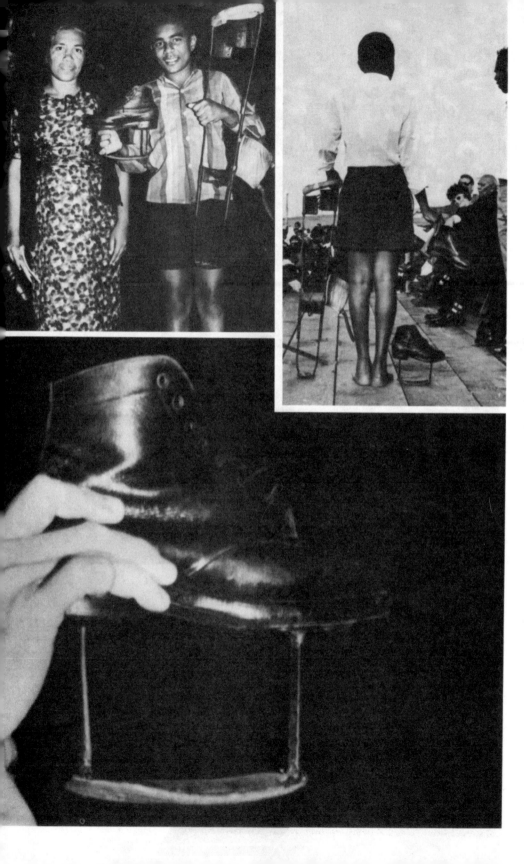

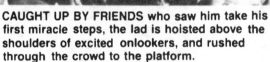

CAUGHT UP BY FRIENDS who saw him take his first miracle steps, the lad is hoisted above the shoulders of excited onlookers, and rushed through the crowd to the platform.

LEFT: As the multitude looked with amazement, the young man, with steel brace and shoes lifted high, marched across the platform to show the miracle God had done for him.

BELOW: While startled onlookers marvel at God's power, this lad tells his miracle story and pledges his life to following Jesus Christ who has made him whole.

OSBORN CRUSADE — Nakuru

T. L. OSBORN holds aloft the crutches and braces of a miraculously healed polio victim, as he affirms: "This Jesus of the Bible is unchanged. He never cripples, wounds or destroys. He lifts the fallen, forgives sinners, heals the crippled."

"Some nights, even before we could pray, people would get converted and healed and changed. They would interrupt the sermon to tell what had happened to them. One night, this happened three times — so mighty was the Lord's presence to save and to heal.

I stood there amidst a press of people on the platform, with eleven crutches in my arms. An assistant held up two big braces. Two pastors were holding up an ambulance cot and two others a wheelchair — evidence of Christ's presence at work."

Domtilla Juma was a helpless victim of paralysis. Unable to stand or work, she crawled away from her home, to die in the jungle. She was found by friends. At the hospital, several operations on her spine left her more helpless than before. Carried to the Osborn Crusade, she heard the gospel, believed on Christ and was totally healed. She goes all over her region, showing the people what God's miracle power did for her.

T.L. OSBORN CRUSADE

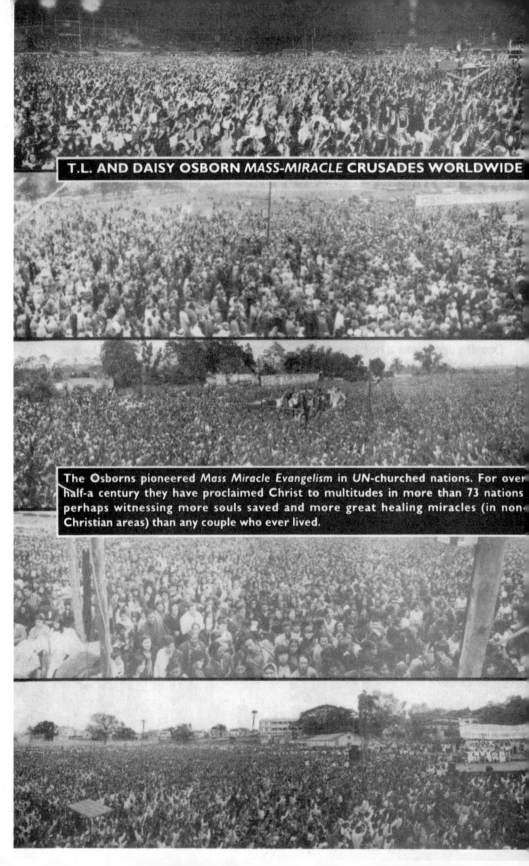

T.L. AND DAISY OSBORN *MASS-MIRACLE* **CRUSADES WORLDWIDE**

The Osborns pioneered *Mass Miracle Evangelism* in *UN*-churched nations. For over half-a century they have proclaimed Christ to multitudes in more than 73 nations perhaps witnessing more souls saved and more great healing miracles (in non-Christian areas) than any couple who ever lived.

S. PACIFIC — Surabaya, Indonesia

EUROPE — The Hague, Holland

AFRICA — Uyo, Nigeria

S. AMERICA — Bogota, Columbia

ASIA — Hyderabad, India

Both T.L. and Daisy are spiritual strategists in ministering to people, lifting them in faith and seeding them with the positive gospel by leading them in confessing the truths of Christ with their lips, then in acting on His word with childlike faith.

Chapter 49

NEW LIFE FACT IV

BELIEVE THAT GOD LOVED AND VALUED YOU TOO MUCH TO LET YOU DIE

God never abandoned His dream for you. God is love and love never quits.

His love went into action the day Adam and Eve sinned. He found a just and legal way to restore humankind back to an intimate relationship with Him.

Although they disavowed His integrity and disbelieved His word, God did not want His beautiful creation to deteriorate and die. And He does not want you to despair and decay in self-destruction and the shame of indignity.

He says:

I have no pleasure in the death of one who dies, so turn yourself and live.

Ezekiel 18:32; 33:11

God was not willing that any should perish, but that ALL should come to repentance.

2 Peter 3:9

God so loved the world that he gave his only begotten Son, that whoever believes in him will not perish, but have everlasting life.

John 3:16

But God showed his great love for you by sending Christ to die for you .

Romans 5:8 LB

It is vital that you realize how much God values you. He created you in His likeness, and you are significant and preeminent to His plan. He made you for life, love, power, prosperity, success, honor and dignity. The seeds of greatness are in you. You are created in God's class of being. God's whole dream is reflected in you. He loved and valued you too much to let you self-destruct.

When you learn to esteem what God esteems and value what he values, then you are ready to comprehend God's salvation plan for you and to reevaluate your own life by the measure of what He has paid to redeem you from death.

Your life is God's life in human flesh. Recognize your roots in God and your value to God. You are His product. His best is in you.

Say this to God.

PRAYER:

O LORD, I thank You for loving me when I did not esteem my own self. Thank You for placing such a high value on me. Though I abused Your trust of life in me and disavowed Your integrity, You valued me too much to let me die in my sins.

Although I deserved deterioration and death, Your love reached out to find a way to save me and to redeem me to Yourself so that we could be friends and partners in life like You originally planned.

Because You are love, You never take pleasure in seeing even the most rebellious and destructive person deteriorate and die. You value me so much that, to have me near You as a friend and a partner, You prefer to pay the full penalty of my sins, in order to justify me and to redeem me.

DEAR GOD, thank You for Your love for me.

Knowing how You value me, I am learning to value myself. I respond to Your love and, here and now, I sincerely thank You for reaching out in love to save me and to lift me out of death, into Your abundant life.

AMEN!

Chapter 50
NEW LIFE FACT V

KNOW WHY JESUS CAME AND DIED AS YOUR SUBSTITUTE

God's salvation plan would end the scourge of death and restore people to life.

What was His plan and how could it restore you to God and legally absolve you from the penalty of death for your sins?

Substitution was the answer.

If someone who is innocent of sin would willingly take the place of one who is guilty and assume full punishment for his or her sins, then the guilty one would be free and could be restored to friendship with God as though no wrong had ever been done.

It was love's idea.

In order to provide you a substitute who had no sin of his own, God gave His own Son.

Jesus Christ, God's Son **was in all points tempted like as we are, yet without sin** (Heb. 4:15). **He did no sin** (1 Peter 2:22).

Jesus was born by a miracle conception. The Spirit of God overshadowed a virgin, and the seed of divine life was created in her womb. In that way, Jesus was not born of human seed that had been infected by sin.

Not only His conception, but His life among people, had to be sinless, in order to be your substitute.

God's Son must be subjected to the same temptations of sin as any human person is. He had to be exactly like you and resist what human persons had not resisted. He had to prove that God's original plan could work — that human persons could choose God's word, and never dishonor His integrity.

Jesus had to be tempted by Satan just as Adam and Eve had been.

This is why as soon as He was mature, He was led into the wilderness where Satan came to tempt Him exactly as he came to tempt Adam and Eve in the garden of Eden.

Every time Satan tried to bring question on God's word, Jesus rejected his suggestion and forthrightly asserted what God had said. (Matt. 4:1-11.)

The Bible says that throughout the earthly life of Christ, He was in every respect tested as you are, yet without committing any sin. (Heb. 4:15.)

That explains why He was able to be your substitute. Since He had no sin in Him, and committed no sin, He could assume your sins and give His life as a ransom for you.

Being made perfect, Jesus Christ became **the author of eternal salvation** (Heb. 5:9).

If your penalty of death was assumed by Him, you would be legally absolved of the penalty.

Since no debt can be paid twice, or no crime punished twice, you would be restored as though you had never done wrong.

Since Jesus Christ suffered the penalty you deserved, and since He did it on your behalf, *you are no longer guilty before God and need never be judged for any sin you have ever committed.*

The judgment you deserved was put on your substitute, in your place, and *that judgment can never be imposed on you again.*

This is the heart of God's plan in the Bible that we call salvation.

Now you can understand these Bible verses. I have personalized them for you.

> **Jesus Christ bore your sins in his own body that you, being dead to sins, should live in righteousness.**
>
> **1 Peter 2:24**

> **When you were utterly with no way of escape, Christ came and died for you when you had no use for him.**
>
> **Romans 5:6 LB**

> **God showed his great love for you by sending Christ to die for you while you were still a sinner.**
> **Now God has declared you not guilty. Now he will save you from all wrath to come.**
>
> **Romans 5:8,9 LB**

> **Now you can rejoice in your wonderful new relationship with God all because of what your Lord Jesus Christ has done in dying for your sins — making you a friend of God.**
>
> **Romans 5:11 LB**

> **Now, since you have been made right in God's sight by faith in his promise, you can have real peace with him because of what Jesus has done for you.**
>
> **Romans 5:1 LB**

So say this to God.

PRAYER:

DEAR LORD, I am so thankful to understand why Christ came and died for me, as my substitute.

I understand that the penalty of sin is death and that death passed upon all persons because all have sinned. But because of Your love, You gave Your Son, Jesus Christ, to die in my place.

NOW I UNDERSTAND that Jesus assumed my guilt and suffered the judgment of my sins. By doing that, He redeemed me and restored me to You, O Lord. Now it is as though I had never sinned. I am no longer guilty. My condemnation is gone forever.

No debt can be paid twice and no crime punished twice. My sins have been paid for. There is nothing against me anymore. The judgment I deserved was assumed by Jesus as my substitute.

THANK YOU, LORD, for Your plan of salvation. I believe that You bore my sins, in my place.

AMEN!

Chapter 51

NEW LIFE FACT VI

UNDERSTAND THE REASON FOR CHRIST'S DEATH, BURIAL AND RESURRECTION

You are restored to God's life again when you realize what Jesus Christ did and believe that He assumed all judgment for your sins in your place. These wonders of God's grace take place in your life:

1) The righteousness of Christ is transferred to you and you are free of all guilt and judgment. 2) Jesus Christ comes and lives the life of God in and through you. 3) You become a new creation. 4) You are restored to God according to His original plan. 5) A supernatural power is given to you which makes you a child of God.

A. *When Jesus Christ DIED*, your old life of sin died with Him. Understand and believe that His death was for you.

I have been crucified with Christ.

Galatians 2:20

B. *When Jesus Christ was BURIED*, your old life of sin was put away forever. Understand and believe that Christ's burial was on your behalf.

We are buried with Jesus Christ unto death.

Romans 6:4

C. *When Jesus Christ was RAISED from the dead*, you were raised up with Him. Understand and believe that His resurrection included you.

God has raised Jesus Christ from the dead and has quickened you together with him, having forgiven you all trespasses.

Colossians 3:12-13

D. *When Jesus Christ arose in a NEW LIFE*, you arose to walk in that same new life of God. Understand and believe that the new life of Christ can now be imparted to you.

You are risen with Christ.
Christ is your life.

Colossians 3:1, 4

Say this to the Lord.

PRAYER:

O FATHER IN HEAVEN, I am so glad that I now understand the reason for Christ's death, burial and resurrection. Thank You for sending Your Son to give His life for me. I now identify myself with Your sacrifice for me, O Lord.

*When You **died** in my place, my old life was crucified with You.*

*When You were **buried**, my old life of sin was buried too.*

*When You were **raised** up from death, I was raised with You by new life in Christ and I can now walk in that same new life. It is the miracle life.*

TODAY, I have come to understand the significance of what You did for me. I relate myself to what You have done for me.

I am thankful for Your great plan of salvation.

AMEN!

Chapter 52

NEW LIFE FACT VII

BELIEVE THE GOSPEL AND RECEIVE JESUS CHRIST IN PERSON NOW

God's plan of salvation is based on faith in the integrity of His word and on your right to choose to believe.

Believe on the Lord Jesus Christ and you will be saved.

Acts 16:31

All who trust God's Son to save them have eternal life.

John 3:36 LB

What specifically are you to trust or believe?

A. That Jesus was sinless and perfect;

B. That He died on your behalf and bore the judgment you should bear;

C. That He did it because God loves you and wants to live in you;

D. That God values you so much that He paid this infinite price to make that possible.

These remarkable facts are what is called the gospel or good news:

• He suffered the penalty of your sins so that you can be saved from death and live eternally as He planned for you, with *honor* and *dignity*.

• He suffered the consequences of your sins so that you can be forever absolved from *guilt, condemnation* or *judgment*.

• He took upon Himself your pains, infirmities and sicknesses, so that you can be free of them and live in *health* and enjoy *longevity*.

• He bore your insecurity, shame, inferiority and loneliness, so that you can live in *fellowship with God* again.

• He died so that you can *live*.

• He assumed your guilt so that you can receive His *righteousness*.

267

God made Jesus Christ who knew no sin to be made sin on our behalf so that in Him we might share the righteousness [or life] of God.

2 Corinthians 5:21

The record of your sins was credited to Christ's account. Then He assumed your guilt and bore the judgment you deserved.

In exchange, His righteousness was credited to your account and you were declared righteous in God's eyes, forever.

When does this happen?

When you decide to believe the good news of what Jesus Christ did, and accept the fact that He assumed all of the judgment for your sins in your place. When you do that, you experience a miracle. This is what takes place in you:

• The righteousness of Christ is transferred to you, and you are free of all guilt and judgment.

• Jesus Christ comes and lives the life of God in and through you.

• You become a new creation.

• You are restored to God according to His original plan.

• A supernatural power is given to you which makes you a child of God. It is a miracle.

Christ opened the way for God to come to you and for you to come to Him. He is your link with God, your way to the good life, to success, to happiness, to total health and to abundant living.

It all happens when you believe the gospel and receive Jesus Christ into your life, by faith.

These results can take place in you today now, because the Bible says, **Now is the accepted time. Now is the day of salvation** (2 Cor. 6:2) — for you.

1. You are reborn, recreated, restored to God, made new. You become a child of God.

When you receive Jesus Christ, God gives you the miracle power to become his child.

John 1:12

2. You receive a new spiritual life, the miracle life of God through Jesus Christ in you.

If you are in Christ, you are a new creature. All things become new.

2 Corinthians 5:17

268

Jesus said, I am come that you might have life more abundantly.
John 10:10

3. You receive total peace. Anxiety, hypertension, fear, guilt and condemnation are gone forever.

Jesus said, **Peace I leave with you, my peace I give to you** (John 14:27).

Being justified by faith, you have peace with God through your Lord Jesus Christ.
Romans 5:1

4. You are restored to friendship, fellowship and life with God — the way you were designed to live on this earth.

Truly your fellowship is with the Father, and with his Son Jesus Christ.
1 John 1:3

5. Your physical body is affected so much by this new inner peace with God that your sicknesses disappear and you experience new physical and mental health.

You will serve the Lord your God, and he will take sickness away from the midst of you.
Exodus 23:25

The Lord forgives all of your iniquities; he heals all of your diseases.
Psalm 103:3

Say this to the Lord.

PRAYER:

O HEAVENLY FATHER, I am so thankful to know and understand the gospel and to believe what it says.

I believe on Jesus Christ and, by faith, I receive, You, dear Lord, as my personal Savior — now.

You were without sin, yet You died for my sins. You took my place, assumed my judgment and suffered my penalty in order to ransom me and to restore me to God as though I had never sinned.

You took my sins and now, by accepting You, You impart to me Your righteousness.

I have come to realize what a price You paid to prove how You value me. Your blood was shed to make me clean. (Rom 5:8-9.)

O, JESUS, MY LORD, since You paid the full price for my transgressions, there can never be any further for me to pay.

I believe that I am saved here, now and forever because of the good news of what You accomplished when You died in my place.

Now I am restored to God my Father through Jesus my Savior. I have recovered the dignity You planned for me.

I do believe that You have now come back to live in me like You originally planned when You created me.

I believe I am saved. You and I are one again because of what Your Son, Jesus, did in my place.

The blood of Jesus Christ cleanses me. (1 John 1:7.)

The life of Jesus Christ regenerates me. (1 Peter 1:23.)

The joy of Jesus Christ fills me. (John 15:11.)

I am of infinite value. (1 Peter 1:7.) Thank You that You love me. I am Yours. (John 6:37.)

You have made my body Your temple. I am redeemed and accepted. I am commissioned in the Kingdom to represent You in this life. (1 Cor. 6:19-20.)

MY SINS ARE PUNISHED. They can never be punished again. My debt is paid. No debt can ever be paid twice.

I am saved — here and now.

I believe, and I am free. Thank You for the power that makes me a new creature, now that I have welcomed You home to live in me.

I am as valuable to You as anyone. I am as beautiful in Your eyes as anyone. I have Your nature. I am loved. I can love others. Whatever I sow in others, I will reap. (Gal. 6:8.)

Thank You that I am part of Your plan. I have a place no one else can fill. (Eph. 2:10.)

No longer will I condemn myself. No longer will I destroy what You value. (Acts. 10:15.)

Now I am accepted. I can do Your work. I am born again. I am a new creature. I have repented of my old values. I have changed my mind about myself and about other people.

Knowing how You value each human person has given me a new value of human life.

I SEE YOU, O Lord, with new eyes. I see others as You see them. I see myself in Your image.

Together we can never fail. Father, everything is possible for You. (Mark 14:36.) Thank You, Lord, that You now live in me.

In Jesus' name.
AMEN!

Chapter 53

THANK YOU, LORD!

Now you are restored to God.

Your dignity is regained.

A miracle life has begun in you.

That is why I included these seven wonderful facts in this book.

You are a new person, with new dignity and new life.

Jesus proved how much God values you.

He paid for you by giving His life in your place.

You are worth what God paid for you.

Now you will never again *condemn* what God has paid so much to redeem.

You will never again *put down* what cost God so much to raise up.

Now you will be a blessing to others who need what you have received.

Jesus showed us God by what He did for others. We show our faith by what we do for others.

When we value people like God values them, we will *heal* them rather than bruise them. We will *lift* them rather than put them down. We will *esteem* them rather than criticize them. We will *forgive* them rather than judge them.

Jesus showed us God by what happened to people who came in contact with Him. We show what God is like in our lives by what happens to people who come in contact with us.

You *grow* as you help others grow. You *prosper* as you help others prosper.

You *learn* by teaching. You *gain* by giving. You *reap* by planting. You *receive* by giving.

What a change takes place in life when you discover God, at home again in you, sharing His lifestyle and His abundance with other lives, through you.

You discover God at work in you, carrying out His kingdom business through you.

He values everyone. *He proved it by what He paid for each one.* He works through you showing His love and His value of people. You discover that He is manifested through you and that gives your life value.

The songwriter said:

> *A bell is not a bell 'til you ring it;*
>
> *A song is not a song 'til you sing it.*
>
> *Love in your heart is not put there to stay;*
>
> *Love is not love 'til you give it away.*

Write to Daisy and me. We will reply. We can be mutual friends in helping other people discover the way of restoration to God's lifestyle.

From the day we hear from you, Daisy and I, with our staff of believing people, will be earnestly praying for God's best to come to you and your house.

We will send you a list of other books we have written to help you. One is titled, *The Good Life*, over 300 pages of terrific, power-filled ideas to help you experience life's best.

We have recorded some remarkable cassette albums which can be a great help and inspiration to you. One of our greatest albums is called, *Super Living*. It contains five hours of total uplift and encouragement.

Chapter 54

OUR FOUR VITAL
VISIONS

I was born on a farm near Pocassett, Oklahoma, the seventh son in a family of thirteen children. I was raised on the farm and schooled in the country.

At the age of twelve, my brother, who had just been converted a few weeks earlier, took me with him to attend a revival meeting, being conducted down by the railroad tracks in Mannford, Oklahoma. Dressed in my country-style overalls, I went; and when asked to play the piano for the singing I very nervously but happily agreed. When the lady evangelist made the call for sinners that night, I was joyfully converted.

I Was "Called" at the Age of 14

From that time, I loved going to the little church; but many times the work on the farm kept me in the field until too late to attend the meeting. Many nights I wept from disappointment at not being able to go to church.

At the age of fourteen, while walking in the woods hunting for the milk cows, I began to weep. It seemed foolish to me, and I wondered why I should be crying. I stopped and prayed, kneeling beside some sandstone boulders. The Lord Jesus spoke to my spirit and made me to know that He had chosen me to preach His gospel.

At the age of fifteen, I left the farm to accompany a fine minister of our community, in conducting some church revival meetings.

I shall never forget the night when I walked out of my home leaving my father and mother in tears. The last of seven sons was leaving.

I knew there were many responsibilities on the farm and far too much work for Dad to do alone, but I knew, also, that the Lord had spoken and I must obey. I knew that the harvest field of a world was so much more important than those acres of land we were farming. I knew that the God who had called me would make a way for my parents, and He did.

At 17, I Met Daisy Washburn

For two and one-half years, I accompanied this minister in many wonderful meetings, which took us through Arkansas and Oklahoma, and finally to California. It was there that a beautiful young lady named Daisy Washburn from Los Banos, California, attended our meetings. One year later, we were married.

For two years Daisy and I traveled in California, preaching the gospel of Jesus Christ.

On March 25, 1943, our daughter, Marie LaVonne, was born, but lived only seven days. The grief and disappointment of this was almost unbearable, but we determined to press on with the gospel of Jesus Christ and to recompense our loss with spiritual births in the kingdom of heaven.

In the spring of 1944, we drove to Portland, Oregon, to conduct a revival, and there accepted the pastorate of a struggling church.

While in Portland, on January 20, 1945 our son, Tommy Lee, Jr., was born.

Our First Ministry Overseas

Three weeks after his birth, we resigned as pastors of that growing church and began nine months of ministry across several states, preparing to sail for India as missionaries.

Nearly a year was spent in India, during which time we experienced the greatest confusion and disappointment of our lives. We had invested everything we owned and had dedicated our lives to go to the other side of the world to win souls, only to find that we could not convince the Hindus or the Moslems that Jesus Christ was the Son of God, that He had risen from the dead, nor that He is alive today as the world's only Savior.

We had the *Bible,* but when we tried to convince the Moslems about Jesus Christ by showing them scripture verses, they showed us the *Koran* which, to them, was God's word given by the mouth of His holy prophet Mohammed.

Both the Koran and the Bible were lovely black books, embossed in gold. Both were revered as God's word. We could not give evidence that the Bible is the true word of God.

We did not know the truths which I have presented here in this book. We did not understand about miracles which prove that Christ is alive. We could not persuade the people to receive Jesus Christ. We felt helpless and defeated.

Although a few were saved in our meetings, after a long siege of sickness during which our son almost died of cholera and I despaired of life for six long weeks with typhoid fever, in the fall of 1946, we returned to the United States and accepted the pastorate of a thriving church in McMinnville, Oregon.

On March 13, 1947, we were blessed with the gift of our daughter, LaDonna Carol.

They Were Dead — We Were Alive

During our time of pastoring at McMinnville, God dealt with us in many wonderful ways.

It was at this time that a lady in our church happened to inform Daisy and me of the death of Dr. Charles S. Price. We had never met the man, but had read scores of his wonderful sermons while we were in India. We loved the man dearly.

When we heard of his death, I went to the church and began to pray and weep. It seemed as though I could not contain my grief. The faith heroes and heroines of previous years began to pass before my mind like a panorama. I thought of Wigglesworth, of McPherson, of Woodworth-Etter, of Gypsie Smith, of Kenyon, of Price, and of others — not one of whom we had ever met or heard preach.

They were gone forever from this world's scene of action. We would never meet them here. The world would never again feel the impact and marvelous influence of their ministry. We would only talk of them and hear of their exploits of faith.

It all seemed very strange to me as to why this should affect me like it did, when I did not even know these people.

I said, "Lord, those great heroes of faith are gone now, and millions are still dying. Multitudes are still sick and suffering. To whom will they go for help. Who will stir our large cities and fill our large auditoriums with the magnetic power of God, healing the sick and casting out devils? What will this world do now?"

The Turning Point for Us

God heard and answered my questions in a marvelous way, though not immediately.

A few days after this, during the month of July, 1947, we attended the camp meeting at Brooks, Oregon, where Rev. Hattie Hammond was ministering.

She preached a dynamic message on the subject: *If You Ever See Jesus, You Can Never Be the Same Again.* We walked out of that meeting in tears, and as we drove home, we talked about her message. I said, "Darling, maybe that is what we need. Maybe if we could see Jesus, our lives would be changed."

Only God knows the depth of our search. We were sincere in our love for Christ. We believed in the power of the Holy Spirit. We were respected in our organization as some of the finest, most effective pastor-evangelists.

We methodically prayed for the sick. But there were few if any results. Others praised us, but we felt helpless. We had gone to India to convince the non-Christians. We were unable to cope. We felt we had failed. We were lonely, frustrated, unsatisfied. Maybe if we could see Jesus, that would be the key. We were in a desperate search for reality.

The First Vision

The next morning at six o'clock, I was awakened by a vision of Jesus Christ as He came into our room. I looked upon Him. I saw Him like I see anyone. No tongue can tell of His splendor and beauty. No language can express the magnificence and power of His person.

I lay there as one that was dead, unable to move a finger or toe, awe-stricken by His presence. Water poured from my eyes, though I was not conscious of weeping, so mighty was His presence.

Of all I had heard and read about Him, the half had never been told me. His hands were beautiful; they seemed to vibrate with creative ability. His eyes were as streams of love, pouring forth into my innermost being. His feet, standing amidst clouds of transparent glory, seemed to be as pillars of justice and integrity. His robes were white as the light. His presence, enhanced with love and power, drew me to Him.

After perhaps thirty minutes of utter helplessness, I was able to get out of bed to the floor, where I crawled into my little study and lay on my face on the floor in full surrender of my entire life to Him whom I had come to know as LORD.

I lay there on my face until the afternoon. When I came out of that room, I was a new man. Jesus had become the Master of my life. I knew the truth: *He is alive; He is more than a dead religion.*

My life was changed. I would never be the same. Old traditional values began to fade away, and I felt impressed daily by a new and increasing sense of reverence and serenity. Everything was different. I wanted to please *Him. That is all that has mattered since that unforgettable morning.* The first vital vision had come.

I had seen Jesus IN A VISION.

The Second Vision

With that vision still fresh before me and the realization that so many of the great men and women of faith had passed away, we sought earnestly to know God's perfect plan for our lives.

In the month of September, 1947, we again became the pastors of the church in Portland, Oregon, which we had resigned before going to India. We settled down for what we expected to be a lifetime of ministry in the beautiful *City of Roses.* But God had this planned only as a short step in His design for our lives.

Soon after the awesome experience of seeing the Lord, a man of God came to our area. He had a most perfect gift of the word of knowledge, coupled with an amazing healing ministry.

As we attended his meetings, we saw hundreds accept Christ; and, right before our eyes, we watched him cast out devils and lay hands on the sick in Jesus Christ's name. The blind, deaf, dumb, and cripples were healed instantly.

I can never express the emotions of my heart in response to the operation of the gifts of healing in that great meeting.

For three or four years, I had been deeply concerned about the traditional methods we had been using in praying for the sick and demon-possessed. We would call the whole church to pray for one person, hoping that someone might be able to pray *the prayer of faith* on behalf of the sick person.

As I watched this evangelist minister to the sick, I was captivated by the deliverance of a deaf-mute girl, over whom he prayed a very simple prayer.

In a quiet but authoritative voice, he spoke: "You deaf and dumb spirit, I adjure you in Jesus' name, leave the child." Then he snapped his fingers, and the girl heard and spoke perfectly.

When I witnessed that and many other miracles, there seemed to be a thousand voices whirling over my head, saying over and over, *"You can do that! That's the Bible way! Peter and Paul did it that way! That's the way Jesus did it. That proves that the Bible way works today! You can do that! That's what God wants you to do!"*

We went home in total awe and reverent exuberance. *We had witnessed the Bible in action.* It was the thing I had always longed for. At last, I had seen God do what He promised to do *through a human person*. Our entire lives were changed that very night.

We had seen the second vital vision.

We had seen Jesus IN A PERSON.

The Third Vision

Many days of fasting and prayer followed. Daisy and I went before God, determined to be channels through which He would minister His mighty works of deliverance to our generation.

We sat down with our Bibles and talked about the wonders we had beheld. We reflected upon our apparent failure in India. We knew this was the answer.

We made a pact between us and with God. We would read the New Testament — especially the Gospels and the Acts of the Apostles, as though we had never read them before.

Everything Jesus said He would do, we would expect Him to do it.

Everything He said for us to do in His name, we would do it.

Days of intense reading of the teachings and ministry of Jesus Christ followed. The Bible, which had been little more than a religious book in India, had become a living, vibrant, message from God to us.

It was during this search that we began to discover all of the dynamic and personal promises of God and the commitments He has made to us when we only believe.

We saw the third vital vision.

We saw Jesus IN HIS WORD.

There was no question about it. Jesus and His Word became one. He was speaking to us personally by the written gospels.

(Be sure to absorb Chapter 32 of this book, titled *The Believer's Authority*, in which I have shared many of the Bible discoveries we made during those days of special research.)

We were so thrilled about seeing the living Christ *in His word*. We knew what He had promised to do, He would do. And we were ready to do what He told His followers to do.

We discovered that all of the wonderful promises and commitments Jesus had made to His followers and to His disciples were made to us. We were His followers. We were His disciples. **If you continue in my word, *then* are *you* my disciples indeed** (John 8:31).

He had plainly told His followers: **Into whatever city you enter, heal the sick that are there** (Luke 10:8-9).

When He called them, **He gave them power against unclean spirits, to cast them out, and to heal all manner of sicknesses and all manner of diseases** (Matt. 10:1).

What could be plainer?

We accepted it — literally.

> **Jesus gave them power and authority over all devils, and to cure diseases.**
>
> **Luke 9:1**

We knew that was for us, too.

Those followers **departed, and went through the towns, preaching the gospel, and healing everywhere** (Luke 9:6).

That is what we would do.

Jesus said, **Fear not; believe only** (Luke 8:50).

We were not afraid. We *did* believe. We were confident. We would do what Jesus told *us* to do. We knew He would do what He had committed Himself to do.

The Fourth Vision

Yet, in spite of this revelation, I wanted the Lord to speak to me in some audible way. I learned later that when He speaks through His word, *that is His voice*, but I was simply overcharged with the desire to hear Him talk to me audibly.

Finally, I notified the church that I would see no one nor speak to anyone personally, nor by phone, until I had heard from God.

Daisy assumed the pastoral responsibilities and I went into an upstairs room alone, to remain until God spoke to me. In the middle of the third day, the Lord spoke to me very clearly and distinctly, and resolved my questions concerning the death of so many heroes and heroines of faith and the need that existed throughout the world for the great ministry of healing faith.

The Spirit of the Lord said to me: *"My son, as I was with Price, McPherson, Woodworth-Etter, Wigglesworth, and others, so will I be with you. They are dead, but now it is time for you to arise, to go and do likewise. You cast out devils; you heal the sick; you raise the dead; you cleanse the lepers. Behold, I give you power over all the power of the enemy. Do not be afraid. Be strong. Be courageous. I am with you as I was with them. No evil power shall be able to stand before you all the days of your life as you get the people to believe My word. I used those people in their day, but this is your day. Now I desire to use you."*

We began to send advertisements near and far, telling the people to bring their sick, diseased, crippled, blind, deaf and dumb. We began to teach the promises of Christ to heal, to save and to deliver *all* who had needs, and to pray for the sick and to cast out devils.

Needless to say, God began immediately to confirm His word which we proclaimed, with miracles, because we had simply taken Him at His word. We had begun to act on the word. If God said it, then it was so. If God promised to do it, then He would do it.

The most marvelous miracles took place.

They brought a girl who was born deaf and dumb. What a joy it was for Daisy and me to draw her close to us, to place our hands on her and to allow Jesus to heal her through our act of faith.

As I placed my fingers in her ears, I only prayed a brief prayer:

"You deaf and dumb spirit, I charge you, in the name of Jesus Christ whom God has raised from the dead according to the scriptures, to come out of this girl, and to enter her no more."

Then in the quiet hush that followed, I snapped my fingers behind her head and she jumped and looked. I quietly whispered words in each ear and she repeated them clearly. The evil spirit had gone. The girl was healed. It was like Bible days. Jesus was unchanged.

That was when we had our fourth vision.

We had discovered Jesus AT WORK IN US.

Now we had finally seen the vision God wanted the world to see when He sent Jesus, His Son, to us.

Jesus said, **Anyone who has seen me has seen the Father** (John 14:9). Later He said, **As my Father has sent me, so I send you** (John 20:21), and promised, **Lo, I am with you** (Matt. 28:20); **I will dwell in you and walk in you** (2 Cor. 6:16).

Jesus came and showed the Father to the world.

Now we show Jesus to the world. He is at work in the believer. We are His body. He is our life. He continues His ministry in and through us.

We had made the grand discovery. We had seen the greatest vision. *We saw Jesus alive and at work IN US.*

That discovery was the key that unlocked our future success with God.

It was not many weeks before the will of God was determined very definitely in the matter of again resigning the church in Portland to take the gospel of the kingdom to the ends of the earth for a witness among all nations and peoples. That was the summer of 1948.

Unprecedented Ministry

As the very latest edition of this book goes to press, I can witness that, for over five decades in eighty nations of the world, Daisy and I have gone in Jesus' name and have acted on the written word of God. We have preached to multitudes of from 20,000 to over 250,000 souls daily in these mass crusades. We have probably reached and led to Christ more non-Christians and may have witnessed more great healing miracles than any couple who has yet lived.

We have been able to lead tens of thousands of previously unevangelized people to Jesus Christ.

We have seen deaf-mutes by the hundreds perfectly restored.

We have seen great numbers of the blind instantly receive their sight — as many as ninety cases in a single gospel crusade.

We have seen the hopeless cripples restored — those in wheelchairs as long as forty-two years, arise and walk. Those on cots and stretchers have arisen and have been made whole.

We have seen crossed eyes go straight, stiff joints loosed in a moment, goiters and tumors leave.

We have witnessed eardrums, lungs, kidneys, ribs, and other parts of the body, which have been removed by operations, recreated and restored by God's creative power.

We have seen incurables made well, cancers die and vanish, lepers cleansed, even the dead raised.

In a single campaign which we have conducted, as many as 125 deaf-mutes, 90 totally blind, and hundreds of other equally miraculous deliverances have resulted.

Happy and joyful confessions of Christ as Savior have numbered as many as 50,000 in one crusade, often many thousands in one night.

What we have seen our Lord accomplish in the past is an example of what He yearns to do in every nation under heaven.

Our Gospel Is for All Nations

One of the most challenging statements in the Bible concerning the last days is in Matthew 24:14. Jesus said: **And this gospel of the** kingdom shall be preached in all the world for a witness unto all nations; and then shall the end come.

More literally rendered from the original text, He said: **This good news shall be proclaimed with evidence to all nations of the world, then shall the end come.**

This prophecy from the lips of Jesus Christ foretells a great era of flaming miracle evangelism that proclaims Christ as Lord, **with evidence,** to this generation. It indicates a worldwide demonstration of early church methods in which **God also [is] bearing them witness, both with signs and wonders, and with divers miracles, and gifts of the Holy Ghost** (Heb. 2:4).

The Big Question — And the Answer

I have never understood how the church expects to convince the non-Christian world that Jesus Christ is the living, resurrected Son of God unless they preach to them that part of the gospel which turned the masses to Christ in Bible days. The following is an example of what I mean.

When we arrived in Colon, Panama, to conduct a gospel campaign there, I preached the opening message, then invited the unconverted to accept Christ as Savior. Instead of their responding as I expected, a ripple of half-smothered laughter swept the audience.

It was clear that they were not convinced about Jesus Christ.

Quickly I said: "I ask no one to commit your life to follow Christ until you are convinced that He is the living Savior, and that He will do exactly as He promised to do in the Bible."

Then I continued: "This book contains God's promises, one of which is to heal the sick. I, therefore, invite those who are deaf, blind, paralyzed, or sick, and who believe in Christ and believe the promises in the Bible, to come forward. I will pray for you according to the Bible and, if what I preached tonight is true, God will do miracles which will prove that Jesus is alive."

Several responded, and we prayed for a half-dozen people. All of them were instantly healed in the presence of the audience.

Needless to say, this astonished the multitude in the arena, as it astounded the multitudes in Jesus' days.

The next night, the arena was packed. I preached, then repeated the invitation to all unbelievers to accept Christ. Over 400 people came forward in tears, giving their lives to Jesus Christ who had demonstrated

His power before their eyes. It was true in Colon, Panama, as it was in the city of Samaria: **And the people with one accord gave heed to those things hearing and seeing the miracles which [Jesus] did** (Acts 8:6).

From Calcutta to Calabar

From Alaska to Argentina, from New York City to New Caledonia, from Trinidad to Timbuktu, from Calcutta to Calabar, wherever we have proclaimed the gospel we have discovered one fact: *The masses will gladly follow Christ if they can see Him confirm His word with signs and miracles.*

Whether the people are red, brown, yellow, black, or white; whether they are educated or illiterate; whether they are rich or poor, I know one thing: They all respond to Christ when they see His unchanging compassion in healing the sick.

From the days when Elijah accepted the challenge at Mt. Carmel and the people turned from the worship of Baal to Jehovah, until our present age, people are ready and are glad to serve the God of miracles.

Regardless of what religious professors may teach, the undeniable fact remains that there is no substitute for the **demonstration of the Spirit and of power** (1 Cor. 2:4).

Paul repeatedly attributed the success of his ministry to the fact that God always confirmed his message with miracles. (Heb. 2:3-4; Rom. 15:18-19.)

The masses all over the world are waiting for the church to return to her knees in fasting and prayer, asking God as the early church did: **Grant to your servants, that with all boldness they may speak your word, By stretching forth their hand to heal; and that signs and wonders may be done by the name of your holy child Jesus** (Acts 4:29-30).

Go To 331

Chapter 55

OUR WITNESS

When I came to you, I came not with excellency of speech or of wisdom, declaring to you the testimony of God.

For I determined not to know any thing among you, save Jesus Christ, and him crucified.

And I was with you in weakness, and in fear, and in much trembling.

And my speech and my preaching was not with enticing words of human wisdom, but in demonstration of the Spirit and of power:

That your faith should not stand in the wisdom of people, but in the power of God.

1 Corinthians 2:1-5

* * *

And [we] went forth, and preached every where, the Lord working with [us], and confirming the word with signs following.

Mark 16:20

February, 1949, Kingston, Jamaica: People gathered from early afternoon to get into the big auditorium. The mass of humanity could hardly be controlled by the police.

We prayed for a throng of people out in the street, since there was no hope of their getting inside, and marvelous things were done. Then we inched our way through the press of people to get inside and after preaching, several hundred accepted Christ as Savior. Deaf mutes, paralytics, blind people, those with crossed eyes, goiters, tumors and all sorts of diseases were instantly and miraculously healed tonight.

We prayed for a 17-year-old lad named Wilberforce Morris. At the age of 9, he had suffered typhoid fever for six long weeks. It completely destroyed his hearing nerves and vocal cords, leaving him stone deaf and mute.

Later his parents both died and he was left as a roving orphan, alone. He had learned to read and write so he could communicate by writing little notes. He always carried a piece of paper and a pencil.

A nice woman discovered his plight and, because he was a fine lad, took him in. Before going deaf, he had learned to play the clarinet, so,

285

despite his illness, the lady paid for his lessons at school so he could continue to try to play. The school music teacher accommodated him as a special favor, and let him continue with the mechanics of playing, even though he was deaf and mute.

Then Wilberforce found out about our meetings. He came and watched. He had seen so many miracles that he decided that God could heal him too. Each night he would struggle to get nearer the front.

Tonight he got my attention and jumped on to the platform and knelt before Daisy and me. It was so touching, we could not refuse him.

I placed my hands on his head with my forefingers in his ears (there was no way to communicate), and I commanded: "You deaf and dumb spirit which has been sent to destroy this lad's hearing and speech, I adjure you to leave him, in the name of Jesus Christ."

Still on his knees, the lad looked up at us so vibrant and sure of a miracle, but when we checked him, he heard nothing. Yet I *knew* he had perfect faith, and I *knew* that the spirit of deafness had obeyed me.

The lad started to weep, and I pulled his chin upward and motioned for him to get up.

As he arose, he heard noises around him. Then his tears turned to joy. I asked the musicians to play. He was thrilled. Then we all sang as he was simply ravished by the singing and the music.

But still no sound came from his mouth. I wrote him a note: "Only believe. God healed your ears. He is healing your voice. Keep trying to talk."

He clutched my note and disappeared.

I'm writing some of this later because I want to share what happened to him.

The next morning, when Wilberforce arose, he had a perfect voice. His miracle was complete.

He went to the EXPRESS newspaper. They published his entire story and, as a result, he got a good job, went on studying music, became a top clarinet player and one of the excellent male voices in his choir.

Hundreds believed on the Lord because of his miracle.

A poor woman whose husband was totally paralyzed, arrived tonight, carrying her husband on her back. She had carried him nearly four miles. The auditorium was packed, the yard was full, police were guarding the gates, and the streets were full. But that woman had faith.

Like the four men who carried the paralytic to Jesus, she did not let the crowd stop her.

She selected a dark place where she would not be noticed, shoved her husband over the wall, climbed over herself, picked him up on her back again, and started pressing through the crowd to the entrance.

Everyone seemed to have mercy on her and gave her space to get through.

Finally, she arrived at the platform in the prayer line. When we saw them, we knew there was real faith. I told her to put her husband down, that she had carried him far enough. Taking him by the hands to steady him, I asked: "Do you believe on the Lord Jesus Christ with all your heart?" He replied in tears, "Yes, sir, I do."

Then I asked, "Do you believe that you will be healed in Jesus' name?"

"Most certainly I do, sir, or I would not have come here," he answered.

"Then," I commanded, "walk in the mighty name of Jesus Christ."

He walked, was healed, and the press of people literally screamed for joy.

After praying for the sick until we were almost ready to drop, I slipped out the back door, jumped over the wall and started down the street, when a poor old woman grabbed me with a desperate expression on her face. She cried, "You are Rev. Osborn, aren't you?" I replied, "Yes ma'am, I am." (A friend was with her.)

"Oh, Rev. Osborn, don't leave me," she begged, "without praying for me. I know that if you will just touch my eyes, I will be healed. I am totally blind. I cannot even see the light. Oh, I must be healed tonight. I know God will heal me."

I said, "Woman, I am so tired. We've prayed for so many hundreds tonight. I do wish you would try to come back tomorrow night and we'll pray for you."

She wept as she said, "Rev. Osborn, I can't come back. I am a poor woman and my friend has brought me here. I must be healed tonight."

Christ's compassion gripped my heart, and I knew He wanted to heal her then.

I held her hands in mine there in the dark and said, "Mother, do you believe with all your heart that if I touch your eyes in Jesus' name, He will give you your sight?"

She answered, "Oh, Rev. Osborn, I know He will heal me now."

Then I laid my hands on her eyes and said, "Woman, in the mighty name of Jesus Christ whom God raised from the dead, I command your blind eyes to be opened, and to receive sight."

She almost pushed my hands from her eyes as she began to look up. Suddenly she exclaimed, "Oh, thank God! Yes, I can see. I can see everything. The moon, the stars, my hands. Oh, thank God. I knew He would do it."

No words can express the joy that floods one's soul in such moments. As she walked away in the dark that night, healed by the compassionate Christ, I said, "Oh Lord! I thank You that You are using us to bring Your compassion and healing power to these precious people. Help us to always be vessels through which Your mercy can flow to bless the peoples of the world for whom You died."

* * *

February, 1950, Ponce, Puerto Rico: Tremendous things are happening in this city. Newspaper reporters have been present, questioning people who have been healed and the whole island is astir. Their articles have been very well written.

A man in the plaza was showing everyone how he can bend his knee. It had been stiff for years. One of the pastors told us that people are crowding the market areas, the fire station, the newspaper offices, the main stores, talking excitedly about the miracles taking place.

The mayor has granted us the use of the great ball field and multitudes are coming. We have been forced to pray for the people *en masse* because the whole field is packed.

I decided to teach them about Jesus Christ being the same. First, I lead them in a mass prayer to accept Christ as Savior. They all repeat the prayer. Then I instruct them to forsake their past lives, to follow Jesus, to read the teachings of Jesus Christ, to go to church, and to share the gospel with others.

After I finish with the message, the salvation prayer and the instruction to the field of new converts, I instruct them in how to have faith for healing — to know that Jesus is healer and that His life in them is healing life, to realize that it is His will for them to be well, that His promise is for everyone, that they must ask in faith, that they must thank God for what they believe they have received, that they must put their faith in action by doing whatever they could not do before, then that they may come up on the platform and tell the multitude about their miracle and show the people whatever God has done as a witness that Jesus is alive and unchanged, and to help others to have more faith to believe on Christ for their own salvation and healing.

The crowds have been so massive and the weather so hot that many were overcome by the press of people, so something wonderful happened. The owner of the radio station sent word that, if we cannot gather the people in the afternoon, he would give us free time to preach and to teach and to pray for the people over the radio. We did that and it is amazing what has resulted.

They sent policemen to guard the radio station from being invaded by the press of people in the street.

During the first broadcast, the president of the station drove through the city to see if the idea would prove helpful. He came back excited and amazed. (Because of the hot weather, the houses are wide open, and most are built pretty close to each other and up against the sidewalks or road.) He said that every radio he heard in every house or car or store was turned up loud, and was tuned to the Osborn Crusade broadcast. (Later, hoards of letters and testimonies were received.)

The station president said that as he drove down the narrow streets, it was overwhelming to see how people were huddled around radios. He said near the market there was a small stand surrounded by a crowd with several policemen. He thought it was an accident, but discovered they were listening to the broadcast.

Shop and house radios were turned up loud so the teaching could be heard everywhere. He found one area where there was a distance between radios, and there, a car was parked with its radio turned very loud, and a group had swarmed it to listen.

Then the time came to repeat the salvation and healing prayer. This was what amazed the man. He said everyone repeated the prayers. Then miracles started happening.

He saw a man drop his crutches and run up and down the street with a crowd following him. He said he was so glad that he did not stay in the studio but had gone out where the miracles were taking place.

After the broadcast, Police Lieutenant Martinez burst into the studio. (I wondered if we were going to be arrested.) But the interpreter finally told us, "No! He is telling what he saw."

He said he had never seen anything so wonderful. He was looking out across the street and saw a woman who had been bedfast for six years. She had jumped up from her bed and ran out onto the street to thank God. She had been an invalid for six years. Her neighbors knew her case.

Wherever we walked on the streets, people stopped us to tell us of miracles. One man was so excited about his miracle. He had been brought to the crusade crippled. One of his feet was twisted like a club foot and the leg had been paralyzed so that he dragged the club foot, hobbling with a big cane. The heel of that shoe was rubbed away.

He kept jumping and walking back and forth, talking fast. He had something in his hands. Suddenly, he stopped and said, "Look here," and opened the package. He had just bought a new heel and some shoe tacks; he was going home to repair his shoes.

The owner of a small, open restaurant nearby came out excitedly and said, "I have known this man for years. He is my friend. It is a fact. He has received a miracle. He has been bringing people into my restaurant all day, and he tells them how he has been healed. It's a miracle!"

A pastor said that a woman next door to him was healed of paralysis. Her leg and arm had been drawn up for many years. In a moment, she was made whole. She is going about testifying to the neighbors of her marvelous healing.

Six deaf mutes were healed during this service, one of which was 55 years of age and had been born in this condition. One young man, who was going to commit suicide, was gloriously converted. Several hernias, growths, and various classes of sickness and paralysis were instantly healed. To God be all the praise!

* * *

March, 1951, Ponce, Puerto Rico: I started to preach early, but after greeting the audience, was told that Juan Santos was present. He had been healed here in our last crusade the night I preached on the healing of the cripple from Mark chapter 2. So we asked him to give his testimony of his miraculous healing. He testified for about thirty minutes. There are few cases in the Bible as dramatic and marvelous as this one.

He had been shot through the spine, destroying his spinal column and the nerves below the waist. It left him totally paralyzed in both legs. For fifteen years he was crippled. Both legs were dead, drawn double, and withered. They were just skin and bones and were completely stiff. One arm was partly paralyzed. The other shook constantly so that he could hardly feed himself.

His head also shook because he had attempted suicide by hitting himself with a club; but the blow only caused the palsy. He could hardly talk because his tongue and throat were partially paralyzed. He dragged himself on the ground with his hands, his drawn and withered legs resting in the dirt between each swing of his body. He was instantly healed and is now as perfect as any man could be. His testimony is known by thousands in Puerto Rico as an undeniable miracle of God's power. He has become a radiant Christian witness.

When Mr. Santos finished his heart-moving testimony, which was more convincing than a thousand sermons, an old lady mounted the platform, anxious to tell what God did for her in our last crusade. She had been healed of total blindness. This is what she told the people:

"Friends told me about a man who was performing miracles. I tried to get someone to take me to the meeting but no one would guide me. I decided to go myself. I finally found my way there. They told me the service began at 5:00 p.m., so I went at 12 o'clock. I listened, but was not healed that night.

"Then I tried to get home in the dark. I got lost. I took a box of matches out of my pocket and struck some and cried, 'Ciega!' (Blind!) A man heard me and came to help me, but I became fearful of him that he was leading me astray in the night, so I told him to leave me and that I would stay there by the road and sleep that night. He left me, and I was alone again. I finally found my way home at 4:00 in the morning.

"The next day I went again and got near the platform and purposed if I could touch the evangelist's trouser legs, I would be healed.

"I listened closely to the message; and when the prayer was offered, I believed. The people all around me were standing tightly together. I finally managed to get some space to move a bit, and I reached out my hand around the edge of the platform, trying to touch the man of God. After a long time, I was begging God to help me touch His servant; and, finally, I heard him moving near my side of the platform. I reached for him and found his legs and grabbed his trousers.

"Then my eyes were restored and I could see everything clearly. I shouted, 'Hallelujah! Hallelujah! I can see! I can see!' It was a very great miracle. I can see you people tonight! I go about telling of God's miracle on my poor blind eyes. I am so happy and thankful to God."

It was not the trouser legs that healed this woman's eyes, no more than it was the garment of Jesus that healed the woman in the Bible. It was the woman's faith. By touching the garment, she set a time in which she would herself believe and have faith for God to do the miracle. As soon as we believe, God does the work.

After these two testimonies, I instructed the audience about ten minutes, as I did not need to preach. These two testimonies were living sermons. Then we led the audience in a prayer. Hundreds accepted Christ as Savior, then the people began receiving their healing. A man totally blind came to the platform so happy. He could now see, "Very clear! Very clear!" A paralyzed man was restored and stomped his feet for joy. Many others were set free. The crowd rejoiced as miracle after miracle was reported for almost two hours.

January, 1952, Camaguey, Cuba: Psalm 105:1 says: **Make known God's deeds among the people.** We are witnessing a glorious demonstration of God's miraculous power here in Camaguey, Cuba.

I can hear ringing in my ears the shouts of "allelujah!" from the masses of people who pack the old baseball stadium and field. As we walk the streets, merchants are triumphant. Clerks in the banks and post office greet us with a "gloria a Dios!" Waiters and cooks in the restaurants do the same.

Numbers of times I have listened as a policeman, a hotel employee, a street-car conductor, or a bus driver explains to some eager person that "Mr. Osborn is no healer: only God is the healer. Listen to God's word. Believe His promises."

Two weeks before we were to leave for Cuba, we laid our needs before our Father and committed our obligations to Him in faith. What followed was a constant miracle as God sent the needed funds to our hands by most amazing means.

After arriving in Camaguey and working hard to get everything ready, I went to my room and dropped on my knees and prayed: *"Oh, God, You have never failed us. You cannot fail us now. We are here to be channels through which Your word shall bless this city. I have done all within my power, and have not spared anything to notify the people of this province that we have come to help them. You must now send Your Spirit and reveal to the people the truth of Your gospel."*

I paused to meditate on His promises, and God spoke to me so clearly these words:

"Have I forgotten that I called you by name? Have I forgotten my promises? Have I forgotten to be faithful? Have I forgotten to be gracious? Do My promises fail today? Is My mercy gone forever? The prayer which has been on your heart for this great city, I have heard and have answered. You are about to see it. Remember the works of My hand and meditate on My doings in other cities where I have sent you. This victory shall be greater, as though lightning had lighted all this Republic with the light of My word, and My blessing shall be like torrents of rain pouring down upon the people. Only have faith, I have heard your desire."

God had spoken to me. His message poured into my soul, through His still small voice, with such clearness that I knew every word He spoke.

All that God promised is coming to pass as we proclaim His good news to the multitudes that come. At the close of the service tonight, more than a thousand accepted Christ. Then we prayed for the sick in a general, mass prayer, since there was no way to pray individually. A mass of miracles were reported.

A woman who had been totally blind came joyfully to the platform showing how she had been healed. A man testified at length, in perfect speech, whom at least one hundred persons in the audience knew to be a bad stutterer, and he was perfectly free.

A woman was exuberant when she found that her stiff knee was healed. Another whose neck had been totally stiff for many years discovered it was free. Three paralyzed men threw down their crutches and were healed. It seemed there was no end to the miracles.

A woman brought her totally deaf boy, who was 12 years old. He was healed so perfectly that he could hear and repeat whole sentences spoken by anyone in a whisper to his back. Asthmatics were healed. A woman found her large goiter gone from her neck. Several hernias disappeared. Many growths and tumors vanished.

We have had 21 glorious days of seeing God's wonders here. Great crowds of thousands have gathered twice daily, to hear the word of God, to surrender their lives to Christ, and to be healed of their diseases.

The sick and crippled have been brought to the meetings on bicycles, carts, wagons, jitneys, carriages, tongas, buses, cars, ambulances, in chairs, in wheel chairs, carried on back, on cots, in beds, led on foot, and every other conceivable manner. Buses have been chartered from all parts of the Republic. Taxis constantly bring loads of sick from opposite ends of the thousand mile long island.

From 1,000 to at least 5,000 persons, and more, have professed to accept Christ as Savior in every service — twice daily. No less than 50,000 persons have made this profession. Miracles have been the talk of this city. When a restaurant man was asked if he knew about the campaign, he exclaimed, "I've heard of no less than a hundred miracles just today."

The tide of faith has continually risen through the steady preaching of God's word twice each day. Everywhere we go, we hear of more miracles. Only a small percent of those healed during the services are able to get to the platform to tell of it.

A banker told us the other day how he had worn thick glasses since he was a child, but now his eyes are well and strong. He told us about his neighbor who had two children, both of them unable to walk. Now they are both healed and able to walk and run normally. Also his own mother had been paralyzed for years. Now she is perfectly healed.

Tonight a young lady wept as she told how that when she was two years old, she had polio and it had left her right leg withered. It became three inches shorter than the left. She is now healed and she walked back and forth, perfectly, with not the slightest limp or difference in either leg. She held her face in her hands as she walked, weeping for joy at what God had done for her.

A mother told how her son had been unable to walk for four years. Tuberculosis of the hip bones had resulted from a bad fall, and his hips had become stiff. Tonight the boy walked perfectly.

A lady, who for 14 years had walked with crutches, was perfectly healed. On the platform and across the city, such testimonies continue to be reported.

One man, blind from birth, was led to the meeting today. As he listened to the message, he fell to the ground, having seen the Lord in a vision. He lay there for some time, and those around him thought he died. Suddenly he regained consciousness, stood to his feet declaring, "I have seen the Lord, and now I can see. I was blind, but now I see." He could see to read fine print. His eyes were perfect. The multitude was hysterical with joy when they heard this report.

Six deaf mutes were healed during the meeting tonight. One was fifty-five years of age, and had been born in this condition. One young man who was going to commit suicide was gloriously saved.

A lady who had a large cancerous growth in her left breast found it completely gone after prayer tonight.

She cried out, rubbing her side, "It is all gone, not a trace of it is left." Also an old man who had a double hernia for many years was completely healed. Scores of other miracles were wrought.

After the great meeting tonight, we went to the car rejoicing over what God had wrought through the power of His word. We noticed that we were followed by a poor family asking for prayer. The man was totally deaf. We prayed for him, after the family assured us that they had faith that if we would only pray, he would be healed. But nothing happened.

After some brief but careful instruction, we prayed again and while we were praying, the man grabbed my hands which I had placed over his ears, and cried out, "Stop! Stop! I'm hearing! Oh! Stop! Talk to me! I'm healed! I can hear!" I don't believe I've ever seen a man so thankful for his hearing as this man was. The family lifted me from the ground hugging me.

Then, abruptly and apprehensively, the man asked, "Will I be deaf again when you leave here?" "No!" we assured him, and he grabbed me again and lifted me from the ground with joy.

As we went home, an old man walked up and said, "I'm so thankful that you folks have come. I was crippled, and walked with canes for years, but now I am perfectly healed."

Psalm 107:20 says, **God sent his word and healed them**. That is being demonstrated in every meeting here. No individual prayers are offered. Just mass instruction, and everyone doing their own believing of the promise, accepting Christ and acting on His word. **The gospel is the power of God to every one that believes.** Any person can turn any promise of God into power equal to what it promises, on their behalf, whenever they will believe that promise and act on it.

* * *

February, 1952, Punto Fijo, Venezuela: Here we have a large open field that is surrounded by a wall. The road was jammed all the way from town to the location of the meeting. There were hundreds of cars and buses. The meeting was thrilling, as over 2,000 professed to accept Christ and promised to join a church in the area.

The miracles were amazing tonight. An old man who had been blind for many years was partly healed the other night, and tonight God finished the job; his eyes were completely healed tonight. He was so happy. Another old man totally blind for six years was healed tonight, too. It is impossible to record all details of the stories told by those so miraculously healed. A girl who was born with badly crossed eyes was completely healed; her eyes became straight and normal. A boy with one deaf ear was healed and could then hear the ticking of a watch. Scores of others were healed who could not possibly get to the platform to tell us about it.

* * *

March, 1952, San Jose, Costa Rica: We arrived at the Mendoza Stadium and found thousands of people jammed in the street in front of the stadium grounds unable to get inside because of the multitude in the arena. Some people who arrived when we did asked, "Aren't they going to open the gates tonight and let the people in?" The answer came, "The gates were opened. The place is packed with thousands inside, and now no more can enter." The property owner was angry, and pastors feared the authorities would stop the meeting on the basis of public safety.

The crowd finally completely broke down one big door and flowed in like a river until the audience just swayed like a field of grain in the breeze. We announced that we would move to the huge bullring tomorrow.

At least 2,500 accepted Christ as Savior after the message. Then we prayed for the sick, and it seemed like all heaven opened up on us as miracle after miracle was reported for nearly two hours.

A boy, who was dying with tuberculosis of the spine and could not bend his back or even move his head, was healed. The mother was in tears as the boy walked normally. At least eight deaf-mutes were healed. The father of one of them was so happy that he was reeling to and fro, intoxicated with joy, his face bathed in tears, telling the people to look at his boy. We checked the boy every way, and he was perfect.

The sister of the lady who cooks for us, who has been totally blind for two years, was led to the service and received her sight. A woman was healed of a tumor. A businessman was healed of a big rupture. He had been to the hospitals, but received no help. Tonight he was healed. At least 200 more raised their hands in the audience, signifying that they too were miraculously healed. It was impossible for them to get through the pressed crowd to testify. Words fail to describe the glory of this great meeting tonight. The presence of God filled the place.

* * *

February, 1953, Guatemala City, Guatemala: After the meeting last night, a woman who had been sitting in a car, crippled and unable to walk for over five years due to a broken back, continued praying and suddenly felt that she should walk. She got out of her car and discovered that she had been made whole. Many witnessed this miracle.

Thousands were present in the hot afternoon service. At least 2,500 accepted Christ in tears. Then I prayed for all who were sick. The miracle power of God was present to heal.

The first woman to testify had walked with the aid of two crutches for 15 years. She was made whole and left her crutches. Then a lady of 18 years was healed. She had tuberculosis in her hip, could not bend it, and had to walk with a crutch. She was completely healed and testified weeping. Then a young doctor came to the microphone to confirm her testimony, saying: "I know her; she was incurable. We treated her; she could not walk. It is true. We can only say truly God heals!"

Then a child who had polio was healed. An older man who had walked with a cane was restored after having suffered for 20 years. A woman whose foot was wrapped in cloth because of a cancerous ulcer was healed. The leg had been badly swollen and she walked on crutches, but she was totally and miraculously restored. It was great!

A wealthy lady and her son came running, extremely excited. He fell into my arms weeping, crying out. "Oh, Mr. Osborn, here's my mother; she has been deaf since my birth. She has never heard in 23 years. Now she is healed. She hears. Oh, He is so good." Many people knew her. She testified in tears of joy.

Next was a retired medical doctor who had not been able to walk for several years; he was completely restored. A woman who had a rupture for 20 years was healed. A policeman was healed. An older woman who was carried in arms to the meeting was made whole. A man who was brought in a wheelchair arose and walked, healed by God's power. A woman also was healed and left her wheelchair. Afterwards, over 1,000 people remained in the audience who declared that they were healed; but we did not have enough time to hear their testimonies.

The night service was twice as large, and thousands more received Christ. Among the great number of miracles of healing was a boy who had crossed eyes from birth. He was perfectly healed. A fine, educated young football player from Honduras was healed of epilepsy. For twelve years he had suffered convulsions, but tonight he received Christ. He said that when the prayer for healing was prayed, he felt the evil power leave him like a whirling wind; then peace and freedom came to him. He wept and wept as he testified.

* * *

February, 1954, Santiago, Chile: After five glorious weeks here in the capital city of Chile, we concluded the crusade with a parade. It was the greatest evangelical demonstration in the history of Chile.

At 2:00 p.m. we arrived at the place where the parade was forming, and people were pouring in like a river. Thousands were carrying signs with their testimony on everything from poles and sticks to broom handles. Scores of trucks, wagons, carts, and every kind of animal-drawn vehicle were taking their place. Over 600 musicians were there from one church alone. There were over a thousand bicycles. A huge Salvation Army float was beautiful. A whole unit of police assisted. The parade filled a street extending over 35 blocks. Standing at one point, it took over an hour for it to pass. In all, it took over four hours from the time the parade started moving until the last of the parade reached the park.

The headlines of the evening paper read: *300,000 Evangelicals March in Osborn Parade.* Then the entire center spread of the paper was a huge picture of the audience, together with other pictures and articles about the parade, stretching across both pages. The whole city is talking about Jesus, His miracles, and the celebrations of praise. To God be the glory!

* * *

July, 1954, Djakarta, Java, Indonesia: 30,000 to 40,000 people were jammed together on the Lapangan Bantang grounds in this capital city. I preached on *The Gospel for Everyone,* stressing John 3:16 and Psalm 103:3. The people are so hungry and eager to learn. Actually, it exceeds what we saw in South America. At the least, 8,000 people raised their hands, eager to accept Jesus Christ into their hearts. This sounds fantastic, but it looks even more awesome, especially realizing that Java is 95 percent Moslem.

When we prayed for the sick, Christ confirmed His word. A boy, who had been blind in both eyes, was wonderfully healed and could see everything. A woman, who had been blind in one eye for nine years, was healed. A Chinese woman, who had been crippled for twelve years and who could only hobble on two canes, was miraculously healed. A woman, who had been severely paralyzed on one side for eight years, was perfectly restored. She was so bad that her entire left side had become drawn and stiff. Every part of her body was healed. Another woman, who had been paralyzed on one side for nine years, was completely restored.

Four men testified of how they had been crippled and were healed. One had not walked in over four years. At least eight or ten totally deaf people were healed. A woman, whose shoulder had been broken and who had been unable to raise her arm for years, was healed.

A great miracle took place on a little girl who had been the victim of a disease which had destroyed the strength and muscles in her legs. Her little legs and hips were just skin and bones, limp and useless. For over two years, the child had not taken a step. The father brought her and laid her in a rickshaw during our message, and she fell asleep. As I prayed for the sick, the father laid his hands on his child and prayed earnestly. The child awoke and cried out: "Papa, I'm healed!" She was instantly made whole. She walked and ran, perfectly normal. One could hardly believe she had ever been crippled, but many witnesses knew her. How we thanked God for His mercy.

Two lepers were cleansed; one had been a leper for five years and the other for twelve years. Both testified that total feeling had returned to the previously lifeless parts of their flesh. Oh, how they wept as they told what Jesus had done for them, and they promised to follow Him.

* * *

September, 1954, Surabaja, Java, Indonesia: Tonight the meeting was heavenly. Christ showed the Moslems that He is the risen Son of God. He did the same miracles that He did before He was crucified.

Over 4,000 accepted Jesus as Savior after my message on *The Healing of Blind Bartimeaus.* Two totally blind women were healed and could see everything; one of them had been blind for twelve years. A lady totally deaf was healed. At least fifteen other totally deaf people were restored. A woman, who had been so ill with tuberculosis that she had no voice, was instantly healed, and her voice was restored.

A Moslem woman stood listening to the message. Then, suddenly, she saw a great ball of light appear behind me on the podium. It burst, and then a huge open hand appeared behind me with blood dripping from it. She believed on the Lord Jesus Christ and was healed also.

Another person saw a great light cover the field of people and a huge cross appeared. Then two pierced and bleeding hands appeared so large that they covered the entire audience. Blood sprayed from them over the people. Everyone who was engulfed in the flowing blood appeared to be immediately healed and made whole. But others feared the blood and fled from it, dragging their poor, crippled, and diseased bodies in a frantic escape to destruction. Signs and wonders like these and others caused tens of thousands to believe on Jesus Christ and to trust His word for salvation.

* * *

March, 1956, Bangkok, Thailand: As we arrived at the gate where the crusade was being conducted, I found my Thai interpreter talking to a woman who had been healed. For nine years she had tuberculosis of the spine and was bent double. She had suffered terribly. She has been attending the crusade and had accepted Christ as Savior. This morning when she got out of bed, she discovered that she had been perfectly healed. Oh, she was thrilled. Neighbors asked her: "What happened? What medicine did you take? Who healed you?" She told them how she had believed on Jesus and had been healed by Him. They said, "It is better that you remain bent down and die than to give up Buddhism." She answered them, "You have your heart; I have mine. I accepted Jesus and He healed me." All day she testified. She told how one of her neighbors, who was unable to raise her arm, had come and was healed, too.

After the message, hundreds received Christ as Savior. We then prayed for the sick. A little leper woman was healed. The leprosy had affected her hands until they were just rigid and numb clenched fists. Her feet were numb and stiff also. Sores had erupted on her legs and hands. She said: "I was alone. I had no job. My parents died with leprosy. No one would talk to me or come near me or visit with me. I was lonesome. But now I have a friend. I am not alone. Jesus loves me. He is not ashamed to come to my hut. He is not afraid of me. I am healed. I am clean. I will always follow Him."

Many others told of tremendous miracles. It was a great meeting among the Buddhists, and Christ proved Himself to be alive.

* * *

July, 1956, Kyoto, Japan: Here in this seat of Shintoism, a city of magnificent temples, we are seeing great throngs gather on an open field to hear the gospel. Tonight was a tremendous meeting, one of those truly great visitations of our Lord to the Shintoists.

I preached on *Good News for Everyone*. Hundreds accepted Christ. Then I prayed for the sick en masse. People literally ran to the podium to testify. The platform was filled in fifteen minutes. A man who had been blind, carrying a white cane, was healed so perfectly that he could even read the Bible to the audience. It was amazing. Seven deaf mutes were healed. It was absolutely tremendous to see them weep as they embraced each other.

I don't think we have ever seen people so emotional. A man with an itching all over his body was cured instantly. A woman was healed of cancer and coughed it up during the meeting. She was well. Three or four were healed of tuberculosis. A woman, lying on a pallet, arose and was made whole. A boy with paralysis and epilepsy was restored instantly. A woman with one leg that had been paralyzed for several years was healed. A boy was healed of crossed eyes; they became perfectly straight. Another lad was healed of a rupture. It was gone. A man, whose finger was stiff because the leaders had been cut, is now perfect; and he was so excited to show how his hand is now normal. Many other great miracles took place, but I do not have the time to record them all. What a visitation of Jesus to the Shintoists of Japan.

* * *

January, 1957, Ibadan, Nigeria: Oh, what a meeting today. It was amazing. This is the largest all-African city on the continent. I preached on *Why Jesus Came*. A vast company of people believed on Christ as Savior. Then we prayed for the sick. It was amazing what took place. The multitude gave great praise and glorified God.

First to testify was a man who had been blind for fifteen years. His eyes were totally healed. He could see everything clearly. Next was a man who had been paralyzed and unable to walk for more than five years; he was made completely whole. Then there was a woman who had hobbled about on two crutches. Her family had helped her to the crusade. She was totally healed and paraded back and forth, holding her crutches in the air.

Then all of heaven seemed to break loose when a man, who had dragged his body on the ground with his hands for over thirty years, was made whole. He had tied old rubber pads on his knees to protect them and used blocks for his hands to help him move about. His legs looked like poles; but as he walked, they developed. He had been a beggar in the streets, and he was a Moslem. Everyone knew him, and the field of people went wild with joy when they saw him walk. He gave a powerful testimony saying: "If Jesus is dead, how could He heal me? You know me. I have accepted this Jesus because I know He is alive!"

300

We have never seen a miracle so totally shake a city. The King of Ibadan knows him as does every business owner. It took over an hour to calm the multitude after hearing and seeing this miracle. While the crowd glorified God, hundreds of others were healed and believed on Christ.

Suddenly, a woman rushed up to testify. She had been a hunchback without hope. They said she was so disfigured, it looked like she was carrying a child on her back. She was made straight in a second, and the people around her were frightened by the power of God as it straightened her back. She was so crippled that sometimes she scooted on the ground rather than try to stand up enough to walk. The woman was completely restored. Oh, it was glorious.

A woman who had been blind for eight years received her sight. She cried out, "I'm not blind any longer! I can see!" Several deaf persons were restored, and so may scores of miracles took place that it would take a book to contain them. How great God is!

* * *

August, 1958, Rennes, France: We have just come in from one of the greatest days we have witnessed in France. Thousands of Gypsies and their caravans formed a great parade and came singing and marching through the city to the campaign grounds. It was impressive and very large. After the people gathered on the grounds, I preached on water baptism and led them in a prayer for salvation as many received Christ and were born again.

Then the baptismal service began. Our daughter, LaDonna Carol, was the first to be baptized by Gypsy pastors. Then others followed. Many could be seen going down into the water weeping and coming up praising God.

A Moslem from Algeria came confessing that he wanted to be baptized since he had believed on Jesus Christ and had accepted Him in the crusade. He was baptized, and we all rejoiced. He went to the microphone and gave his testimony of faith in Jesus Christ, declaring that his entire life was now dedicated to Jesus.

Then a man, who is a famous Gypsy nightclub singer, came and testified that he, too, had been gloriously saved today and must be baptized. He had on a beautiful suit. He had run to nearby shops to see if he could buy clothes to be baptized in, but could not, so he returned quickly to keep from missing his opportunity. He confessed that he had been a very unclean man and a terrible sinner, but now he is completely saved and so happy. His wife was by his side in tears, and together they were baptized. It was wonderful.

Many others came and testified and were baptized, too. I was particularly impressed by two outstanding Gypsy violinists who had played in the Gypsy orchestra. They came to be baptized. One is old, effervescent, an excellent musician. As a young musician, he played for President Woodrow Wilson. The other one is considered to be the best Gypsy violinist of our time. He was converted a few days ago. Both of these great musicians went into the baptismal tank together.

Before they were baptized, I asked the orchestra to play a beautiful Gypsy hymn as these two great musicians followed the Lord in water baptism. Hundreds of people wept as the orchestra played their sweet music. When they came out of the water, the crowd rejoiced and glorified God. Hundreds were baptized. Only God knows the glory of this occasion today. Rennes, France, and the Gypsy communities of Europe will never be the same.

* * *

August, 1958, The Hague, Holland: This crusade is truly historic — the greatest crowds ever in Europe's history to receive the gospel face to face. Police claimed that from 120,000 to 150,000 were gathered on the Malieveld grounds tonight. There were at least a hundred policemen present. I do not know how many scores of Red Cross nurses and staff with stretchers, and trucks were on duty. They have gathered all spare wheelchairs, stretchers, and cots from this entire area in order to get the invalids to the meetings. To watch them was like watching an ambulance corps on the frontlines, serving the wounded and helpless.

The papers, radio, and TV are all very positive in their news coverage.

The executive committee has been uneasy about the chief of police who has been quite stringent in his demand on us. They thought he might be looking for technical reasons to end the campaign. But, today, the committee's secretary was summoned to the office of the chief of police who had also gathered together a large number of his top men. Before them all, he told his men how he believed that this was of God, that he was very, very thankful that such a meeting and such wonders of God could take place in his city, Holland's capital.

It seems unprecedented to me the way this nation is doing everything possible to assure the success of this great campaign. Tonight I preached on John 3:16,17. Never have we seen a mass of people more attentive. Thousands accepted Jesus Christ as Savior and were born again when we invited them to decide for Christ.

Then we prayed for the great mass of people, and miracles of healing were taking place everywhere. There is no way I could convey the glory of this meeting. A girl who was 90 percent blind was completely healed. A man, who had a severe back injury, a cancer on his nose, and a double rupture, was perfectly healed. The cancer simply vanished. No sign of it remained. His back was as free as a child's, and both ruptures disappeared.

A woman who had been in a wheelchair for 21 years was perfectly healed. During the message, she just got up and began to walk and was made whole. Then she ran to the platform to show everyone how she could run, and even jump. Then a funny thing happened: when she went down from the platform, she could not find her wheelchair. At the hotel that night, a government information agency man told me that he saw her running about everywhere so happy, but looking for her wheelchair, and she could not find it.

A lad took off the steel braces from legs which had been paralyzed by polio. He walked back and forth on the platform to show that his legs were perfectly healed. A man on two crutches was marvelously healed and came across the platform, carrying his crutches. Another man, who could only walk with the aid of two canes, was healed. He, too, came rejoicing, carrying and waving his canes. A woman in a wheelchair got up and was healed. She was so very happy. A lady was healed of cancer of the breast. It was gone. Another lady was healed of a hernia. A man was healed of asthma.

An older woman, totally blind, was brought to the crusade in a wheelchair. That dear lady was completely healed. She really raised a ruckus in the camp when her blind eyes came open, and then she got out of her wheelchair. She could see everything clearly and could walk as good as anyone. It was really amazing.

Oh, there were scores of other marvelous miracles; and, as usual, hundreds raised their hands in the audience, saying that they were healed but could not get to the platform. Holland can never forget this day and can never be the same again.

* * *

February, 1959, Lome, Togoland: Tonight I feel more amazed over this campaign than ever before. It is among the greatest. Such power. Such conversions. Such miracles. Every day more and greater miracles are taking place. And as for conversions, there never seems to be anyone who refuses to accept Christ. It is mass conversion and mass healing.

Tonight I preached on *Acting Faith.* Four lepers claimed complete healing already. Two of them had sores all over their hands and feet; in a few days, all of those sores have dried up. One of them had the type of leprosy where all his flesh burned like fire. Now his flesh never burns, and he feels well. The other was the painful type, and she is free of all pain.

An older lady who was totally blind for over five years was healed and could count the fingers of people in the audience. Then there was a girl who was carried by her father from a far-away village. For some years she had not walked a step. Tonight she could run and jump like any girl. A young man was carried by his father to the meeting from a distant area. He had been unable to walk for about six years. He had tried all of the native doctors and fetishes, but to no avail. Then he heard about the campaign, and his father carried him here. He was completely healed tonight and just smiled and wept and rejoiced as he testified.

Another young man was healed who had been bedfast for three years. From far away in his village, he heard about the campaign. He said that he heard that the Son of God had come down to earth and was healing the people. I told him that was right; but that I was not the Son of God, that His name is Jesus. He understood and was marvelously converted.

This poor man had been vomiting blood as often as twenty times a day. He was dying of tuberculosis. Over a hundred miles up in the interior, he had heard of the miracles. He had been bedfast for three years and could not walk. He had no voice. His parents were so poor that they only had enough money to pay the transport driver his one-way fare to Lome. They knew if he was not healed, he would die. If he was healed, he could walk.

They carried him to the old truck, paid the fare, and put him in the care of the driver who helped him during the trip. Upon arrival in Lome, the truck driver carried him and laid him on the ground under a tree near the platform. He had a few precious coins with which he bought some rice from a woman who occasionally went to the grounds. Three days he had lain there, and tonight he was healed. As he testified, his voice grew stronger. He was one of the happiest persons I have ever seen.

The Lord's mercy never fails. We are thankful that He has allowed us to be His instruments to bring the gospel to these dear people. Over fifty towns and villages have already sent invitations begging us to come preach the gospel to them or send someone in our place. It is so touching to hear different people testify of coming from afar, then to hear them begging us to come or to send a teacher to them. Another chief has sent a letter and is even here in the audience, begging us to send someone to his people.

One man testified whose right leg was smaller than the other. Now he is well, and the leg is normal. An older man was healed of total blindness. A young man was perfectly healed of a deaf ear. A woman was healed of a large rupture and just cried out with joy: "My man is so proud of me now." It is truly amazing what God is doing in Togoland!

* * *

February, 1960, Lucknow, India: Fourteen years ago, Daisy and I left India in what seemed to be failure. We sought God for the answer; Jesus revealed Himself to us, and now I take up my pen to try to set down what our eyes have seen on this second night of the Lucknow, India, crusade. Words are inadequate to record the glory of the meeting.

Early in the afternoon the people were crowding onto the grounds near the stadium. By early evening the multitude was packed tight and stretched far out across the field, past our large light installation, out into the darkness. Officials estimated 50,000 to 75,000 people were present. They were very reverent and well behaved.

One could not imagine the looks on the people's faces. Some of the strange characters present were beyond description. For example, right in front of the platform, not three feet from me, there stood an old Hindu holy man in a dirt-smeared robe. His long, squalid beard and his frizzled hair shrouded desperate inquiring eyes. Yellow paint was smeared on his forehead. Mixed mud and dust covered his face and hair. He was standing erect. In his right hand was a large Neptune spear as his staff. What a joy to give out the powerful gospel message. How marvelous to see the power of Christ penetrate, not only that man, but hundreds of other equally strange and superstitious people in our midst.

I preached on Mark 9:23, urging them to **only believe**. Thousands did believe; and when I finished my message, we called upon them to accept Christ. It looked as though everyone raised their hands into the air to receive the Savior. It was overwhelming — a sea of hands, a tidal wave of response. As in the Bible, **multitudes were added to the Lord**.

Then we prayed for all the sick. When finished, we have seldom seen anything like it. Hundreds were miraculously healed and began trying to reach the platform to show us.

The first person up the steps was an elderly Hindu man, carrying two crutches above his head. He was radiant. His long hair and beard were flowing. For five years he had been crippled. Now he paraded back and forth, so happy. By that time, another older man with a large red turban came bounding across the platform. He, too, was healed completely. A man, whose foot and leg were crippled, was perfectly healed. He had walked on one side of his foot, which was turned directly inward with the ankle twisted over. Both feet were perfectly healed and completely straight. He ran and jumped as the people glorified God.

Two men who were blind came to the crusade together. Both of them were healed. Their eyes were so bright and clear that one could hardly believe they had been blind. Oh, they were both so happy! A child with one arm bent double, so that he never had been able to stretch it out, was perfectly healed. He was very happy. Two brothers, totally blind, came and were healed. It was a most wonderful sight to see them look at each other and touch each other in admiration. Then a girl was healed of blindness and could see everything. A 70-year-old woman, who had been nearly blind for seven years, was healed and could see clearly.

A most touching thing: A little old woman, clad in a dirty cloth, testified in tears. She would praise Jesus, then place her open palms together and bow to me in East Indian fashion. Then she would bow to my feet and touch them, then repeat it again and again. She had been a beggar and had no one to help her. Her children and her husband were dead. She was left alone in life to beg.

She said that she had become terribly sick until she was too weak to beg. Each day that she could not beg, she had no way to get a little rice, so she became sicker and weaker.

Then she would cry and touch my feet again to say how thankful she was that she was not lying in the bushes anymore, sick and hungry. Someone had found her in her dying state and told her about Jesus and about this meeting. Somehow she had managed to come. Now, Jesus was her friend, and she was healed. "Now," she said, "I can go back on the street and beg, because I am not sick and weak. I can talk loud enough to ask for alms and get a few coins a day to eat." Oh, it was touching.

How thankful we are to have come again to India, just for her. There were at least twenty blind people healed tonight. My wife counted six people healed of crossed eyes. Numerous cripples and lame people walked. Several deaf mutes were healed. What a difference in the response to the gospel of Jesus with signs, wonders and miracles. Fourteen years ago we left India because we were powerless in convincing the Hindus and Moslems that Jesus is the Son of God, risen from the dead and alive today. This time we came in the power of the Holy Ghost and the authority of Jesus. India has not changed. Jesus has not changed. But T. L. and Daisy have been transformed. We have seen Jesus!

February, 1963, Manila, Philippines: Tonight was a very wonderful service. The multitude was vast. I preached on *Four Steps to Healing*, closing with great emphasis on the fact that salvation includes healing and that to receive healing, one must receive the healer. The Lord surely confirmed His word to the people as they cried out to God for salvation.

Then we prayed for the sick, and God confirmed His word. A man who had been deaf for over thirty years was healed. A woman who was deaf for ten years was healed completely. A child, healed of polio, took off a steel leg brace and shoe and walked perfectly. A lady was healed of a large goiter. A woman with one leg two inches shorter than the other felt God's power go through her, and both legs were perfectly equal. Another woman was healed of a goiter and a blood disease. It was an outstanding case.

A man carried both of his crutches above his head as he came to the platform and testified. He can walk as well as anyone. A man, who had a cancerous growth on the side of his neck the size of two fists, was perfectly healed. They had sent him home from the hospital to die. Nurses were afraid to touch him. The huge growth simply disappeared. It was astounding! He walked back and forth, pounding the side of his neck, shouting: "Look. It's gone. It's gone. The cancer is gone." One of the pastors knew the man and was amazed. A local pastor grabbed me and, in tears, said, "He's staying in our church. We know how he was. The cancer is gone. It was as big as two fists and was an open, odorous sore. It's gone. It's amazing."

What a tremendous meeting. Scores of great miracles took place. The multitude will never forget what they saw tonight.

* * *

April, 1965, San Fernando, Trinidad: The crusade here in San Fernando, Trinidad, has been one of the greatest we have ever seen in our lives. The entire city has been attracted to hear the gospel. Upwards of 50,000 to 75,000 people, perhaps even 100,000, have poured onto the great crusade grounds at the edge of the city from all over this island-nation.

Tonight I preached on what Jesus did for every individual at the cross. I emphasized His substitutionary work for each one and stressed Romans 1:16 — that the gospel is the power of God to everyone that believes. When I finished the message and gave an invitation to accept Christ, at least 5,000 people raised their hands to believe on Jesus Christ and to receive Him as Savior. Then we prayed for the sick, and there was an avalanche of miracles. All over the crowd rejoicing could be heard, and one could see people here and there being healed.

At the edge of the crowd, groups were running after different ones who had received miraculous healing. Before we knew it, the platform was being engulfed with people who wanted to testify of what God had done for them. They were shouting and praising God. Some were jumping; others were crying.

A young man was weeping and rubbing his eyes. His left eye had been badly crossed, and he was nearly blind. Twice he had undergone surgery to straighten the crossed eye and to restore his sight, but both operations failed. Tonight his blind, crossed eye was completely restored.

Then an old woman touched me on the arm, wanting to testify. For over three years her right eye had been totally blind. She was completely healed. A thirteen-year-old lad, who had been born deaf, was healed. His ears were perfect. A little baby, which had been born crippled, was brought in the arms of its mother. There was no sign of knees or of knee-caps. Both legs were rigid and doubled flat against its chest. Doctors forced the stiff legs down and bound them in casts. The mother attended the crusade and believed for a miracle. The next morning both legs were normal. Pain was gone, and the child had two knees that functioned perfectly. Those who knew the child's condition were astonished at this creative miracle of God.

A dear man was healed of a paralytic stroke which had left him dumb and helpless. His wife had to feed and dress him. But in the meeting tonight he was completely restored. He could walk, jump, run, and talk normally. It was a great miracle. A dear lad was healed of a totally deaf ear. There was a large scar behind his ear that showed where a radical mastoid operation had been performed in which his hearing faculties had been removed. God performed a creative miracle. Now, he can hear the faintest whisper.

A little boy, whose left eye was totally blind after being hit in the eye with a stone, was completely healed. He had also been bitten by a poisonous snake, and his right leg was swollen and painful. But it also was made whole. There was a girl who walked very awkwardly because her left leg was curved and her foot was twisted. But tonight the bones in her leg and foot became perfectly normal and straight. A dear old woman who was totally blind and deaf was healed. Those around her were delighted that her sight had been miraculously restored.

A dear man who had come to the crusade hobbling on crutches was made whole. He had prayed to God for a miracle and he had been completely restored.

Another precious man was carried to the crusade on a bed because he was paralyzed and unable to move his legs. He was instantly healed. He got up from his bed and began to walk, swinging his arms and moving his hands. He was made perfectly whole. An older woman, who had been totally blind for several years, was led to the great campaign. She listened intently to the message of the gospel and believed on Jesus Christ. During the healing prayer she placed her hand on her blind eyes, then acted her faith. Her sight was restored, and she was overwhelmed at being able to see clearly again.

There was a woman who had been totally deaf for 32 years. During the prayer, her ears seemed to pop open, and she could hear the faintest whisper. A beautiful lad about twelve years old was healed in his legs. One leg was twisted inward, and the foot was malformed. Some might call it a club-foot. He walked on the side of his foot, and the knee was twisted inward. With childlike faith, this lad asked God to heal him as we prayed for the mass of people; and he received a creative bone miracle. The club-foot was straightened out, and his leg that had been twisted was also made perfectly whole.

Perhaps the greatest miracle of all was the healing of Harold Khan, who was a Moslem lad. When he was only twelve years old, he was injured while playing football. His right leg was damaged so that all growth ceased. An incurable bone disease resulted, affecting his left leg, too.

Harold is 14 now; and since the accident, his body has grown as any robust youth's, except for his right leg which never developed after the injury. It had already become 5 1/2 inches shorter than the left one and was much smaller. Harold walked with the aid of a special shoe for his dwarfed right leg, elevated on a 5 1/2-inch platform. His left leg was bound in a steel hip-to-heel brace because of the bone disease affecting it.

News reached the Khan home of the campaign. Mrs. Khan wanted to take Harold, but was forbidden by the strict Moslem father. But while he was away, she took her son at the risk of family disfavor and attended the great meeting. Both she and her son believed on the Lord Jesus Christ tonight as we expounded the simple dynamic message of the gospel.

Before we prayed for the sick, Harold believed that God was seeing him, and he wept before the Lord as he listened to the message. As we were praying, he took off the elevated shoe from his right leg and the steel hip-to-heel brace from his left leg and accepted Jesus Christ into his heart. Then this awesome miracle took place. His short leg became normal as the Lord passed his way.

Harold and his mother came weeping to the platform, carrying the steel brace and elevated shoe. When Harold came up the stairs with this strange elevated shoe in his hand, holding the big leg brace above his head, he was weeping. I presumed that he had come to tell us about someone else who had been healed. I looked at him, and his legs were perfectly normal. I could see no reason for his having this elevated shoe and big leg brace, so I asked him: "Who has been healed?"

He was sobbing convulsively. He finally said, "It's me. I've been healed. These are the things I've taken off my legs!" It was incredible to behold. Pondering that pair of perfectly equal legs, one could but wonder at the awesome power of God to do the utterly impossible. He walked back and forth on the platform, and both of his legs were perfectly equal. It absolutely astounded the multitude of people.

Truly Jesus Christ proved again by this great miracle that He is the Son of God and is risen from the dead according to the scriptures. Moslems do not usually believe these things about Christ, but no one could doubt that the Christ of the scriptures lives today when they saw this wonderful miracle that God had performed on Harold. The following day, Harold's entire family accepted Jesus as Savior and Lord of their lives.

A woman, 105 years old and totally blind, was led to the crusade. She received her sight. What a miracle of mercy. Truly there is nothing impossible for God.

There were many other miracles, but I simply do not have enough time to record them all. Truly, Jesus Christ is the same yesterday and today and forever!

* * *

February, 1969, Kinshasa, Zaire: When I take up my pen to record a day like today, I am at a loss for words to express the glory and wonder of it all. A great multitude heard the word as I preached on Psalm 103:3. When we prayed the prayer of repentance, everyone prayed. There seems to be no one who refuses. It is just overwhelming to witness.

After the prayer for healing, an avalanche of people ready to witness of a miracle converged onto the platform. It was so thrilling. There is no way to record them. It was the same as in Bible days. The dumb and deaf, the blind, lame, crazy and sick were all healed. The people cried and laughed and rejoiced.

As we were closing the meeting tonight, a mother placed two of her children up on the platform with a bucket. I've never seen anything so precious. Those two children reached up to tell me to look. Then they set the bucket on the platform, took off the lid, and pointed. There was a spotless white cloth covering a clean pan with a lid on it. They lifted it out, removed the lid, and there were eight clean white fresh eggs.

The children smiled sweetly and wanted me to take them. I took my hat and squatted down as the children placed each egg in the hat, smiled, then replaced their pan in the bucket and put the lid back on it. Then they got up, and the larger one, about four years old, reached out to shake my hand, then went back to the edge of the platform to their mother.

I thank God that we can be among these people. It is an extraordinary experience. We quickly ate a roll of bread in the car and drank some fruit juice, then went to the large hall where 1200 preachers were waiting for us to share with them the secrets of evangelism.

* * *

December, 1974, Benin City, Nigeria: This is an enormous crusade in this city whose history is so steeped in pagan culture and primitive superstition. There were 50,000 or more attending.

Tonight I preached on Romans 1:16, *The Gospel.* I was able to really convey the message of the good news with an unusual anointing as I told them: "My government in heaven has authorized me, as an ambassador in Christ's name, to announce to every sinner who believes in what Christ did at the cross that you will never be condemned by your sins, that you are forgiven now. I am authorized to pronounce that every captive is free, to announce to all sick people that you are healed and that Satan no longer reigns with authority in your lives if you believe on Jesus Christ. I am sent from God with a special proclamation, and I have been ordered to tell all captives of sin, disease, and devils that the term of your captivity is ended and that you may now walk out of bondage as free persons saved and healed by Jesus Christ, God's Son."

Needless to say, hundreds did walk out of bondage. In all directions, spontaneous outbursts of praise and excitement could be seen as cripples suddenly began to walk and as people began to realize they were healed. Great glory was given to God, and everyone believed that Jesus was truly in their midst.

The message was clearly grasped, and a great wave of reverence gripped the people as they repented of sins and received Jesus Christ. It was a powerful night, and the many thousands present could easily witness the great signs and wonders which God did among them to confirm His word.

The platform was simply flooded by hundreds of people, pushing and crying and rejoicing, wanting to tell what God had done for them.

There is no way that I could record the scores and scores of great testimonies we heard. A boy wept as he confessed that he was a thief.

Now he says he will never steal again. A lad testified whose right heel had never touched the ground because his knee was bent; he had to walk on his tiptoe. He was perfectly healed. His leg became straight, and the foot was flat on the floor. Then a boy came who had one leg quite a bit shorter than the other. He, too, was absolutely perfect and walked with a true, even stride. It amazed everyone.

A woman threw away two canes with which she had staggered along for seventeen years. Tonight she was totally restored and walked perfectly.

A man came carrying two heavy sticks. For years he had only been able to stagger along by bracing himself with these two canes. Now he tossed those heavy sticks away and walked as well as anyone. An old blind woman was healed. She could see everything and was so happy. A young woman with one blind eye was completely recovered. At least three deaf mutes were healed, and many who were deaf in one or both ears were restored.

We examined so many that we finally had to say, "Praise the Lord" and pass them on. It's impossible to tell how great God's presence and power were.

* * *

February, 1976, Uyo, Nigeria: Tonight we have beheld the glory of God in a way seldom seen. The newspaper estimated that at least 200,000 were present. How merciful is our God to these dear people to move among them and perform such wonders!

I preached on the healing of the leper in a narrative style, expounding as I read the story. Each time I emphasized a point, the multitude would break out clapping. This area seems so receptive to the gospel. As usual, we directed them in a prayer for salvation, accepting Jesus Christ and confessing faith in Him. Hundreds wept freely. It's very touching to see them and to hear them pray. You could see different ones smiting themselves on the breast, as the sinner did in the Bible. God must be moved with great compassion when He sees a multitude like this crying out to Him for mercy.

After a long period of prayer and thanksgiving, I began to announce to them that it was time to accept the answer by faith and to put faith into action. Some most remarkable miracles took place. A handsome lad, about fifteen years old, had been deaf since he was two years old when he had a bad fever. Tonight he could hear the faintest whisper and the ticking of my wristwatch from either ear.

Suddenly, a dear man mounted the stage, looking so happy. He had crawled on his hands and feet in a pitiful way. His knees had been stiff.

It seems that a deadening, stiffening paralysis, mixed with perhaps arthritis, had crippled him. His hands had been twisted and gnarled. To show us how he had managed to move about, he bent over and walked across the platform on his hands and feet. It was really sad. But then he rose to his feet and raised both arms heavenward and praised the Lord in such a precious way that hundreds of us wept for joy. He could now walk, bending his legs, and could do anything in a normal way. He was made whole — a wonder of God. The multitude cheered and clapped for joy.

The next one who testified was quite an old man who, for the past eight years, had only been able to move about by scooting on his haunches with his hands at his side. He pushed himself along in a most painful way. He showed us on the platform how he did it. Then the dear old man rose to his feet and showed everyone how he can walk upright, which he hadn't done for eight years.

Then a dear woman bounded up on the other side of the platform, crying: "Look at me. I was a leper. See my feet. Now I am healed. Look at me walk. Look. My feet are healed. I can feel them. They are well. I am healed." It was a marvel of God. She stomped her feet. There had been angry open sores on them, but they were clearly dried up. She was overjoyed. She left, crying out: "I'm healed. My feet are healed. I can feel them. They are not dead. They are alive." No one could doubt what God had done for her.

Then a man came who had been totally blind for several years. He was able to see everything. Next, a woman who had been blind came rejoicing because she could see everything clearly. She had been led to the crusade. Now she rejoiced as she pointed out all the people. She could count the fingers of anyone who raised a hand out in the audience. It was marvelous.

A dear mother brought her child paralyzed by polio. She was crying and thanking God because the child was healed and could run and jump and walk perfectly. Then an older man, who had been a witch doctor, came up the steps. He was ashamed of the curses he had put on people and the deaths he had brought on through fear. Now he wanted to receive Jesus so that he would never be a witch doctor again. I commanded the evil spirits of witchcraft to leave him and to never torment or possess him again. The people were astonished; and then, as though someone had defeated a great enemy, they cried out in joy and clapped for a long time. It was touching. The old man was delivered, and everyone was amazed.

Suddenly, Daisy brought up a young man about twenty-five years old. He had no hair. For eight years, he had been a raving maniac. It took four men to bring him and to control him during the meeting. He had been in the University of Lagos, studying medicine. Then one day he suddenly began to lose his mind and became totally insane. A growth began to develop in his throat and neck. It was large like a mango seed and extremely painful. Tonight during the mass prayer, he began to be calm, his mind was restored, and every trace of the growth on his neck disappeared. Another man on the platform verified his story. We were all amazed. He spoke good English and was a most brilliant young man. He gave a moving testimony, explaining how he became fearful and confused. He could not stop raving. He wanted to hurt people. Nothing made sense to him anymore, and he felt that everyone was trying to harm him. Now he says everything is clear and normal. He is amazed that all of the terror that had tormented his mind is gone. He thanked Jesus and pledged to serve Him always.

Then I turned to see a man coming up the steps who had been a leper. He was overwhelmed that the deadness from his feet and hands was gone. His hands had become clenched and motionless. But now he could open and close them well. Every finger was free. He could feel with his feet and his hands. He was amazed and overjoyed and kept on praising God. An elderly man came up the steps carrying a long staff. He was surprised and so happy. He said that he had an operation on his back and hip and had never walked since the operation which was six years ago. He was helped to the crusade by friends, but got there late, just as we began to pray. When the prayer was finished, he could stand up and walk with no trouble and with no pain. He was overwhelmed. All were thankful to see how God's mercy reached out to this dear man.

A young man about twenty years of age came and said: "I was mad. I was crazy. But now, I am healed." We were all amazed by his words. He looked so nice. We wondered if his story was true, so I asked for his name. He announced his name over the loudspeaker. Then I asked if anyone knew him. Suddenly, some hands were raised. I asked the people who knew him to come to the platform. A fellow came and said: "I know him. It's true. He was crazy, and we had to hold him at times. He has been like that for several years." They marveled. He was sane, normal, radiant, and sensible. He talked calmly and coherently. One simply stood amazed at the mercy of God.

An old woman who had been crippled in her back for many years came to testify. She hadn't been able to stand upright, always walking bent over, supporting her back by bracing her hands above her knees. Now she stood perfectly erect, reared back, forward, and sideways; then she waved her arms. She was healed by a perfect miracle. A middle-aged woman who had been blind was led to the meeting, and now she has received sight.

A man about forty years of age came to testify. As he talked, I heard gasps from the audience and expressions of wonder. My interpreter was so awestruck that he quit interpreting for me. I nudged him to keep translating for me. He said: "Wait, wait. What is this!" He was amazed. I had to insist that he tell me what the man was saying. Then the man stretched out his arms with wrists upturned, placing them close together, and I saw big scars and tough calluses on his wrists. Then he showed the people his ankles: they were the same. I asked my interpreter: "What is this? Tell me." He said: "Oh, this cannot be true. This cannot be true."

Then he explained that for eleven years the man had been crazy and possessed by demons. They had to keep his feet and his hands in iron bands with chains. They had kept him locked in a mud hut. He would fight and try to kill people. They could not get near him, so he had to be kept in iron bands.

Again, a pastor said: "This cannot be so." I asked: "Then why are these scars on his wrists? And look at his ankles." They were worse. Deep calluses circling his ankles confirmed the awful story. The dear man looked and seemed so normal that it was difficult to believe he had been insane; so I asked for someone in the multitude who knew him. Promptly a woman came through the crowd, excited and crying. She was shouting: "I know him. I live by the place where they kept him chained and locked up. He screamed. He was dangerous. He tried to kill people. To change his clothes or to feed him, they had to fight with him."

Then the dear man interrupted the woman and opened his mouth wide, pointing at his teeth. Some of them were gone. He said: "They beat me and kicked out my teeth." It was sad, yet it was glorious to witness. The woman kept talking and thanking God for the wonder of his healing. The man was truly delivered. Obviously, the tormenting demons had gone out of him as we had preached the word and prayed for the multitude, and he was healed.

Who could doubt the glory and mercy of God after witnessing such miracles, signs, and wonders? I could write for hours and not tell all that happened tonight. The stories are endless. People were healed everywhere. The platform was filled with people who had been healed. All across the crowd, hundreds of people raised their hands to signify that they were healed but could not get through the tightly packed multitude to testify. It's truly amazing as it was in Bible days when Jesus saw the multitude and was moved with compassion toward them and healed their sick. He is the same yesterday, and today, and forever for those who will have simple childlike faith and take Him at His word, without theological complications and psychological analysis.

* * *

December, 1977, Nakuru, Kenya: Amazing things are taking place in this city. The whole town is talking.

We're hearing of amazing things that took place last night. At the far edge of the crowd, a woman who was born blind and had never seen in her life was suddenly healed. As she began to see, she became so frightened that she screamed aloud and started to run. Then she saw a car moving. It horrified her, and she panicked. She was a simple village woman who had lived sightless. Now she could see masses of people moving about and she was horrified. Her husband called to her to calm her. She knew his voice and turned to him, but seeing him coming toward her, she screamed and turned and ran. They finally caught her and held her until they could help her overcome the shock of seeing for the first time in her life. A leading Christian businessman witnessed it all.

Then another blind woman was sitting in a car at the edge of the multitude. Her husband was standing by the rear of the car. His wife was totally blind. When the prayer was finished, the woman opened her eyes and her blindness was absolutely gone. She was so shocked and overwhelmed that she screamed and jumped out of the car and called for her husband. When he rushed to her and saw what had happened, he fell to the ground, weeping and crying out loud.

Ismael, one of the principal ushers at the crusade, and many local Christians, saw it and verified it as the lady with her husband came to testify.

Then over at one side of the multitude, Ismael had been watching a boy with terribly crippled feet. They turned up so that he walked on the sides of his ankles.

All of a sudden after the prayer, the boy's feet straightened out and he could stand straight on them. Both feet were flat and he was perfectly healed. Ismael took him and tried for over an hour to bring him to the platform, but could not even get near, so great was the press of the crowd. The boy will come tomorrow to show what God has done for him.

Pastors have been coming to our room all day with additional reports of miracles that they know about. The Finnish missionary here, with two of our interpreters, came into our room, almost out of breath.

316

They said that over on Kolingen Street, the police are having to forcibly open a way through the crowd in the streets so the cars can pass. A four-year-old child, who was born totally blind, received sight last night and the street is jammed by people who are amazed. The mother has the child there, showing everyone. What is overwhelming to the people is that many of them know the child and confirm the mother's words that he was born with a white film on his eyes, so thick that it seemed like a skin. Now that film has disappeared and the child is clearly seeing everything.

While I've been writing this, they brought the child to the hotel for us to see, and it is absolutely amazing what is happening to that boy's eyes. It is a creative miracle.

One of the hotel men said to Daisy's interpreter: "I must go today and get my wife from the village. I was standing in the meeting last night, and my own eyes witnessed a great miracle. A woman, who was born blind, suddenly received her sight. She screamed and tried to run from everyone and from everything that moved, and they had to catch her and hold her. I saw it with my own eyes. Oh, I never thought I would ever see something so wonderful as this!" (It was the same woman I described earlier.)

Then one of the pastors pointed out of the hotel window to a woman who was sitting on the wall by the road. A group was with her. We just received word of her miracle last night. She had been crippled in both legs and could barely manage to move about. Her knees were bent and turned inward. She could scarcely walk at all. She had to shuffle herself by moving her legs below her knees, balancing her weight with a heavy stick. Last night the woman was healed. They brought her to the hotel to show us the miracle. It is awesome. Her legs are well. It was a marvel to see the woman showing the crowd that gathered around the hotel what God had done for her. Her legs are restored; they are normal.

The first miracle that reached the platform last night was a lad with crutches and steel leg braces. He and his mother came to the hotel today and gave us a most wonderful testimony. The boy was a healthy eleven-year-old, who went to school. Then he was in a car accident. His right leg was broken above the knee. After the cast was removed, he fell and broke it again and broke the left leg, too. They put both legs in casts up to his waist. Then they discovered that he had a bone disease which made them brittle and weak.

For three months the lad lay flat in bed. In boarding school, he was finally able to walk again by using two crutches. Then he fell and broke his right leg again. One more time he spent three months in a cast. This time, the feeling in his leg was gone, and it seemed to be dead. A creeping paralysis had set in, and there seemed to be no life in his legs. Again, he was put on crutches; but both legs had to be fitted with steel braces. Even so, he could hardly swing his legs along. Without the supports, he could not bear his weight or take a step. But last night he took off his braces and handed his crutches to his mother who gave them to me. Then the lad walked all over the platform, back and forth, while the multitude marveled. Oh, how happy he was. Today his joy is even greater as he is gaining strength by the hour. We are seeing Bible days again. I wonder what else we will hear about before the day is over.

When we arrived at the crusade field this evening around 4 o'clock, it was filling up with people. By the time I began preaching, there must have been 40,000 to 60,000 people present. Every road leading toward the grounds was a river of human beings.

I preached on *Blind Bartimaeus*, then dealt thoroughly with the multitude about salvation and receiving Jesus Christ. What an experience to lead such a multitude in prayer to be saved. I wish the whole world, especially Christians of the world, could experience what we saw today — and what we've seen for over four decades in over 70 nations. No words can describe the sacred and powerful atmosphere and presence of Jesus when a great multitude cries out to Him for salvation.

Thousands and thousands were converted today. And there was great joy in the city. It was like Bible days when Philip preached in the city of Samaria. There is no way to describe the wonder of it all.

After urging them to follow Jesus and to go to church, we instructed them about healing and prayed for them to be healed. Then we led them in a thorough confession of thanks, of faith, and of acceptance of healing.

Then we asked them to put their faith into action, to begin to do what they could not do before the prayer. I must testify here that I do not believe we have seen the equal before, at least not often. It seemed that the healing power of God exploded across the field and, in every section of the multitude, groups at the far edges started running, following cripples who had been healed or who had taken off braces or tossed crutches aside and had begun to walk and run. The field was an explosion of joy. It was one of the most heavenly scenes we've ever witnessed.

Just as I was getting ready to ask them to come to the platform, a lad burst up the ramp, carrying two crutches in one hand and two braces with shoes on them in the other. That dear lad was marvelously healed. Just as I was trying to calm the audience to explain about the boy, a girl about fifteen years old bounded up the ramp, past the excited photographers, carrying two large braces and walking almost perfectly normal. There I was with two crutches and four big braces and shoes trying to get the audience quieted down enough to explain these miracles. Then I saw them handing braces and crutches over the heads of the people, passing them toward the platform in four places at once.

About that time, the multitude realized what was happening and they went wild. They rushed a woman up the right side of the platform, carrying two crutches and one brace above her head. She had been healed, too, and was weeping for joy. Then someone yelled, "Look here." A woman, whose eyes seemed wild with excitement, came yelling and crying, carrying two hip-to-foot braces with shoes on them, and we tried to have her testify. She kept looking about wildly and, finally, she said. "It's not me, it's my daughter. She was healed. She took off these braces and began to run and I've lost her. Can you help me find her?" And she began calling for her daughter. It was pandemonium everywhere as you could see people with crutches, canes, and braces, waving them in the air in no less than a dozen places at a time. Groups could be seen breaking out of the crowd, running, as someone was healed near them.

The platform, by this time, was overrun with people who had been healed by a miracle — and the number kept increasing. A pastor pressed through frantically, with two crutches above his head. He saw a man throw them down and turn around and start running as the people opened up a way before him. The pastor had not been able to get on the platform, and this had happened when he was standing out in the audience. We called for the man, but could not get things quiet enough to find him.

A youth bounded up the ramp, among the crowd of healed cripples. He had been born deaf and dumb, and the lad could repeat every word we spoke. He heard even the ticking of a watch. When the people realized it, they were amazed. I was trying to explain it all when a mother, carrying two crutches high above her head, came rushing up the ramp and across the platform, walking as well as l can. Then a lady who was deaf and dumb and who had spastic paralysis came, looking almost wild with excitement. Some pastors knew her. Now she was completely healed. She could clearly repeat every word I spoke; and by the time we finished checking her, her contortions ceased. Her eyes were filled with amazement as she discovered that she could move her arms and hands up and down, double and straighten them, with no more spasms.

By this time, there was such hilarious joy and boundless happiness that we simply lost control. All ramps — both sides and back — were jammed with miracles. When I asked how many more out in the field were healed but could not come forward, probably 2,000 hands were raised and waved as they praised the Lord to affirm that they were healed.

It would take a great book to begin to tell the wonders God performed this night. Witnessing this day, I can only say, to God be the glory! I thank Him again for letting Daisy and me experience yet another wondrous day. We've been *seeing* God confirming His word with miracles for over thirty years already.

* * *

May, 1978, Monterrey, Mexico: So much is happening so fast in this historic crusade that one can only record a small percentage of what is reported. News keeps coming in about more miracles. Tens of thousands of people are talking about it. A group from Veracruz came by plane. One of them had been paralyzed and was unable to walk. He is up now, feels strong, and walks erect. He walked up to me as I was preaching and wanted to testify.

A woman from Saltillo, with a broken leg and a fractured disc in her spine, was perfectly restored. One man who had been paralyzed for 27 years, hobbling on a cane, was completely healed. Another man, paralyzed since an accident 20 years ago, was healed. He said: "I came for a miracle, and I got it."

Almost everyone that comes here to our room tells of someone else who has been healed. The city is being stirred. Only God knows what will happen this week. We're living a miracle. Why the government has allowed this is still a marvel to us, and we stand in awe before the fact that when God wants to give a witness to a city, or to a nation, the hearts of the leaders are in His hand.

Today the meeting was formidable. Such a multitude came. Such hunger for the word. The poor people are overwhelmed and are so appreciative, seeming to realize that God is giving a special witness and blessing to them. There are many on stretchers, dozens in wheelchairs; others are carried on beds.

Tonight I preached on the healing of Bartimaeus. I stressed the point that God still heals the blind today. I emphasized what an opportunity it is when Jesus passes our way. How Bartimaeus himself prayed. How he prayed the right prayer — for mercy. How all forces unite to keep one from asking for a miracle — to keep quiet and humble — but how he prayed more and how Jesus heard his call. How he was healed and how he followed Jesus.

I never was able to finish my message. Four times during the message I was interrupted by miracles taking place in the crowd. It was amazing how the power of the Lord was present to heal. Early in the message, clapping and rejoicing broke out as someone was healed. Far to the edge of the multitude, we heard another group rejoicing and crying out about a miracle. I got them quieted, then continued preaching.

After a few moments, I heard rejoicing far out to my right. It was like a rustle in the crowd. Two steel leg braces were being held up in the air, and the crowd was opening as the group advanced. I lost control of the multitude and had to pause in my preaching and wait. Up the steps came a girl, walking steady and strong. This dear child's bones had had a disease that caused them to crumble and break. It was impossible to bear her weight as her knees would slip out of joint. Her ankles were brittle, and it caused her excruciating pain. That child was healed. She never looked up, only straight ahead, and marched triumphantly across the full length of the sixty-foot-wide platform, then back, three times. The people wept and rejoiced as the girl walked. It was truly a wonder to behold.

Finally, we restored order and resumed teaching. After another fifteen minutes, another big commotion broke out, and I could see what was happening. Someone far out in front of me had been healed and was moving toward the platform. As they came within range of the powerful floodlights, there was a steel brace being waved over their heads, and someone was walking rather rapidly. I simply had to interrupt the message again as they triumphantly marched up the steps. There was a boy about ten years old. His father was carrying a big steel brace that had been strapped from the lad's waist, up around his chest, to support his neck. The boy had a disease of the bones, which had twisted his body and neck severely and only the brace could hold him straight. Now he was walking upright with his hands in the air, and his father was in tears. The lad was made whole.

Then others started rushing up to testify, and on both sides, miracles were happening. I saw that I would never be able to finish my message if I stopped again. The power of the Lord was present to heal. We finally got the multitude calmed, resumed preaching, and had made several major points when it happened again on both sides of the platform at once. I knew that this time we would never control them, so I refused to let them come up the steps, because I felt it was important to pray the prayer of repentance and to receive salvation. I asked them to wait until I had finished; then I made a call to accept Christ and a multitude repented and received salvation.

As we were thanking God for His new life, they started getting healed again. Then I said: "I have taught enough. So come on up and tell of God's wonders, for His glory."

And they started, from both sides, until the platform was packed with people. What a sight and what a night to be remembered in this great city.

The first lady up the steps just walked past me and ignored me. She paraded to the end of the platform, then came back. I walked along by her side, and all she would say as she was weeping was: "I'm healed. I can walk. I can walk. Look at me. I'm well." Back and forth she marched steadily and perfectly, while the multitude clapped.

Then a lad was healed. The mother was weeping. She said: "My son had meningitis when he was only three years old. He is ten now and has not walked since that attack. He has only lain in bed or sat in his chair." None of the family wanted him to be brought, and they tried to discourage the mother from her "crazy" idea. The mother carried her son to the crusade secretly and he is perfectly healed. He walked as normal as any lad. It was wonderful.

A woman marched about who had not walked for twenty years due to an operation. She was restored. A fifteen-year-old boy, who had never walked without crutches, carried them above his head as he walked back and forth. A farmer, who had been a paralytic, gave a moving testimony. He had numerous gods in his house which he had trusted. He did not know about the reality of Jesus. He had been in an accident thirteen years before and spent nine long years in the hospital because of a broken back. For the last four years he has hobbled on crutches. Tonight he was healed and promised that his whole life was for Jesus now.

Then a lady came to testify who had not walked in twenty-five years. She had received a leaflet announcing the crusade, but did not want to know anything about such a meeting or about Protestants. Finally, she consented to be brought to the crusade tonight, and the family was so happy because she was healed. She was overwhelmed.

A young lady, who had fallen twice and ruptured a disc in her spine, was unable to stand or walk. But during the prayer, she got up and walked and was healed. She was so happy as she cried: "Look at me. Jesus has healed me."

A woman was healed of arthritis in all of her joints. Oh, she was thrilled. She said: "The doctors are going to be amazed to see how I am healed."

One dear man's heart was healed. He was scheduled for surgery because he could not walk more than a few meters without gasping for breath. Now he had walked thirty blocks to the meeting and was well and breathing normally. He was not even tired. It was a great miracle.

A woman, who for seven years had eaten almost nothing because of a cancerous tumor in her stomach, was brought to the meeting by her daughter and was healed. The mother of Daisy's interpreter has had a disease of deterioration of the bones. Tonight she was healed. An old woman shouted because she was healed of heart trouble. Oh, she was happy. A lad about thirteen years old was healed of crippled feet. They were turned in so badly that he could not walk without tripping, and he could not run at all. It was a glorious miracle. Both feet were perfect and absolutely straight. He ran back and forth. I examined his feet, and they seemed to be perfect. He fell into his mother's arms, and they both wept. It was wonderful.

* * *

December, 1979, Nakuru, Kenya: Today was one of those historic never-to-be-forgotten crusade days. An enormous multitude of people were assembled to hear the message of God. Daisy and I knelt as we prayed with the multitude for God to reach into the homes and lives of each of our faith partners at home and for God to bless them with the same miracle power that He is pouring out on this crusade here.

Then I preached on the healing of the lame man in Mark chapter 2 who was carried to Jesus at Capernaum. I was able to get the message across by the anointing of the Holy Spirit, and a great spiritual work was wrought among the people. I finished with a call for sinners to repent, and there was a great move of God among the multitude. Thousands received the Lord in their hearts. I led them in a confession of faith until it was clear that they had understood and received Christ.

They received Him in such a real way that suddenly they began being healed everywhere. I never did get to pray for the sick. They knew Jesus had entered their lives, and His power began healing them everywhere. It was among the very great miracle nights of our whole ministry.

Among the first to mount the platform was a mother with her three children. They had all been born deaf. Each was healed and able to hear perfectly. What a miracle. What mercy from God.

Then a woman bounded across the platform, stomping her feet and waving her arms, carrying crutches above her head. She had been in a terrible accident, and many of her bones had been broken. She had been dragged to the side of the road and left for dead because they could only help those for whom there was some hope of saving their lives. Hours later, someone heard her groan and realized life was still in her. So they put her on an old truck and hauled her to the hospital. But she was so near dead that her bones were never set.

Her recovery was very slow; and by the time she was out of danger, they would have had to re-break the shoulder, rib, and pelvic bones to align her twisted body. Since she was a poor village woman, she was left to heal as she was. She had to walk with crutches. Her left arm was twisted and could not be raised. Her shoulders were deformed, as were her legs and pelvic area. But tonight Jesus came to her and she was miraculously healed. She walked back and forth across the platform, waving both crutches above her head, raising her left arm, weeping aloud, praising God for His mercy to her. It was marvelous.

Following her was a man about twenty-two years of age who had been crippled by polio when he was a child. He was unable to walk without crutches, but was wonderfully healed tonight. He walked carrying his crutches above his head and glorifying God before the multitude.

Then a lad came to testify. He had an injection which had damaged the nerves in one leg. It never grew and was three inches shorter than the other. It had been paralyzed. Tonight he was healed, and the people were amazed.

A young fellow with a full leg brace and built-up shoe for the other foot came walking across the platform, carrying his shoes and the brace above his head. He was healed. It was a miracle.

A lovely girl who had been born deaf and dumb was healed. She had come each night and today, at home, she began to talk. Her parents were astonished. Then tonight the full miracle took place, and she could hear a faint whisper in either ear and repeat every word and phrase in a normal voice. It was one of those awesome deaf-mute miracles.

A fine lad, deaf in one ear since he was born, was perfectly healed; and he gave the most wonderful testimony. He preached like a man. I was so touched. No doubt God will use him as a preacher as he grows up.

A dear woman who had never walked in her life was carried to the crusade in a bed by her friend. She was visited by the Lord tonight, and she got up and began to walk. It astonished her friends. The Finnish missionary knows her. She walked back and forth across the platform to the amazement of all who were present.

Several people suffering with epilepsy were made whole. They accepted Jesus, and devils left them.

We never prayed at all for the sick tonight. The people just accepted Jesus Christ in their lives and understood that, when He comes in, sickness must leave. They believed; they put their faith in action; and according to their faith, it was done to them.

One of the greatest miracles tonight was a young man who had polio when he was a baby and was unable to walk. He tried crutches and canes, but fell and broke his weak legs so often that he finally gave up hope. To move about, he dragged himself backwards on his buttocks, with his hands.

Three weeks ago when our team began conducting film services in the villages, this fellow saw one of our films in his town and he purposed to come to the crusade.

He listened and received Jesus Christ in his heart and was wonderfully healed. He got up and walked alone, back and forth across the platform. He showed us how he had to scoot along on the ground, then he jumped up and paraded his new miracle. He preached a sermon as he testified for no less than fifteen minutes. I was astounded at his words. He is handsome in the face, and has a sharp and sound mind. He spoke for all of Africa, thanking us for coming and for giving his people a chance to hear the gospel of Christ and to see His power.

He talked about others more than of himself. He pled for his people. He felt that we had blessed his country by coming. He longed for all of Kenya to be present and to hear and to see what he had witnessed. He vowed that he would never forget Jesus Christ, and he would always serve Him.

Then God spoke to me and showed me His plan for this fellow's life while he still poured out his heart to the multitude. I heard Africa speak through this man.

When he finished testifying, I told him that Jesus Christ had chosen him and had set him apart to be a preacher to his nation, that God would use him and that people would be blessed and saved and healed wherever he would go. Everyone was amazed. I urged the pastors to teach him and to assist him.

Senator Young from Oklahoma, who was in the crusade, embraced him and promised to buy him a Swahili Bible. We agreed to pay for his room and food so that he could attend our teaching seminar for workers and learn of Jesus Christ and of the faith that is in Him.

Then Doctor Whitaker, a surgeon from Oklahoma, came to his side weeping, touched by what had happened. It was a great testimony to all who were present. God's presence was mighty.

Then a lad came, carrying a steel leg brace in one hand and a shoe in the other. Polio had left him lame but Jesus made him whole.

A woman who had been a prostitute for years came weeping. She was rubbing her abdomen where a large cancerous tumor had been.

Now it was all gone, and she was so overwhelmed that God would show mercy to her. She didn't dream that she could be healed. She wept aloud and finally dropped to her knees, bending her face to the floor. Then with hands raised high and her face bathed in tears, she thanked God for His mercy. All of the multitude was overwhelmed.

I could recount many more cases tonight. They seemed endless. God was glorified and the city was truly stirred to believe on Jesus Christ and to serve Him. What an honor to be used of God, to be part of such a spiritual visitation to a nation.

* * *

January, 1980, Embu, Kenya: Today was a great day indeed. A multitude crowded onto the Moi Stadium grounds. I preached on *Faith, Hope and Love.* It was perhaps the largest crowd ever to assemble for a gospel meeting in this entire region. After the preaching, people began being healed everywhere. Many hundreds received Christ. I commanded cripples to raise their crutches and canes or to toss them aside and to walk in Jesus' name. They did as I said, and soon we could see groups or crowds moving in four or five directions at a time as cripples were healed and crowds followed them. It was a long time before I could gain the attention of the people and get those healed to come up to the platform to testify.

I made the mistake of telling them to go out on the field and to prove what God had done for them, and that is what they did instead of coming up to testify before the multitude of people. But finally, different ones began to come and tell us what God had done for them. They took off braces and threw away canes and crutches. Here and there, they handed them up to us on the platform.

Different outbursts of praise and joy would break out as others began to be healed. While crutches were being raised here and there, all of a sudden a blind man mounted the steps. His eyes were open, and he could see everything. Then an old man with crippled feet was healed. He jumped and stomped across the platform with tremendous joy. He was completely healed.

Then a mother came with her daughter who had been out of school for two years because she lost her eyesight and had to be led about. She had been taken to the hospital in Nairobi, but nothing could be done for her. For eight years, she had no vision. Now her sight was restored. She and her mother were weeping for joy.

One older woman was healed of terrible suffering in her bladder. It was touching to see how she rejoiced. There was a woman who had been bedfast for six years, unable to walk and to help herself. Carried there in a bed and laid where she could hear us, she had been healed. Her friends came up the steps with her, and we all marveled at her testimony. She was so thrilled because she could stand, and even talk. She had not been able to talk for a long time. Now she walked back and forth, and everyone praised God as she told her story of deliverance.

A woman with a deaf ear was healed. She could hear a faint whisper in the ear that had been stone deaf for many years. A man who had suffered asthma for years was healed. A man who had been in an accident, and had been in pain ever since, was healed. All pain left him and he was absolutely restored. An old man came who had suffered in his back and could not bend over, as he said, ".... even to eat, but now I can play like a child." He stooped, squatted, doubled, bent, jumped and ran to show how completely his back was healed. A woman with abdominal pains for seven years was healed and was free of pain. She said: "I've been like the woman in the Bible with the issue of blood, but now I am well. I touched Jesus today." She said a heat had gone through her body and all was well. Then they brought a woman who had been totally deaf. She could hear every word I whispered in either ear. She was really very excited.

An old lady came and threw a walking stick down. She said she had suffered so much and couldn't walk without a cane, but now she is well and she never wants to use that cane again. She marched back and forth and was so happy.

An elderly woman came whose hips were so stiff that she had barely been able to walk. Also, she was nearly blind. For three weeks she had been lying at home. Now she could walk and jump and run and see clearly. Then an old mother told how that, though she lived very near, she had not been able to come to the crusade meetings because of lame feet and legs; so her friends carried her to the grounds. She was healed and walked like a young girl and was so happy.

A lady who had suffered for many years with epilepsy said she knew when the tormenting spirit left her. As I prayed, she knew that she was healed.

A man who had noises in his head and was nearly deaf was made whole. Now all the noises are gone and his hearing is clear.

Daisy came and told about another crippled man who had been healed. He was well known in the town. When he was healed, he took off his braces and threw down his crutches. But, instead of coming to the platform, he and a large group paraded out of the grounds and up the road by the market place to show the city what God had done. They sent an usher to catch him and bring him back to testify, but he said: "No, Mr. Osborn said to go tell the people, so I am doing that."

The whole town is in an uproar and the man is well running, walking, jumping. What a testimony. How like Bible days.

Another man who had been totally deaf for two years was healed and can hear everything. A woman who could hardly breathe and had great pain in her abdomen was healed. She had been to witch doctors and had suffered so much. She had sold some chickens to buy a ticket to come to the hospital, but they could not help her. Then she heard of the crusade. She came and was completely healed. She pointed to her child and said: "Look, even my child is happy because she knows now that I am well."

There was no end to the wonders God did in the lives of people tonight. It is overwhelming to hear and to see such marvels of God. One woman with shaking palsy was perfectly healed, and her hands are as steady as a child's. What a night. What wonders. God is being glorified.

* * *

As this latest edition of *Healing the Sick* goes to press, we can say afresh: **Jesus Christ** [is still] **the same, yesterday, and today, and forever** (Heb. 13:8), and by the grace of God, we are continuing to witness across the world the wonderful things **Jesus began both to do and teach** (Acts 1:1) wherever we proclaim His word.

In every country where we have gone, without exception, we have seen the same hunger and response to mass evangelism. **Great multitudes followed** (Jesus), **because they saw his miracles which he did on them that were diseased** (John 6:2).

Mass evangelism — preaching the gospel with signs following, out in the public places — will always be effective. It is the pattern set forth by Jesus Christ and followed by the early church. It is the order of this generation, too, because neither our Lord nor human beings have changed. Perhaps, our two greatest crusades were conducted in two extreme contrasts of society: In both Holland and Zaire, audiences exceeded 150,000 in a single service. Wherever we go, we find that Christ is still moved with compassion and people are still eager to see the wonders of God.

Our Lord continues to confirm His word with signs and wonders wherever the gospel is preached. Those who believe are made whole physically, mentally and spiritually.

Among the people of these many nations of the world, **with great power** [we] **give witness of the resurrection of the Lord Jesus: and great grace** [is] **upon** [us] **all** (Acts 4:33).

Many signs and wonders [were] wrought among the people; And believers were the more added to the Lord, multitudes of both men and women.

Acts 5:12,14

God also bearing [us] witness, both with signs and wonders, and with divers miracles, and gifts of the Holy Ghost.

Hebrews 2:4

Chapter 56

CHRIST AT WORK IN YOU

Having received Christ by faith into your redeemed life, the kingdom of God is at work in the new you.

You can never again *negate*, reduce or impoverish yourself.

You can never again *condemn* what God paid so much to redeem.

You can never again *put down* what God paid so much to lift up.

You can never again *accuse or judge* what God paid so much to forgive and make righteous.

You can never again *do anything to harm or weaken or destroy* what God paid so much to heal, to restore and to save.

You can never again *depreciate, discredit or disparage* what God paid so much to dignify and to make royal.

You can never again *criticize* or *revile* what God esteems to be of such infinite value.

Having received Jesus in you, you have discovered the real life for which God created you.

Memorize and repeat these lines the Lord inspired me to write to you:

> *The me I see is Christ in me!*
> *Now I can be all that I see.*
> *For now I see a brand new me!*
> *God's embassy is now in me.*
> *All luxury, and discovery;*
> *New melody — my jubilee!*
> *I've found the key. So, I decree,*
> *That the me I see is Christ in me!*

When Christ lives in you, your new life is really His life in you.

You say, Jesus:

Here is my brain; *think* through it.

Here is my face; *glow* through it.

Here are my hands; *touch* with them.

Here are my eyes; *see* through them.

Here are my ears; *listen* with them.

Here are my lips; *speak* through them.

Here is my heart; *love* through it.

Daisy, my wife, says: "Learn to practice the awareness of Jesus in you."

You begin to say:

I am somebody. God and me are partners. We share the same life.

Nothing is too good for us. Nothing can stop our success. We have lift-up power. We are conquerors. We are royal and we are rich.

Say "Yes" to what you see that you want to be.

Say "Yes" to your greatest vision.

See yourself BEING what you want to be, DOING what you want to do, HAVING what you want to have.

See yourself sharing the Jesus-life, forgiven, cleansed, righteous, transformed, justified.

See yourself healed, restored, strong, robust, resilient, energetic.

See yourself happy, confident, at ease, fulfilled, productive.

See yourself prosperous, successful, wealthy, vigorous, blessed.

See yourself free from debt, without mortgages, without fear, anxiety or problems.

See God in you. He is Master. See His kingdom within you.

Chapter 57
SHARE THE GOOD NEWS

You have read this book. I am sure it has been a great blessing to you. Tell your friends about it. Order several copies and lend them where they will help others to be blessed. By doing this, you will be helping those about you. You may be the means of lengthening their lives by merely letting them know these truths.

Withhold not good from them to whom it is due, when it is in the power of your hand to do it.

Proverbs 3:27

Share the blessings and knowledge you are receiving with others who are hurting, who are lonely and who are afraid — with those who have never been taught about their Bible rights to freedom from both sickness and sin.

Help us to spread the good news. See that your pastor and every Bible teacher in your community has a copy of this book.

The world needs this good news, and you can help bring it to them.

Many are being healed while reading these messages, and their testimonies are continually being received. If you are one of them, write us your testimony of healing. Tell us how this book has affected you.

Jesus made a wonderful promise:

If you will confess me before people, I will confess you before my Father in heaven.

Matthew 10:32

The finest way to say thanks to God for the gift of His life is to share this happy information with others.

See yourself as God sees you. See the unlimited possibilities that beckon you.

You are part of a winning team. Nothing can stop you and God together.

It was love's idea not to let you die in emptiness, but to pay for your sins, and to restore you to God's lifestyle for which you were originally created.

Now you are at home with God again. He is blessing you with life's best through Jesus Christ. You have regained dignity. You are restored to God's family and to His lifestyle.

Count on Daisy and me as personal, faithful friends. We care about you and we are with you to help you through our prayers and faith.

We will keep helping you. We will not quit.

About the Authors

The ministries of T.L. and Daisy Osborn have made an unprecedented impact on the world in our time. They are valued among the great soulwinners of this century.

Married at ages 17 and 18, the Osborns were missionaries in India at 20 and 21. In 1949 they instituted the OSFO International Gospel Center – a world evangelism and missionary church organization.

Their life commitment: To express and to propagate the gospel of Jesus Christ to people throughout the world.

Their guiding principle: The top priority of the church is the evangelism of the world.

The Osborns have conducted mass crusades in over 80 nations, preaching to audiences ranging from 20,000 to 250,000 nightly and more.

They have sponsored over 25,000 national preachers as full-time missionaries, reaching their own unreached tribes and villages.

They have published gospel literature in 132 languages and dialects.

They have produced documentary films and crusade tapes for public evangelism in nearly 80 major languages.

They have provided airlifts and huge shipments of soulwinning tools for gospel missions and workers worldwide.

They have furnished vehicles with films, projectors, screens, generators, P.A. systems, audio cassettes and cassette players, and great quantities of literature for evangelism abroad.

They are energetic and prolific writers. T.L. Osborn's living classic, *Healing the Sick* — now in its 43rd edition — has been a faith-building best-seller since 1951.

Their big 512 page Classic Documentary--*The Gospel According to T.L. & Daisy*, is unmatched among Christian Publications. Dr. Daisy's five major books (see listing opposite page) are unequaled in Christian literature for women, helping the female members of the Body of Christ to discover their own Identity, *Dignity, Equality & Destiny* in God's redemptive plan for their lives.

The Osborns have probably reached and led more unreached souls to Jesus Christ in non-Christian lands, and may have witnessed more great healing miracles, than any other couple who has ever yet lived. Their team efforts in world evangelism are truly pace-setting as they proclaim the good news to the world: that Jesus Christ is the same yesterday, and today, and forever. (Heb. 13:8.)

To contact the author write:

Osborn Ministries • P. O. Box 10 • Tulsa, OK 74102 • USA

Please include your prayer requests
and comments when you write.

Books by T.L. and Daisy Osborn

Choices for Women Who Win

God's Love Plan

Gospel According to T.L. and Daisy

Healing the Sick (A Living Classic)

How To Be Born Again

Modern Miracles in Mombassa

New Life for Women

Outside the Sanctuary

There's Plenty for You

Power of Positive Desire

Receive Miracle Healing

Soulwinning

The Best of Life

The Good Life

The Woman Believer

Woman Without Limits

Women and Self-Esteem

You Are God's Best

Available from your local bookstore.

HARRISON HOUSE
P. O. Box 35035
Tulsa, Oklahoma 74153

Teaching Audio Cassettes
by Daisy Osborn and T.L. Osborn

Winning Our World I – 13 Lessons

Winning Our World II – 13 Lessons

Ministry of Healing I – 12 Lessons

Ministry of Healing II – 9 Lessons

Ministry of Healing III – 9 Lessons

Trinidad Crusade – 5 cassettes

Faith To Change Your World – 5 cass

Super Living – 5 cassettes

Healing by Christ – 4 cassettes

Believe the Man Jesus – 3 cassettes

Christ Unchangeable – 7 cassettes

The Believing Church – 5 cassettes

Freedom for Everyone – 10 cass

Contact for Impact – 3 cassettes

Anointed/Appointed To Act – 12 cass

Jesus Life for Indonesia – 13 cass

Power of Positive Desire – 4 cass

Receive Miracle Healing – 6 cass

Soulwinning – 4 cassettes

Power for Your Hour – 2 cass

Gospel Dynamics – 4 cassettes

Healing the Sick – 12 cassettes

Yes to God's Success – 2 cass

You Are God's Best – 4 cassettes

Behold the Son – 40 cassettes

Be Alive – 5 cassettes

Big Love Plan – 4 cassettes

If I Were a Woman – 2 cassettes

It's Great To Have Faith – 3 cass

Kingdom of Freedom – 4 cassettes

Live From Mexico Crusade – 4 cass

4 Healing Principles – 6 cassettes

Miracle Christ Life – 13 cassettes

Miracle Living – 13 cassettes

Biblical Relationships – 13 Lessons

Creation Realities – 13 Lessons

Old Testament Discoveries – 13 Lessons

Believers in Ministry – 5 cassettes

Demise of Religion – 3 cassettes

Go for the Climb – 2 cassettes

Choosing Is Never Losing – 2 cassettes

God of Miracles – 3 cassettes

Unchanging Christ – 2 cassettes

Test of Discipleship – 2 cassettes

Faith Makes the Difference – 2 cassettes

Hope for the Hampered – 2 cassettes

Person, Power, Product – 3 cassettes

Marks of a Believer – 2 cassettes

Paris Seminar – 7 cassettes

Always Succeed, Here's How – 7 cass

God's Call to Women – 2 cassettes

Living the Jesus Life – 4 cassettes

5 Choices – Women Who Win – 2 cass

Guidelines for Living – 5 cassettes

Biblical Submission – 4 cassettes

7 Facts for Miracle Prayer – 1 cassette

Power for You – 1 cassette

Look Up! Look Up! – 1 cassette

Mombasa Crusade Live – 16 cassettes

Kampala Crusade Live – 12 cassettes

God's Husband/Wife Team – 2 cass

Jesus Visited Our House – 2 cassettes

Miracle Prayer – 2 cassettes

Hope, Health & Happiness – 1 cass

Prayer of Salvation

A born-again, committed relationship with God is the key to the victorious life. Jesus, the Son of God laid down His life and rose again so that we could spend eternity with Him in heaven and experience His absolute best on earth. The Bible says, **"For God so loved the world, that he gave his only begotten Son, that whosoever believeth in him should not perish, but have everlasting life"** (John 3:16).

It is the will of God that everyone receive eternal salvation. The way to receive this salvation is to call upon the name of Jesus and confess Him as your Lord. The Bible says, **"That if thou shalt confess with thy mouth the Lord Jesus, and shalt believe in thine heart that God hath raised him from the dead, thou shalt be saved. For whosoever shall call upon the name of the Lord shall be saved"** (Romans 10:9-10,13).

Jesus has given salvation, healing and countless benefits to all who call upon His name. These benefits can be yours if you receive Him into your heart by praying this prayer.

Heavenly Father, I come to You admitting that I am a sinner. Right now, I choose to turn away from sin, and I ask You to cleanse me of all unrighteousness. I believe that Your Son, Jesus died on the cross to take away my sins. I also believe that He rose again from the dead so that I might be justified and made righteous through faith in Him. I call upon the name of Jesus Christ to be the Savior and Lord of my life. Jesus, I choose to follow You, and ask that You fill me with the power of the Holy Spirit. I declare that right now, I am a born-again child of God. I am free from sin, and full of the righteousness of God. I am saved in Jesus' name, Amen.

If you have prayed this prayer to receive Jesus Christ as your Savior, or if this book has changed your life, we would like to hear from you. Please write us at:

Harrison House Publishers
P.O. Box 35035
Tulsa, Oklahoma 74153

You can also visit us on the web at
www.harrisonhouse.com

The Harrison House Vision

Proclaiming the truth and the power
Of the Gospel of Jesus Christ
With excellence;

Challenging Christians to
Live victoriously,
Grow spiritually,
Know God intimately.